RED GUIDE

North Wales
(Northern Section)

Llandudno Colwyn Bay Rhyl
Conway Penmaenmawr Bangor
Anglesey Betws-y-Coed Llanrwst
Capel Curig Caernarvon etc

Edited by Reginald J. W. Hammond

Fifth edition

WARD LOCK LIMITED
116 Baker Street, London W1M 2BB

© 1975 Ward Lock Limited

ISBN 0 7063 5500 8 Casebound

ISBN 0 7063 5499 0 Paperback

Published in Great Britain
by Ward Lock Ltd
116 Baker Street, London W1M 2BB, a member
of the Pentos Group

Reprinted 1979

Printed Offset Litho in Great Britain by
Cox & Wyman Ltd,
London, Fakenham and Reading

Contents

CONTENTS

Illustrations

Town Plans

Introduction

This Guide deals with that part of North Wales lying north of a line drawn from Chester to the Nevin Rivals and following the roads from Chester to Ruthin and from Betws-y-Coed to Beddgelert. The district has long been famous for its combination of seaside, mountain, and wooded, rocky glens; but modern transport facilities have made more widely known its wealth of scenery of a softer nature and transformed many a formerly remote hamlet into a popular little resort. Much of the area is now part of the Snowdonia National Park, thus protection is afforded for the natural beauty of this lovely region.

The majority of visitors prefer to combine the joys of mountain and sea, and for their accommodation a whole chain of resorts stand along the northern shore. Of these the most popular are **Llandudno, Colwyn Bay** and **Rhyl,** with **Prestatyn, Abergele** and **Rhos-on-Sea** as satellites. No less famous in their own way are the resorts west of the Conwy river—**Conwy** itself, **Penmaen-mawr, Llanfairfechan, Bangor** and **Caernarvon.** Quieter but with scenic attractions all their own are the inland centres such as **Betws-y-Coed, Capel Curig, Llanberis** and **Beddgelert.**

"Farthest north" in the district is **Anglesey,** a wonderful holiday island combining magnificent coast scenery and pure air with easy access to the finest part of Snowdonia.

Pwllheli, Criccieth, Corwen, Bala, Llangollen, Barmouth, Aberystwyth, and other centres in the more southerly part of North Wales are dealt with in a companion volume—*North Wales (Southern Section).*

APPROACHES TO THE DISTRICT

By Railway. The main line of the **London Midland Region system of British Rail** skirts the coast and serves all the more important resorts. Through trains do the journey from Euston to Rhyl in about $4\frac{1}{2}$ hours and there are similarly good services from the important Midland and northern centres.

Buses connect the railway with such places as Capel Curig and Beddgelert, and resorts along the Anglesey coast.

By Motor Coach. During the season daily coach services are maintained between the North Wales resorts and the principal Midland towns, and also London. Current announcements should be consulted for details.

By Steamer. During summer months occasional day excursions are made by steamers of Messrs. P. & A. Campbell, Limited from Liverpool to Llandudno. The time occupied by the voyage is about $3\frac{1}{4}$ hours. The trip is a delightful one, the coast being visible all the way, while during the latter part of the journey the Snowdonian mountains form a noble background. Full particulars can be obtained on application to the Company at 4 Dock Chambers, Bute Street, Cardiff, or any agency.

Road Routes to the District

Chester and Shrewsbury are the gates by which the majority of motorists and cyclists enter the Northern Section of North Wales.

The road westward from Chester follows the coast and the railway practically all the way to Caernarvon. That from Shrewsbury is much to be preferred by those seeking scenic beauties: indeed, the run from Llangollen on to Betws-y-Coed is one of the most beautiful in Wales if not in Britain, and the high level of the scenery is maintained to the coast, whether one goes northward from Betws-y-Coed down the Conway valley or north-eastward *via* Capel Curig and Nant Ffrancon. An alternative route is northward from Shrewsbury to Wrexham, Mold and so to the coast road.

Chester is 17 miles from *Liverpool* by way of Birkenhead; 38 miles from *Manchester* by way of Northwich. *Leeds* is 70 miles distant by the same route, and *York* is 89 miles from Chester. From *Sheffield* the shortest way (69 miles) lies through Glossop, Stockport and Altrincham. The routes from *Nottingham, Derby, Leicester,* and neighbouring towns, pass through Newcastle-under-Lyme and Nantwich. Motorists from the *Birmingham* area can proceed either *via* Wellington and Whitchurch to Chester or use the southern "gateway" and enter the district *via* Shrewsbury and Llangollen.

The fastest route from **London** is by the M1 motorway to Coventry, or the equally direct but slower A5 via St. Albans, Dunstable, Stoney

Stratford, Daventry and Coventry, then by Tamworth, Lichfield and Stone to Newcastle-under-Lyme and Chester (196 miles). A more pleasant route, avoiding much of the industrial area of the Midlands, is that *via* Oxford, Worcester, Kidderminster and Bridgnorth to Shrewsbury (154 miles from London, 174 from Southampton), or again that via Aylesbury, Bicester, Banbury, Stratford-upon-Avon and Kidderminster. Motorists from the south and west will probably make their way northward by Gloucester, Worcester and as above.

Those who enter the district by way of the road running from—

CHESTER TO CAERNARVON

have a choice of ways as far as Abergele. There is the coast route through Flint, Mostyn and Prestatyn; there is the route through Hawarden, Northop, Holywell (turn off at Newmarket for **Rhyl**) and Rhuddlan, and there is a third way through Mold, Bodfari and down the lovely Clwyd valley to St. Asaph and thence past Bodelwyddan and St. George to **Abergele.**

A mile or so beyond Abergele, road and rail unite and run practically side by side throughout the remainder of the journey to Caernarvon. **Colwyn Bay** and **Rhos-on-Sea** are passed (40 miles); then **Llandudno Junction** (45¾ miles). Over the Conwy Bridge to **Conwy** town and on to **Penmaenmawr** and **Llanfairfechan.** Then on past Aber to **Bangor** (61 miles); and a further run of 9 miles terminates in **Caernarvon** (70 miles from Chester). Additional notes on the road westward of Conwy (including routes in Anglesey) will be found on a subsequent page.

THE ROUTE VIA SHREWSBURY

The first 25 miles of this route run northward to the lovely Vale of Llangollen, where a more westerly direction is taken.

From Llangollen the route continues through **Corwen** and out on to the moors by **Cerrig-y-Drudion** ("stone of the heroes"). Corwen stands at the head of the Vale of Clwyd, at the other end of which is the popular resort of **Rhyl.**

By Pentrefoelas the Holyhead road descends to **Betws-y-Coed,** affording fine views of the mountains clustered around Snowdon. Crossing Waterloo Bridge, and leaving Betws-y-Coed behind, the road soon runs past the Miners' Bridge and Swallow Falls and so to **Capel Curig.** Turning left here, the road runs through magnificently wild scenery to **Pen-y-Gwryd,** where bear right for Gorphwysfa, at the head of Llanberis Pass. At the foot of the pass are Llyn Peris, the villages of old and new **Llanberis** and Llyn Padarn. The route now lies past Llanrûg to **Caernarvon** (90 miles).

For **Llandudno** do not cross Waterloo Bridge at Betws-y-Coed, but continue northward down the Conway Valley, through Llanrwst and Tal-y-Cafn. For **Conway** and **Penmaenmawr,** cross the Waterloo Bridge, but in half a mile turn to right across Pont-y-Pair (disregarding Capel Curig road on left). Some visitors prefer to approach Penmaenmawr and Llanfairfechan by way of Capel Curig and Bethesda, turning abruptly to right opposite the gateway of Penrhyn Castle: the mileage from Betws-y-Coed is but slightly greater, and the road certainly provides better going, though there are some rather dangerous bends between Ogwen Lake and Bethesda. For **Bangor** and **Anglesey** turn *left* at the gateway of Penrhyn Castle, some 4 miles beyond Bethesda.

TRAVEL WITHIN THE DISTRICT

Travel within the district is facilitated by excellent road and rail transport services. The roads are good and almost every one is served by buses. The **Railway** links the important towns, and with careful forethought and combination of rail, bus and coach services the tourist can cover most of the ground and visit all the places of beauty and interest with little trouble.

Sunday is observed in Wales more strictly than in some other parts of Britain; tourists who propose making use of trains or buses on that day should, before setting out, consult the time-tables. Restricted services run almost everywhere, but in some cases restriction amounts almost to cessation of traffic.

Cycling is popular in the district, though the wise cyclist avoids as much as possible the roads most used by coaches.

Llandudno is the seaport of North Wales so far as tourist steamer traffic is concerned. Visitors may be reminded that enjoyable circular tours may be made by combining steamer with train or bus. A delightful way of journeying up the Conwy valley is by the boats which run between Conwy and Trefriw, as described on pp. 95–98.

Hotels and Accommodation

Throughout the area there are establishments of every grade from the palatial hotels of the popular resorts to the tiny inn or farm of the remote hamlets. Selective lists are given under the various descriptions of places concerned. Fairly comprehensive lists of all types of accommodation can generally be obtained on enquiry to the local authority.

Youth Hostels

Youth hostels vary from cottage to mansion, but all provide simple accommodation at very reasonable prices. Information on membership at a small annual subscription may be obtained from Y.H.A., Trevelyan House, 8, St. Stephen's Hill, St. Albans, Herts.

Maeshafn. Holt Hostel, Maeshafn, Mold, Clwyd.
Colwyn Bay. Foxhill, Nant-y-Glyn, Colwyn Bay, Clwyd.
Oaklands. Oaklands, Llanrwst, Gwynedd.
Penmaenbach. Near Penmaenmawr, Gwynedd.
Roewen. Rhiw Farm, Roewen, Conwy, Gwynedd.
Lledr Valley. Lledr House, Pont-y-Pant, Dolwyddelan, Gwynedd.
Capel Curig. Plas Curig, Capel Curig, Betws-y-Coed, Gwynedd.
Idwal Cottage. Idwal Cottage, Nant Ffrancon, Bethesda, Bangor, Gwynedd.
Bangor. Tan y Bryn, Bangor, Gwynedd.
Llanberis. Llwyn Celyn, Llanberis, Gwynedd.
Snowdown Ranger. Snowdon Ranger, Rhyd Ddu, Gwynedd.
Bryn Gwynant. Bryn Gwynant, Nant Gwynant, Gwynedd.

Camping and Caravanning

The best camping in North Wales is inland, notably in the Conwy and Lledr valleys, both above and below Betws-y-Coed. The hills are high and steep, but there are numerous level grounds within easy reach of streams and with trees affording shelter and a certain amount of privacy. The Llanberis Pass is too sternly rugged to appeal to campers, and for a similar reason the Bethesda-Nant Ffrancon-Capel Curig route is not recommended; but there are places with possibilities between Capel Curig and Pen-y-Gwryd, and thence to Beddgelert and Portmadoc the country is ideal camping-ground.

Generally speaking, the seaside sites are few, and except in Anglesey they are not particularly attractive owing to the fact that the railway runs within a few yards of the sea nearly all the way from Rhyl to Bangor. Anglesey, however, has numerous coves and bays that are quiet and sheltered and eminently suitable for camping.

Those who like organized camping-places will find several near the coast road on either side of Prestatyn; at Kinmel Bay and Towyn; between Rhyl and Pensarn; and on Conwy Morfa.

Within half a mile of the coast there are excellent camping-grounds practically all the way from Prestatyn to Caernarvon. Behind Rhyl are the meadows bordering the Clwyd; along towards Colwyn Bay the ground becomes more hilly, and really

11

excellent pitches can be found by those who take the trouble to seek them. There is no camping on the Great Orme's Head, but the Gloddaeth hills have possibilities. At the back of Conwy mountain is some very delightful camping country, and there is more at the back of Llanfairfechan and on towards Aber.

Angling

North Wales is highly attractive to the angler, as there is good trout fishing, free or almost free, in nearly all its lakes and streams, while in the Dee, Clwyd, Conway and Seiont excellent salmon catches are made. Particulars of waters available will be found in the descriptions of the various centres given in this Guide.

Visitors are reminded that, whether fishing in free or preserved waters, River Authority Licences are necessary. Those concerned are the Dee and Clwyd River Authority, Chester, and the Gwynedd River Authority, Caernarvon.

Mountain-Walking

A few suggestions are offered to walkers unfamiliar with the conditions in this part of Wales. Boots should be nailed. Many of the best walks are over grass-covered slopes, and during dry weather ordinary leather soles become slippery to danger-point. Rubber soles, preferred by many climbers, may prove dangerous on wet grass or rock. Map and compass are essential for safety. The new-comer should take an early opportunity of getting his bearings by climbing to some viewpoint on a clear day and identifying the peaks and, if possible, familiarizing himself with the direction of the various valleys and watersheds. Such knowledge may be invaluable in mist. A practical way of showing appreciation of the cairns which have been erected along many of the routes is to *add another stone*.

The routes described in this book are all well within the powers of the average walker, and in clear weather are free from danger, but the novice would be well advised to keep to the beaten tracks and to gain experience before attempting routes or climbs which may be beyond his powers of endurance. The greatest danger is from mist. If overtaken suddenly, it is best to remain still for a while, for the mist may pass as quickly as it came. Needless to say, no actual climbing should be undertaken without experience, and then always with at least one companion. Finally, in view of a possible hold-up (owing to mist or sprained ankle, for instance), it is well always to keep some food in reserve. Chocolate and dates make an easily carried emergency ration.

HEIGHTS OF MOUNTAINS

With distances to summits from nearest centres

SNOWDON, 3,560 ft.
  Llanberis, 5 m.
  Capel Curig, 9 m.
  Pen-y-Gwryd, 5 m.
  Beddgelert, 6½ m.
  South Snowdon
    (Rhyd ddu), 3½ m.
  Snowdon Ranger, 3½ m.

CARNEDD LLEWELYN, 3,484 ft.
  Aber, 7 m.
  Bethesda, 4 m.

CARNEDD DAFYDD, 3,426 ft.
  Aber, 9 m.
  Bethesda, 5 m.

GLYDER FAWR, 3,278 ft.
  Pen-y-Gwryd, 2 m.

GLYDER FACH, 3,262 ft.
  Pen-y-Gwryd, 2¼ m.

Y GARN, 3,107 ft.
  Llanberis, 4 m.

Y FOEL FRAS, 3,094 ft.
  Aber, 5 m.
  Bethesda, 5 m.

TRYFAN, 3,010 ft.
  Capel Curig, 5 m.

CADER IDRIS, 2,927 ft.

MOEL SIABOD, 2,860 ft.
  Capel Curig, 2 m.

ARENIG FAWR, 2,800 ft.

MOEL PERFIDD, 2,750 ft.
  Bethesda, 3½ m.

PEN HELIG, 2,731 ft.
  Capel Curig, 4 m.

PENLLITHRIG-Y-WRACH,
    2,621 ft.
  Capel Curig, 3 m.

MOEL HEBOG, 2,566 ft.
  Beddgelert, 2½ m.

CARNEDD GOCH, 2,301 ft.
  Nantlle Station, 4 m.

CNICHT, 2,285 ft.
  Beddgelert, 5 m.

The Welsh Language

Numerous grammars and dictionaries exist to aid the holiday student. Pronunciation becomes easier if certain rules are observed. With the exception of *y* every character has a constant sound, which it retains in every variety of combination, and no letter is ever mute, although it may be so rapidly passed over that the untrained ear may fail to catch it. The accentuation, too, is governed by one general rule, which is this: all words of more than one syllable have the accent on the last syllable but one, excepting only a few instances, in which the last syllable, being either aspirated or circumflexed, takes the accent.

It should be noted that the initial letters of certain Welsh words are changed (or mutated) when they follow certain other words or occupy a certain position in a sentence; thus *M* some-

13

times becomes *F*, so that Mawr (great) means the same as Fawr; and *C* sometimes becomes *G*, so that Croes (cross) means the same as Groes. The mutations most frequently met with in place-names are, *C* changed into *G*, *P* into *B*, *T* into *D*, *M* into *F* and *D* into *Dd*.

The pronunciation of most of the Welsh letters is more or less similar to their English pronunciation, but *f* takes the sound of *v* (the English *f* is *ff* in Welsh), *ch* resembles the Scottish *ch* in *loch*, *dd* has the sound of *th* in *thee* (not as in *thick*), while *ll* has no English equivalent. *Y*, in any other syllable except the last, is pronounced like the *u* in *but*, *chum*, *hunt*, etc., in the last, like *i* in *din* or *sin*. These two sounds are well exemplified by the word *sundry*, the *u* and *y* of which represent the *y* in its relative positions. When circumflexed, *y* is exactly the same as *ü*.

The following six letters are not found in the Welsh language: *J*, *K*, *Q*, *V*, *X* and *Z*. *J* is supplied by *si* or *i*. *K* is supplied by *c* or *ch*. *Q*, in words taken from other languages, is *e* preceded by *cw*, as Cwellyn—Quellyn. *X*, in foreign words having this letter, is indicated by *cs*, as *Ecsodus—Exodus*. *Z* is supplied by *s*.

Welsh Place-Names

Some knowledge of the meaning of a few Welsh place-names will add to the visitor's interest, for many of them are vividly descriptive; for example, Pwll-du is a black pool, and Careg-wen a white stone.

ABER, the place where a river discharges into the sea or into another river.

AFON, a river.

ALLT, a cliff, or side of a hill.

BACH (or FACH), little.

BANC, platform, tableland.

BECHAN (or FECHAN), small—the lesser.

BEDD, a grave (beddau, graves).

BLAEN, extremity or beginning: used as a prefix in the name of a place at the head of a valley.

BRON, the slope of a hill.

BRYN, a mound or hill.

BWLCH (or FWLCH), pass or gap.

BYCHAN (or FYCHAN), small—the lesser.

CAE, an enclosed field.

CAER (or GAER), a camp or fortress.

CANOL (or GANOL), the middle one.

CARN (or GARN), a prominence.

CAPEL (or GAPEL), a Chapel.

CASTELL, a castle or fortress.

CEFN, a ridge.

CELLI (or GELLI, sometimes GELLY), a grove or copse.

CIL, a recess or retreat.

COCH (or GOCH), red.

COED (or GOED), a wood.

CORS (or GORS), a bog or marshy place.

CRAIG (or GRAIG), a crag.
CROES (or GROES), a cross.
CRUG (or GRUG), a heap or mound (e.g. Crickhowell, or Crughywel).
CWM, valley.
CYMMER, a junction or confluence.
DIN (or DINAS), a town or hill fort.
DREF (or DRE), a dwelling-place or village.
DU (or DDU), black.
DWFR (or DŴR), water.
DYFFRYN, vale or valley.
EGLWYS, a church.
ESGAIR, a long ridge.
FACH, little.
FAEN, a stone.
FAES, a field.
FAN, a fence.
FAWR, great, large.
FELIN, mill.
FFORDD, way, road.
FFRID, a plantation.
FOEL, a bare hill.
FFYNNON, a well or spring.
FYNYDD, a mountain.
GAER, a camp or fortress.
GARTH, hill or headland.
GELLI, a grove or copse.
GLAN (or LAN) bank or shore.
GLAS (or LAS), blue (if water), green (if fields).
GLYN, a glen.
GOCH, red.
GOED, a wood.
GOITRE, a home in the wood (from Coed and Tre).
GRAIG, a crag.
GROES, a cross.
GWAITH, work.
GWAUN (or WAUN), a common or moor.
GWERN (or WERN), a swamp or bog.
GWYN (or WYN), white.
HAFOD, a summer dwelling: in olden times this signified a hill-residence used during the summer, in contrast to the main homestead, *Hendref* or *Hendre*, in the valley, occupied during the winter months.
HÊN, old.
HIR, long.
ISAF, lowest.
LLAN, primarily an enclosure; its secondary meaning is a sacred enclosure or church-yard—hence the present meaning, a church.
LLECH, a flat stone.
LLWYD, grey, sometimes venerable.
LLWYN, a grove.
LLYN, a lake.
LLYS, a court or hall.
MAEN (or FAEN), a stone.
MAES (or FAES), an open field, in contrast to a closed field, CAE.
MAN (or FAN), a place.
MAWR (or FAWR), great, large.
MELIN (or FELIN), a mill.
MERTHYR, a martyr.
MOEL (or FOEL), a bare hill.
MWYN, a mine, ore.
MYNACH, a monk.
MYNYDD (or FYNYDD), a mountain.
NANT, a brook.
NEUADD, a hall.
NEWYDD, new.
OGOF, a cave.
PANDY, a fulling-mill (used in wool manufacture).
PANT, a hollow place, a valley.
PEN, head, or top.
PISTYLL, a spouting waterfall.
PONT (or BONT), a bridge.
PORTH (or BORTH), a port or gate.
PWLL, a pool, pit, or hollow.
RHAIADR, waterfall or cataract (in English, often spelt Rhayader).
RHIW, a slope, or ascent.
RHOS, an open moor.
RHUDD, reddish.
RHYD, a ford.
RHYG, rye.
SARN, a causeway.
SYCH, dry.
TAL, a headland, brow of hill.
TIR (or DIR), land—soil.
TRE (or DRE), a dwelling-place or village.
TREF (or DREF), same as TRE.
TY (or DY), a house.
TYDDYN, tenement or small holding.
UCHAF, higher, highest.
UWCH, above.
WAUN, a common or moor.
WYN (WEN), white.
Y, YR, the, of the.
YN, YM, in.
YNYS, island.
YSTRAD, low flat land by a river.
YSTWYTH, winding, flexible.

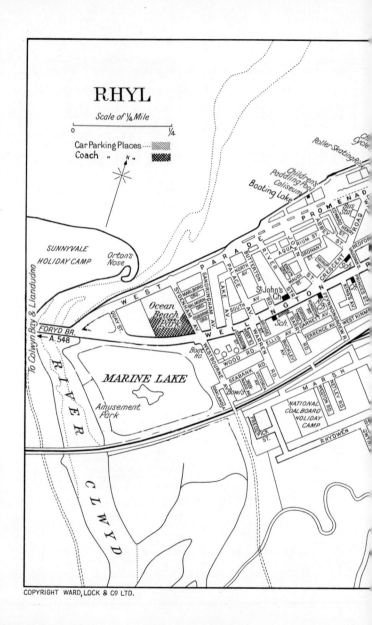

RHYL

Scale of ¼ Mile

0 ——————— ¼

Car Parking Places ----
Coach " "

N

Roller-Skating Rink

Children's
Paddling Pool
Coliseum
Boating Lake

SUNNYVALE
HOLIDAY CAMP

Orton's
Nose

P R O M E N A D E

Bus Stat.

Edward Henry St.

ABBEY ST.

GRONANT ST.

P A R A

BITTERTON AV.

A Q U A R I U M ST.

CRESCENT

MAUDE
ST.

BEDFO

SYDEN

LACE

MARLBORO
GRO.
ST. BALMORAL
GRO.
OSBORNE
GRO.

NORTH
AV.

St. John's
Ch.

KINGS AV.

PRINCES

WEST

QUAY ST.

Ocean
Beach
Park

SANDRINGHAM RD.

SOUTH
AV.

WELLINGTON

Sch.

BRIGHTON

PLYNMONYDD AV.

GARNETT AV.

WEST KINMK

S I D N E Y   A V E.

WARREN

ELLIS
AV.

BRICKLEY
RD.

TERRENCE AV.

KINMEL

R

To Colwyn Bay & Llandudno

FORYD BR.

A.548

Boat
Ho.

WESTBOURNE AV.

WOOD RD.

VICTORIA RD.

M A R S H

NETLEY RD.

MISSION RD.

R I V E R

MARINE LAKE

Amusement
Park

Bow's

SEABANK AV.

MARSH RD.

GARLAND

OAKLAND

NATIONAL
COALBOARD
HOLIDAY
CAMP

FREDERICK
ST.

RHYDWEN

GWIN

D

C L W Y D

COPYRIGHT WARD, LOCK & Cº LTD.

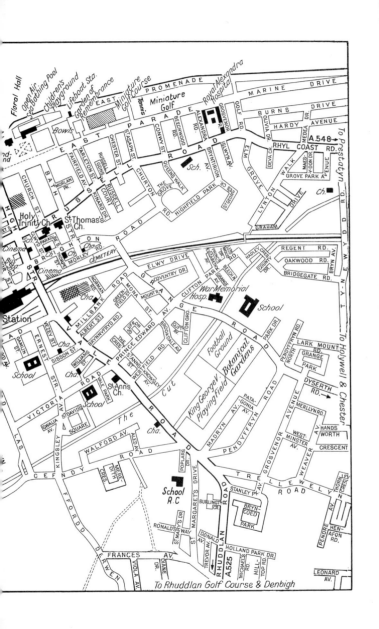

Rhyl

Access.—All express trains call at Rhyl. There are through carriages from the principal towns. By the fast trains the run from Chester takes only 40 minutes; from Liverpool about 1½ hours; from Manchester, 1½; from Birmingham, 3; and from London (Euston), about 3½ hours.
Road routes.—See p. 8.

Amusements.—Bathing, boating, fishing, bowls, tennis, golf; concerts, band and theatrical performances, cinemas, a model yacht lake, paddling pool, large amusement parks, coach tours, Sports Centre.

Banks.—*Barclays; National Westminster; Lloyds; Midland; Trustee Savings.*

Baths.—Open-Air Swimming Pool, near the Pier, is open daily during the season, including Sunday, from 10 a.m. to 8 p.m. Indoor Pool.

Boating.—On the Marine Lake, consisting of 40 acres of open water, there is perfectly safe boating, for the maximum depth is 4 feet.

Bowls.—Public crown greens on the Promenade east of pier and in the Botanical Gardens, Grange Road, Weekly tournaments. The Rhyl Bowling Club greens are in Seabank Road.

Buses between Rhyl and Rhuddlan, Bodelwyddan, St. Asaph, Abergele, Betws, Denbigh, St. George, Kinmel, Prestatyn, Meliden, Dyserth, Holywell, Hawarden and Chester; also to Newmarket, Colwyn Bay and Llandudno.

Dances.—Dixieland Show Bar, Titos, and Downtown Club.

Distances.—Abergele, 6; Bangor, 30; Betws-y-Coed, 27; Bodelwyddan, 6; Cefn Rocks, 9; Chester, 30; Colwyn Bay, 12; Conwy, 16; Denbigh, 12; Dyserth Waterfall, 4; Gwrych Castle, 7; Holywell, 14; Kinmel Park, 6; Llandudno, 20; London, 211; Pantasaph, 12; Prestatyn, 3½; Rhuddlan, 3; Ruthin, 18; St. Asaph, 6.

Early Closing Day.—Thursday.

Fishing.—Good sport is obtained in the Clwyd and the Elwy. In the Clwyd, between the sea and Rhuddlan, fishing is free, except for salmon and trout, *see* below. A portion of the River Elwy beyond Rhuddlan is preserved by the Rhyl Angling Association (31 Sussex Street). Season, weekly and daily permits. Fishery Board licences necessary. Permits for a 2-mile stretch at Llanfairtalhaiarn, can be obtained from 31 Sussex Street. Permits to fish in the local Reservoirs: Llyn Aled (coarse fishing); Plas Ucha and Dolwen (trout) from Rhuddlan Borough Water Office, Russell Road, Rhyl. The sea-fishing from the pier and at the mouth of the River Clwyd provides good sport. Information from the Fishing Secretary, 31 Sussex Street.

Golf.—On the shore between Rhyl and Prestatyn is a 9-hole course of true seaside character, with a comfortable clubhouse. There is also an 18-hole course at Rhuddlan.

Hotels.—*Crescent*, Crescent Road; *The Grange*, East Parade; *Titos*, Marine Drive; *Morville*, East Parade; *Sandringham*, West Parade; *Palace*, West Parade; *Queens*, West Parade; *Westminster*, East Parade; *Ye Windsor*, Windsor Street; *Haven*, West Promenade; *Sunholme*, Marine Drive; *Panshanger*, West Parade; and many others.

Information Bureau.—Central Promenade.

Libraries.—Public Library in the Town Hall block of buildings, with a Reading Room and a Reference Room.

Newspapers.—*Rhyl Journal* (Wednesday).

Parking Places.—For coaches: Marine Lake, Greenfield Place. Car park- East Parade.

Places of Worship, with hours of Sunday services: *Trinity Parish Church*, Russell Road (Welsh services 11 and 6.30); *St. Thomas's*, Russell Road, 8, 11 and 6.30; *St. John's*, Wellington Road, 9.30 and 6.30; *St. Ann's*, Vale Road, 8, 11 and 6.30; *Roman Catholic*, Wellington Road, 8.30, 9.30, 12 and 7; *Presbyterian*, Princes Street, 11 and 6.30; *United Reformed*, Water Street, 11 and 6.30; *Baptist*, Sussex Street, 11 and 6.30; *Methodist*, Bath Street, 11 and 6.30; *English Presbyterian*, Kingsley Avenue, 10.30 and 6.30. Several Welsh churches.

Population.—About 23,000.
Post Office.—Chief Office is in Water Street. Open weekdays from 9 a.m. to 5.30 p.m. Bank Holidays, 9 to 12 noon.
Putting Greens on Promenade and in Botanical Gardens.
Roller Skating.—Open-air rink on the promenade.

Tennis.—Hard courts on Promenade, and in Botanical Gardens, Grange Road.
Theatres, etc.—*Gaiety Theatre, Coliseum*, on the Promenade; *Little Theatre*, Vale Road; two cinemas in High Street, *Astre Triple Cinema* in Brighton Road.

"Breezy, Bracing Rhyl," and "Sunny Rhyl," as residents have good reason to call it, is one of the chief holiday places in the Principality, a position it has attained with almost startling suddenness. In 1820 the place consisted of only a few detached dwellings: almost exactly a century later, in 1921, the population was 13,398, and since then the number has grown to the neighbourhood of 23,000. Rhyl has become a resort appealing to a great variety of visitors, who in the aggregate exceed a million in the course of each season.

One of the chief recommendations of Rhyl to holiday-makers is its accessibility. It is but a short run from Manchester and Liverpool, and is the nearest seaside town to the manufacturing centres of the Midlands, while the excellent main-line train service makes it readily accessible to Londoners.

The Sands

Rhyl's beaches are magnificent. There are no cliffs to place young children in danger, but firm, smooth, golden sands, that extend for miles and form a veritable children's paradise; while young and old alike, who regard a daily dip as one of the chief pleasures of visits to the seaside, hold Rhyl beach in high esteem for the facilities it affords for safe and pleasant bathing.

At low tide when the water recedes a great way and the edge becomes shallow, swimmers have **The Open-Air Swimming Pool** on the Promenade. The Pool is 110 yards long and 30 yards wide. There is a Café and weekly Bathing Beauty contests are held throughout the season. There is also an Indoor Pool and Recreation Centre.

The Marine Drive and Promenade

extends along the entire front of the town from east to west, a

19

distance of some three miles. At the eastern end the road runs behind rock gardens and grassland, but the promenade continues along their seaward side.

The Promenades serve a double purpose, as is well seen when high tide and stormy weather coincide, for at such times the dash of the waves upon the wall is a splendid spectacle, watched often by great crowds. A feature of the Promenade is its unusual width, with attractions such as the Paddling Pool for children, a large Paddle Boat pool, a Children's Cycling Track and a line of trampolines.

Near the *Gaiety Theatre* is the open-air **Swimming Pool,** already described. Here, too, protected by glass-walled shelters, are bowling greens and tennis courts and a number of sunshine chalets.

An interesting attraction on the Promenade is the **Royal Floral Hall,** with its colourful collections of tropical plants and flowers.

The Foryd Bridge

(Foryd means the *Ford of the Sea*) spans the estuary of the River Clwyd, and carries the main road westward from Rhyl to **Kinmel Bay** and **Towyn,** with a number of holiday camps, and on to Colwyn Bay.

The bridge commands a view of a large portion of the **Vale of Clwyd,** through which the stream flows. This Vale, which has been described as "the Eden of Wales," is very extensive compared with the size of its river, being some 24 miles in length and from 5 to 7 miles in breadth, while the greatest width of the river is usually barely 10 yards. The banks, however, are low, and after heavy rain the swollen stream floods the adjacent lands and rolls onward to the sea with destructive force. In the Vale are the three towns of St. Asaph, Denbigh, and Ruthin. The first-named is the nearest to Rhyl, and the tower of its cathedral is one of the objects in the prospect from Foryd Bridge. A more conspicuous object is Rhuddlan Castle, to the left of the Cathedral, while to the right is the lofty spire of Bodelwyddan Church. Then away to the left again, and barely visible, are the scanty remains of Dyserth Castle, over which rises Newmarket Cop, famed for the view it commands, and for the great tumulus on its summit. To the right of the Cop are Moel Hiraddug and, farther away, Moel Fammau. The view from the bridge is finest at high tide, as then the estuary is full of water.

Just southward of the road that crosses Foryd Bridge is—

The Marine Lake

a sheet of ornamental water covering 40 acres, and having a safe depth of 4 feet. Here pleasant boating and yachting may be enjoyed in perfect safety, while there is a special boating pool for children. The ground around the lake is laid out as an amusement park.

Towards the eastern end of the Marine Parade is the **Royal Alexandra Hospital**. It was under the direct patronage of Queen Alexandra, who laid the foundation-stone in 1894, being then, of course, Princess of Wales. The late Duke of Westminster took a deep interest in the Hospital, and, in addition to other donations, gave to the building fund the Eclipse Stakes (£10,000), which he won with his horse "Flying Fox," a fact commemorated by the weather vane, which is a representation of a fox.

In Grange Road, east of Gladstone Bridge and the railway station, is another of Rhyl's recreation grounds—

The Botanical Gardens,

now developed by the home authorities and a favourite rendezvous for visitors and residents. There are eight acres of delightfully laid-out grounds, tennis courts, crown bowling green, putting, and a children's playground. There is a café and a car park.

As Rhyl is of quite modern growth there are no noble piles with historical associations or examples of ancient architecture. The town, however, is by no means destitute of notable buildings, prominent among which is—

St. Thomas's Church,

in Russell Road. It is a conspicuous building, in the Early English style, with accommodation for about 1,000. The tower is surmounted by a shingled spire, (203 feet high) and has a peal of eight bells. The church was designed by Sir Gilbert Scott, and was erected mainly through the exertions of the Venerable Archdeacon Morgan, the first Vicar of Rhyl.

Westward of St. Thomas's, and actually sharing the same churchyard, is **Trinity Church**—the parish church of Rhyl. The services here are in Welsh.

At the junction of Queen Street and Wellington Road, and, therefore, in the centre of the town, is an important block of buildings comprising the **Town Hall** and **Public Library.**

The erection of the Library was facilitated by a gift from the late Andrew Carnegie. It includes news and magazine rooms, a splendid reference library, and a well-equipped lending library.

In Wellington Road is **St. John's Church,** of unusual design incorporating a central dome.

PRESTATYN

Banks.—*Barclays; Midland; National Westminster; Trustee Savings; Williams and Glyns*—all situated in the High Street.

Bathing and Swimming.—Royal Lido Outdoor Heated Swimming Pool (Summer season); Pontin's Indoor Heated Swimming Pool (open to general public in winter); Sea bathing at Ffrith, Central and Barkby Beaches.

Bowling Greens.—Bryn Newydd; Coronation Gardens; Highbury Avenue, and Roundwood, Meliden.

Car Parks.—Council Offices (rear); Kings Avenue (adjacent to Head Post Office); Fern Avenue, High Street, Victoria Avenue; Station Road; Lower High Street (rear of Railway Hotel). Also extensive accommodation in all beach areas.

Early Closing Day.—Prestatyn, Thursday; Meliden, Wednesday.

Entertainments.—Dancing, Cabaret, Concerts; Competitions throughout the season at the Royal Lido, Central Beach Cinema/Arts Centre; Scala, High Street.

Golf.—Prestatyn Golf Course (18 holes); St. Melyd Golf Course (9 holes); Ffrith Beach Golf Course (miniature 12 holes).

Hotels.—*Royal Victoria; Nant Hall, Grand; Prestatyn Holiday Camp, Bryn Gwalia, Pontin's Holiday Village; Presthaven Sands Holiday Centre.*

Places of Worship.—*Parish Church,* High Street; *Meliden Parish Church,* Meliden; *Roman Catholic Church of St. Peter and St. Francis,* Plas Avenue; *English Presbyterian,* Nant Hall Road, *English Methodist,* Trinity Church. Pendre Avenue; *English Methodist,* St; John's Church, Station Road; *United Reformed,* Victoria Road, *Rehoboth C.M. Church* (Welsh), High Street; *Bethel Methodist* (Welsh), High Street; *Welsh Congregational,* Victoria Avenue; *Horeb Methodist* (Welsh), Marine Road; *Mission Church* (Church in Wales), Victoria Road; *Holiday Camp R.C. Chapel,* Camp Entrance, Victoria Road; *Seion C.M. Church* (Welsh), Meliden; *Salem Methodist* (Welsh and English), Meliden.

Population.—15,000.

Post Offices.—Head Post Office, King's Avenue. Sub Post Offices at Marine Road; Meliden Village; Meliden Road; Victoria Road; Ffrith Beach.

Sailing.—Jetty and car and Boat Park, Barkby Beach.

Tennis.—Municipal Courts, Gronant Road.

Prestatyn is a popular family resort, situated four miles east of Rhyl at the head of the Vale of Clwyd and within easy travelling distance of the industrial areas of Lancashire and the Midlands. The town has long been popular with visitors from these areas, and in recent years has attracted holiday makers from further afield with its numerous attractions and entertainments for young and old alike. The three sandy beaches have patrolled bathing areas for safe swimming, and are linked to each other by a promenade, with a miniature railway running between Ffrith and

Central Beaches. Ffrith Beach has a large amusement area, which includes motor boat and canoe pools, a miniature golf course, go-karts, astroglide, a supervised continental play area, round-abouts, etc., and also has two large self-catering tea pavilions which are available for hire to parties visiting Prestatyn. There are also a number of amusements at Central Beach, as well as the Royal Lido, a large complex housing cafés, restaurants, bars, a swimming pool, and the recently modernised ballroom where entertainments are presented every night of the week. The newly developed Barkby Beach is ideal for the sailing enthusiast with its jetty and car and boat park, and also to be found there is one of the most pleasantly situated picnic sites in North Wales.

The hills overlooking the town centre offer quite a number of interesting and attractive walks through the surrounding country-side, and also round the Nature Trail, within the town's bound-aries. Prestatyn is situated at the northern end of the Offa's Dyke Footpath, which closely follows the Dyke itself, along the bound-ary between England and Wales.

Historically, Prestatyn dates from Neolithic times, and many discoveries have been made in the area relating to this period. Other discoveries have also pointed to a Roman settlement, possibly connected with lead mining activities at Meliden, having been situated in the town. During the 11th Century a castle was built by Robert Banastre, a Norman baron, but during the following centuries, this was attacked on a number of occasions, and was finally destroyed in 1282 by Llewelyn, Prince of Wales. The foundations are situated in a field on the eastern outskirts of the town. Another important building in Prestatyn was the palace of the Bishops of St. Asaph, which was destroyed by Owain Glyndwr in the 15th century, and the site is now occupied by a farm.

The font in the Church of **Gwaenysgor,** rather more than a mile south-east of Prestatyn, resembles that of Lincoln Cathedral, and is one of the best specimens of Norman work in North Wales. The chalice is Elizabethan and is inscribed "The Cuppe of Gwaynisker." The registers date from 1538. They are the oldest in the diocese of St. Asaph.

Excursions from Rhyl and Prestatyn

This section deals with particulars of only those places within a few miles of Rhyl and Prestatyn. The index will guide the reader to information respecting those places which, like Conwy, Llandudno, Colwyn Bay, Betws-y-Coed and the summit of Snowdon, are easily accessible from this part of the coast, but are either more closely connected with other centres or are themselves important resorts.

As already noted, Rhyl stands at the mouth of **The Vale of Clwyd,** which is itself worth exploration. Approaching its interesting spots from the coast, we come first to—

RHUDDLAN,

a small town on the Clwyd, less than 3 miles from Rhyl by road, or 2½ miles by a path striking across the fields. (Hotels: *Castle, Marsh, New Inn.*) Its **Bridge** appears to have been either built or repaired in 1595 as the abutment of one of the arches bears the arms of the Bishop of St. Asaph at that time. Another ancient structure, known as the **Old Parliament House,** is in High Street. Upon it is inscribed:—

"This fragment is the remains of the building where King Edward the First held his Parliament, A.D. 1283, in which was passed the Statute of Rhuddlan, securing to the Principality of Wales its judicial rights and independence."

The statute was really a code of laws assimilating the Welsh laws with the laws of England.

Rhuddlan Castle

Open, *daily, charge.*

A castle was founded at Rhuddlan early in the tenth century by the Prince of North Wales, who made it his principal residence. It was taken and burnt in 1063 by Harold, the "Last of the Saxons". It was rebuilt by the Welsh, but, before the end of the eleventh century a new one of the motte and bailey type was erected by Robert of Rhuddlan, nephew of the Earl of Chester, by command of William the Conqueror.

More than half a century later it was retaken by the Welsh, and was alternately in the hands of the Welsh and of the English. After the defeat of Llewelyn, Edward I gave instructions for the erection of an entirely new castle a little to the north-west and this began in 1277.

The present castle is constructed of native red and yellow sandstone and is a rectangular building with a tower at each angle and two at the entrance gates. The present entrance, by way of an earthen ramp across the northern end of the moat, is a modern development, there having originally been no break at this point in the moat.

It was in Rhuddlan Castle that Edward succeeded in inducing the Welsh to acknowledge his infant son, born at Caernarvon, as Prince of Wales. The King's offer to the Welsh chieftains, to give them a prince born amongst them, who had never spoken a word of English and whose life had been irreproachable, is well known, as well as the Welshmen's acceptance of the offer in ignorance of its hidden meaning. The Castle was the birthplace of Edward's second child, the Princess Eleanor. In 1399 Richard II dined in the Castle, on his way to Flint, where Henry, Duke of Lancaster, by whom he was deposed, awaited him. During the Civil War the stronghold was garrisoned for the King, and, on being captured by a Parliamentary force, was dismantled.

Rhuddlan Marsh, which lies between Rhyl and Rhuddlan, was the scene in 795 of the utter defeat of the Welsh by the Saxon forces under Offa, King of Mercia. Such of the Welsh as escaped the sword were drowned by the returning tide, while the prisoners were put to cruel deaths, without regard to age or sex. In commemoration of this tragic event was composed the plaintive Welsh air of "Morfa Rhuddlan," which is supposed to express the weeping and wailing of the bereaved women.

Quite close to Rhuddlan Castle, and believed by many to be connected with it by a subterranean passage, is the **Old Banquet**

House. Also near the Castle, and reached by a short walk along the river bank, is **Abbot's Hill** (known locally as *Bonc Hill*), which commands a panoramic view of the surrounding country. It is said to be the site of an ancient stronghold. A quarter of a mile south-east is **Abbey** or **Plas-Newydd Farm,** on the site of an ancient Priory of Dominican friars. Remains of the Abbey form part of the outbuildings. The inscribed slabs of the Abbey are now preserved in Rhuddlan Church.

There are bus services from Rhyl, St. Asaph or Abergele which pass **Bodelwyddan Marble Church,** described on p. 56.

Bodrhyddan Hall lies 1½ miles eastward from Rhuddlan off the Dyserth road. The seventeenth-century manor house, home of Lord Langford, contains interesting portraits, armour, pistols and furniture (*open Tues and Thurs, June–Sept., 2–5.30, charge*).

Eastward from Bodrhyddan Hall is—

DYSERTH,

some 2½ miles from Rhuddlan, 3½ miles from Rhyl, *via* Gladstone Bridge. It is romantically situated, as its name signifies, on a very "steep" declivity commanding an extensive view, though the appearance of the hillside has been spoiled by mining.

The **Church,** which is quite ancient, contains a ninth-century cross, formerly in the churchyard, the pedestal of a cross which apparently belonged to the eleventh century, and a fine fifteenth-century "Jesse" window, one of the many traditional monastic relics found in Welsh churches, it being said to be part of the spoil of Basingwerk Abbey. Unfortunately, the lower panels, on which the patriarch was represented in a recumbent position, disappeared many years ago. In the churchyard are curious arched tombstones and old yew-trees.

Near the centre of the village is a **Waterfall,** formed by a stream from *Ffynnon Asaph,* or St. Asaph's Well, in the adjoining parish of Cwm. It leaps down the face of a limestone rock 40 feet in height. The amount of water discharged is about seven tons per minute. In former times the spring was in great repute for its sanctity and supposed healing properties, and was therefore the object of pilgrimages.

Dyserth Castle formerly stood on a rocky promontory about half a mile from the village. From the site there is a wide and delightful prospect. At the foot of the north side of the rock is the **Talargoch Leadmine,** which has been worked practically without cessation from the time of the Roman occupation until recent years. The excavations are of enormous extent and numbers of Roman coins have been found in the district.

In a field adjoining the Castle site on the south are the remains of a fifteenth-century **Manor-House** of a shape and size common in many parts of Ireland, but rare in Wales.

Proceeding up the Vale of Clwyd, we come to the village-city of—

ST. ASAPH

Some 5½ miles by road from Rhyl. Next to St. Davids, it is the smallest of cities, having a population a little over 2,200. It occupies a slight eminence between the rivers Clwyd and Elwy, and from the church built on the latter derives its Welsh name of Llanelwy, "the church on the Elwy." (Hotels: *Oriel House, Plas Elwy, Talardy, The White House*. Early Closing.—Thursday).

The city claims great antiquity in ecclesiastical history, its origin being due to Kentigern, better known as St. Mungo, first Bishop of Glasgow, who, having been driven from his see by persecution, fled for refuge to Wales, and on the pleasant site of St. Asaph built a monastery and a church about the year 560. Being recalled to his charge in his native country on the cessation of the persecution, he nominated a pious scholar, called Asa or Asaph, as his successor, after whom both the church and the place came to be named. In later days, the monastic church became the cathedral of the diocese.

St. Asaph Cathedral

Services.—*Sundays*—8.15, 11 and 3.30. *Weekdays*—7.40, 8 and 5.30.

Of the earliest building, or of those by which it was successively replaced during the first seven centuries of the history of the diocese, there are no remains, for, as was customary in those days, the first edifice was of wood, as were probably others which took its place. The oldest portions of the Cathedral are a doorway and other parts of the chancel. They are remnants of the Norman church, which was burnt to the ground by an English force during the invasion of Wales by Edward I. The work of rebuilding was undertaken by Bishop Anian II, who held the see from 1268 to 1293. In 1402 the Cathedral was burnt by Owen Glyndŵr. The Chancel lay in ruins until 1482, when it was repaired under Bishop Redman. The next great event in its history was its restoration, 1870–80, from designs by Sir Gilbert Scott, the beautiful reredos, the Bishop's throne and the pulpit being then added. More recently it has undergone extensive repair owing to a subsidence in the foundations of the Tower and the ravages of the death-watch beetle. New roof timbers have been placed in the North and South Transepts.

The Cathedral is the smallest of the ancient Cathedrals in England and Wales. Its principal dimensions are: extreme length, 182 feet; breadth of nave and aisles, 68 feet; length of transepts from north to south, 108 feet; height of central tower, 100 feet. It is a plain cruciform structure, chiefly in the Decorated style, but with Early English windows in the chancel. The principal feature of the exterior is the low square **Tower**. This is entered from the North Transept.

In the interior, the visitor should not fail to notice the **Stalls** in the chancel. They are specimens of the Perpendicular style, and the oldest portions are the work of Bishop Redman. The **East Window**, an example of the Decorated style shows scenes from the life of our Lord. It is a memorial of Bishop Carey (1830–1846) and Mary, his wife. The reredos is of Derbyshire alabaster. The two eastern windows on either side are in memory of Bishop Short (1846–70) and his wife. The middle window on the north, above the stalls, contains subjects suggested by the songs of Miriam and Deborah, and is a *Memorial of Mrs. Hemans*, the poetess, who is commemorated also by a tablet in the south aisle of the nave. Next to this window, representing Joshua and St. Paul, is a window in memory of Bishop Joshua Hughes (1870–89). On the south side the central window, "the Magdalene and Mary," is a memorial to Susan Maria Sisson, d. 1865, and the three-light window to the west, with scenes in our Lord's life, commemorates Dean Bonnor (1859–86).

The **South Transept** contains the *Lady Chapel* and a chantry chapel recently restored.

In the South Aisle are two ancient monuments: (1) a fine effigy, thought to be that of Bishop Anian (*see* p. 28); (2) a massive slab, probably fourteenth-century, of which the history is unknown. It has carved on it a shield bearing fleurs-de-lis and a lion rampant, with a sword passing diagonally underneath; also a hare chased by a hound.

In front of the Cathedral stands a handsome **Monument**, dating from the tercentenary commemoration of the translation of the Bible into Welsh by Dr. Morgan, who became Bishop of St. Asaph in 1601. It is an "Eleanor Cross," 30 feet high, with eight figures upon it, the chief being that of Bishop Morgan. The others represent scholars who assisted him. Against the west door of the Cathedral is the tomb of *Bishop Barrow* (d. 1680), with an inscription containing a request for the prayers of passers-by which was used in a lawsuit as evidence of the lawfulness of prayers for the dead.

To the west of the Cathedral is the Bishop's House. The Deanery is on the south side of the Cathedral. The Old Deanery, now a hotel, is about a quarter of a mile distant, on the west bank of the Elwy.

To the south-west of the Cathedral is the Chapter Room and *Cathedral Museum*. It contains several objects of interest, including one of the oldest of hornbooks; a copy of the Petition of the Seven Bishops to James II (the Bishop of St. Asaph was one of the signatories); the earliest edition of the New Testament in Welsh (1567); a "Breeches" Bible; a "Vinegar" Bible, three copies of the first Prayer Book of Edward VI, one of which belonged to Roger Ascham, Queen Elizabeth's tutor; a sealed Prayer Book (1662); a small bronze figure of a horse taken out of a grave at Gwaenysgor; a manuscript Lexicon in Welsh, Greek and Hebrew, made by the self-taught Dick of Aberdaron. (see below)

The *Breeches Bible*. published in 1579, is so called because Genesis iii 7 is rendered: "The eyes of them bothe were opened . . . and they sewed figge-tree leaves together and made themselves breeches."

In the same version there is also a curious rendering of Judges ix. 53, where it is said of Abimelech that a certain woman cast a piece of millstone upon his head and brake his "brain-pan."

The *Vinegar Bible* was printed at the Clarendon Press in 1717, and owes its name to the heading to Luke xx. being given as the Parable of the Vinegar (instead of Vineyard).

The **Parish Church**—dating from 1524—stands at the bottom of High Street. It is an ancient and beautiful building, mainly in the Perpendicular style and is a good example of the "Clwydian" type of church, consisting of two parallel aisles separated by an arcade. Local tradition connects the two aisles with the names of St. Kentigern and St. Asaph respectively.

In the south-west corner of the churchyard, near the road, is a stone with a Welsh inscription, marking the grave of the eccentric person named Richard Robert Jones, who became better known as **Dick of Aberdaron,** the village of Aberdaron, on the south coast of Caernarvonshire, being his birthplace. He acquired thirteen or fourteen languages, but could make no profitable use of them. He was always in great poverty, and used to parade the streets of Liverpool dirty and ragged, with some mutilated books under his arm. He was born in 1788, and died at St. Asaph in 1843.

About half a mile from the Cathedral is the house called *Rhyllon,* where Mrs. Hemans lived with her mother. Mrs. Hemans resided also at "Bronwylfa," between "Rhyllon" and St. Asaph, but that house has been pulled down and another bearing the same name has been erected on a neighbouring site.

South-eastward of St. Asaph are the villages of Tremeirchion (bus service) and Caerwys.

Near **Tremeirchion Church** is a house called *Brynbella,* built by Mrs. Piozzi, better known as Mrs. Thrale, the friend of Dr. Johnson. She was buried in a vault on the north side of the nave: there is a wall tablet near by.

On the road leading north along the hillside, at a mile from the village, is **St. Beuno's College,** built in 1848 for theological students of the Jesuit order. On the way will be seen *Capel y Craig*, a tiny chapel of striking beauty, looking out over the valley from the summit of a great rock. It stands on the college estate and was built in 1866 to the plans of a church student who had been an architect. Dedicated to the Virgin Mary, it sustains a tradition expressed by St. Mary's Well at Cefn (*see* below) and other ancient shrines in North Wales. In the entrance court of the college stands a fourteenth-century cross acquired from the churchyard of Tremeirchion.

In the reverse direction, at the south end of the village, is *Ffynnon Beuno*, an ancient well dedicated to the uncle of St. Winefride and patron of the college (*see* under Holywell, p. 39).

Caerwys, 3 miles eastward, though now an insignificant place, was originally the site of a Roman station. Near it are beautiful woods, through which visitors usually walk when approaching Caerwys by way of the ancient village of **Bodfari,** which stands nearer the river, and also farther south.

Cefn Rocks and Caves. In the bend of the Elwy some 2½ miles southwest of St. Asaph are the **Cefn Rocks,** with caves which have yielded articles left by primitive man, and bones of the bear, bison, reindeer, hyaena and other animals not now existing in the British Isles. The caves are approached by terraced and zigzag paths up the face of the cliffs, and are open to visitors daily from April to September, free of charge. There is nothing to see, and the caves are of interest only on account of what was found in them, but the view from their vicinity is charming. The caves may be visited in the course of a delightful motor run through hilly wooded lanes. From St. Asaph take the lower road to Denbigh and at the sharp bend at end of town turn up the lane on right, keeping to left at fork in a quarter of a mile. Soon after passing the modern church of Cefn, on the right, the road turns sharp to left, and at a farm soon after to the right. The path to the caves begins at gate on left about 200 yards down the hill.

To continue the ride, follow road down through woods, over bridge and then up to left, with lovely views across the valley. The first turning on left leads back to the Denbigh main road, or one can continue to Henllan and Denbigh.

It is worth while, however, to strike westward from Henllan along the Llansannan road and then to turn off on left by one of the lanes crossing to the Denbigh-Pentrefoelas road—charming country on the edge of wild moorland with grand views of the distant mountain.

Trefnant, about 2½ miles south of St. Asaph, is notable for a handsome memorial church in the Decorated style, erected in 1855.

St. Mary's Well. Less than a mile below the Cefn Caves is St. Mary's Well, or Ffynnon Fair, in a field by the side of the Elwy, at a spot about two miles from St. Asaph Cathedral. In olden days the well was accounted holy, and was used for baptismal purposes. It was also at one time noted for the clandestine marriages performed in the chapel above. This chapel was very like that of St. Winefride at Holywell. Only the main walls are now standing, but the stonework of the well is still perfect.

DENBIGH

Banks.—*Barclays*, Hall Square; *Midland*, Vale Street; *National Westminster*, Vale Street.

Distances.—Betws-y-Coed, 24; Mold, 16; Ruthin, 8; St. Asaph, 6; London, 203.

Early Closing Day.—Thursday.

Golf.—Denbigh Golf Club (9-hole course), one mile from town centre.

Hotels.—*The Bull; Crown; Yeoman; Hawk and Buckle.*

Library.—Public Library, open 10–7; Thursdays, 10–1; Saturdays, 9–12.

Market Days.—Wednesday. Livestock on second Tuesday of month.

Population.—8,420.

Post Office.—Head Office in High Street.

Denbigh is an important market town in a pleasant situation in the centre of the Vale of Clwyd, 12 miles from Rhyl by road and about 30 miles from Chester via Mold. To lovers of historic sites, it is of great interest and it is equally delightful to those who enjoy fine scenery, for the surroundings are of great rural beauty. The town is attractive also to anglers, being in the centre of good fishing in the Clwyd ($1\frac{1}{2}$ miles), the Elwy ($4\frac{1}{2}$ miles) and their tributaries. Stretches of the rivers are under the control of the Dee and Clwyd Fishery Board.

Trout fishing is also available on other stretches of the rivers, but permission must be obtained.

The prosperity of this town depends upon the trades and industries ancillary to agriculture and the frequent markets, fairs and sales of stock. There is, however, a large new industrial development. Schools include a comprehensive school, the well-known Howell's School (girls) and the Brigidine Convent School for Girls.

Denbigh Castle

(Open daily from 9.30, Sundays from 2. Charge.)

Prominent for miles around are the ruins which crown the steep hill under which the town of Denbigh nestles, and in turn the ruins afford splendid views of the Vale of Clwyd and its enclosing hills. There are several ways from the High Street, Bull Lane, Temple Bar Steps and Love Lane.

When in the course of his contest with Edward I, Llewelyn, Prince of Wales, had been surprised and slain near Builth, his brother David regarded himself as the sovereign of the Welsh, and summoned the chieftains to a consultation at Denbigh, at that time a small hill fortress. It was resolved

Esplanade Gardens, Rhyl

At Llandudno

Llandudno from the Cable Cars

The Esplanade, Llandudno

to continue the war, but the capture of David and the complete subjugation of the Welsh soon followed. Then Denbigh was granted by King Edward to the Earl of Lincoln, who surrounded the town with a wall, and commenced the building of the Castle in 1282. When complete, the Castle was an extensive and superb structure, largely formed by grouting—that is, two parallel walls were built, and the space between them was filled with a mixture of stones and hot mortar. When the mass had become thoroughly dry, it was like a solid rock.

After the death of the Earl of Lincoln, the Castle became the possession of a succession of courtiers, including Hugh de Spencer, one of the unworthy favourites of Edward II; Roger Mortimer, Earl of March, the paramour of Edward II's consort, Queen Isabella; and Henry Percy—"Hotspur." It was besieged, captured and re-captured by the Lancastrian and Yorkists during the Wars of the Roses. Before this, the town had been partly burned during the wars of Owen Glyndŵr.

In 1643 the Castle was fortified and garrisoned by Col. William Salusbury, at the command of Charles I. In September 1645 Charles I retreated to the Castle after his defeat at Rowton Moor near Chester, but after three days left for Chirk and the Midlands, leaving the garrison at the Castle. Later that year they were besieged by the Parliamentarians under General Mytton who, after many skirmishes, realized that his cannon fire was of little use against the Castle, and decided to starve out the garrison. This plan succeeded. Mytton and Salusbury, however, were old friends, and arranged honourable terms of capitulation, the brave defenders marching out with colours flying.

Denbigh Castle was one of the last Welsh castles to hold out for Charles I. It was dismantled in 1660, and the ruins left to decay. Extensive repair work has been carried out.

The boundary of the Castle is still marked by high walls and towers, most of them much ruined, though the entrance gateway and the adjoining tower are still imposing. The enclosed area is one great lawn.

Just inside the entrance to the Castle is a small **Museum**. The contents include Roman pottery, ancient tiles, cannon balls, coins, swords, pictures, an ancient map of Denbigh, and a model of the birthplace of the famous African traveller, Sir H. M. Stanley (originally John Rowlands).

Just below the entrance to the Castle is the tower of **St. Hilary's Church,** all that remains of an ancient garrison chapel probably erected before 1334 and which served as the town church for centuries.

A short distance from St. Hilary's is a portion of a building commonly called **Leicester's Church.** It dates from 1579, and consists mainly of a long wall, pierced for the windows. The Earl, it is said, intended the building for a cathedral, in place of St. Asaph's, but he died before it was completed. Afterwards the Earl of Essex when on his way to Ireland, borrowed the money raised for the work and neglected to return it. Just below the ruin is an entrance to the **Town Wall** (*admission charges as for Castle*).

In the lower part of the town are the ruins of the **Friary** of White Friars founded in the fourteenth century, and damaged by fire in 1898. The walls have been extensively repaired by the Department of the Environment.

Denbigh's **Parish Church**, dedicated to St. Marcella, is situated a little over a mile eastward of the town centre.

St. Marcella Church, generally known as *Eglwys Wen*, meaning Whitchurch, is in the Perpendicular style with two parallel aisles separated by light octagonal pillars. One interesting monument is a tomb with recumbent figures of Sir John Salusbury of Llewenni (ob. 1578) and his wife. It also contains a monumental brass representing Richard, the father of the famous Sir Hugh Myddelton, with Jane, his wife, kneeling at an altar with their nine sons and seven daughters behind them. It is also the burial-place of other worthies, including Humphrey Llwyd, the Welsh historian, and Thomas Edwards, the writer of witty dramatic "Interludes."

North of the town is **Plas Clough,** built more than three centuries ago by Sir Richard Clough, who assisted Sir Thomas Gresham to establish the Royal Exchange.

One and a half miles from Denbigh and yet forming part of the ancient borough is the lovely village of **Henllan.** The tower of the church is separate from the main building probably on account of weakness in the foundations. Alternatively the slight eminence on which it stands assisted the bells being heard for a greater distance.

About 4 miles due east of Denbigh is **Llangwyfan,** with a large sanatorium erected as part of a Welsh memorial to King Edward VII, the corresponding building being at Talgarth, in mid-Wales. Both establishments were opened by King George V in July, 1920.

At a distance of 7 or 8 miles slightly south of east from Denbigh rises **Moel Fammau** (pronounced *Vamma*), distinguished by the ruins of a lofty pyramidal mass of masonry erected to celebrate the Jubilee of George III and overthrown by a storm in 1862. It is the loftiest point of the Clwydian range of hills, extending from Rhyl to Ruthin, its elevation being 1,823 feet.

A short distance south-west of the castle is the white farmhouse, known as **Galch Hill,** notable as the birthplace of Sir Hugh Myddelton, the great engineer who supplied London with water by means of the New River, which he formed, with King James I as financial partner. In the dingle beyond, called *Dolhyfryd* (beautiful meadows), is a cottage having over its doorway lines attributed to Dr. Johnson, who visited the dwelling during his tour in Wales in 1774, but if the date below them is correct, it is evident either that Johnson is not the author, or that they were suggested by some other place.

Dr. Johnson, who was visiting his friend Mrs. Thrale at Brynbella, near Denbigh, was entertained at **Gwaenynog**, near by, then the seat of the Myddeltons, and he rambled in the neighbouring fields and woods, in which, as he records in his diary, he "delighted to stand and recite verses."

To commemorate his visit, Mr. Myddelton set up a monument in a field beyond the second of the cottages alluded to above, **Johnson's Cottage** as it is called. The memorial consists in part of a Grecian urn with the following inscription:—

"This spot was often dignified by the presence of Samuel Johnson, LL.D., whose moral writings, exactly conformable to the precepts of Christianity, gave ardour to Virtue and confidence to Truth."

It will be remembered that the Doctor did not appreciate the compliment. "Mr. Myddelton's intention," he wrote to Mrs. Thrale, "looks like an intention to bury me alive. I would as willingly see my friend, however benevolent and hospitable, quietly inurned. Let him think, for the present, of some more acceptable memorial."

In the corner of the wood, half a mile or more to the left of Gwaenynog, is **Segrwyd Hall**, the birthplace of Dr. Dolben, Bishop of Bangor in the reign of Elizabeth I. In the hollow between more distant hills is the beautifully situated little village of **Nantglyn** (5 miles from Denbigh), the birthplace of the surgeon, Edward Samwell, who went with Captain Cook on his first voyage round the world, and the burial-place of Dr. Owen Pughe, the grammarian.

Two miles or so south of Denbigh is **Llanrhaeadr,** one of several villages bearing a name which appears generic in Wales (the full name of this one being Llanrhaeadr-yn-Cinmerch). The principal objects of interest are the fine Jesse window and the chancel roof of its church. The window is of the sixteenth century. There is a tradition that it was purchased with the votive offerings of pilgrims to the Holy Well, Ffynnon St. Dyfnog, near the church. The well was in great repute for the cure of skin diseases.

For notes on the mountain road from Denbigh to **Pentre-foelas,** *see* p. 59.

Farther up the Vale of Clwyd, in the fairest of all its fair spots, is the ancient and quaint little town of—

RUTHIN

Ruthin is situated on the banks of the River Clwyd, 18 miles from Rhyl by road. (Hotels: *Castle, Wynnstay Arms, Eagles, London House, Ruthin Castle*.)

The heart of the town is **St. Peter's Square,** used for fairs on the first Tuesday in the month. On the south side the National Westminster Bank occupies what was formerly the **Courthouse** and prison. The building was erected in 1404, and furnished with a gallows, the whole of which has not even yet been removed, the end of a beam belonging to it being visible a couple of feet to the right of the westernmost dormer window, under the eaves. The last of the executions here, however, took place in the reign of Queen Elizabeth I, the victim being a Jesuit priest.

On the east side of the Square a building forming part of the Castle Hotel attracts attention by its singular architecture, there being on its roof dormer windows at three elevations. It dates from the fourteenth century, and was formerly the Myddelton Arms. On the north side of the Square iron gates are at the entrance to the churchyard, and adjoin the main **Post Office.**

On the west side of the Square, at its junction with Clwyd Street, is a fine old timbered structure, occupied by Barclays Bank. It and the adjacent house and shop were originally Exmewe Hall, built in 1500 by Thomas Exmewe, a wealthy London merchant, who, a few years later, became Lord Mayor of London. Its second tenant was Edward Goodman, a mercer, whose son Gabriel, born in it, became Dean of Westminster and a great benefactor to his native town. In front of the building is a rough block of limestone called **Maen Huail** (Huail's stone), on which King Arthur is said to have beheaded his rival in a love intrigue, Huail, brother of Gildas the historian.

Connecting with the Square at its south-western angle is **Castle Street,** leading to the Castle Lodge, and noted for its houses of ancient date. No. 1 was the birthplace, in 1560, of Dr. Parry, Bishop of St. Asaph, and translator of the Bible into Welsh, 1620, his version being still in use. The quaintest house, known as **Nantclwyd House,** has been the Judges' Lodgings for nearly a century.

From Castle Street one may pass by way of Record Street into **Well Street,** which, in the sixteenth and seventeenth centuries, contained the winter residences of the gentry holding estates in the vicinity of the town. It is the site of the *Wynnstay Arms Hotel,* known in other days as the Cross Foxes, and familiar to readers of *Wild Wales* as the inn where Borrow dined with his guide, John Jones, the poor weaver, who then for the first time tasted duck. No. 2, Well Street (the old Post Office), is one of the oldest buildings in the town. It was the only house that escaped destruction during Owen Glyndŵr's investment of the town in 1400.

Ruthin Castle

(Now a hotel well-known for its medieval banquets.)

The ancient Castle was founded, upon the site of an earlier stronghold, by King Edward I in 1281, and was granted by him to Reginald de Grey, Justiciar of Chester, in whose family it remained until the end of the fifteenth century. Its history has been comparatively uneventful. In the year 1400 it was unsuccessfully assailed by Owen Glyndŵr, who, pursuing an old quarrel with Lord de Grey, suddenly attacked Ruthin, sacked the town and fired it. During the Civil War the Castle was held for Charles I, but after a three months' siege in 1646 it was taken by the Parliamentarians, and was soon afterwards demolished. It remained a ruin for 180 years, and then its restoration was begun. On a portion of the site a castellated residence was erected in perfect harmony with the ancient work, the local red sandstone being used for the new building, as it had been for the old. The grounds are so interwoven with the fragments of towers and walls that a scene of exceeding loveliness and charm has been created.

Ruthin Castle was the seat of the late Colonel Cornwallis West, into whose possession it came through his descent, in the female line, from Sir Thomas Myddelton, Lord Mayor of London in 1613, who subsidised the publication of the first cheap Welsh Bible (*Y Bibl Coron*). He was a brother of Sir Hugh Myddelton of New River fame. The Castle is now in use as an hotel.

Ruthin Church

(Open daily 8 a.m. to 8 p.m.)

The Parish and Collegiate Church of St. Peter (Church in Wales—Anglican) was founded in 1310 by John de Gray "as a Collegiate Church for seven Regular Priests . . . which should henceforth be free from the jurisdiction of Llanrhudd and be the parish church of the Vil and Castle of Ruthin." The original Church consisted of the present North Aisle, with a Choir to the east of a central tower. The South Aisle was added c. 1350–60, and Ruthin Church was probably the original of the double-naved churches of Dyffryn Clwyd. The older churches of the Vale, such as Llanrhudd and Derwen, were not so planned. The fine oak roof is the most interesting feature of the church. That of the north aisle, dating from about 1508, and presented by Henry VII, is divided into 500 carved panels, no two being alike. It has recently been restored. In a recess of the north wall of the Chancel is a bust of Dr Gabriel Goodman, a duplicate of which can be seen in Westminster Abbey, where he was Dean from 1560–1601. On the wall of the north aisle is a portrait brass of his father, Edward Goodman, Mercer, died 1560, and another of him with his wife, their three sons and five daughters. The church was restored c. 1859, when the Spire was added to the tower, and the pitched roof placed over the nave. There are eight bells, and the Curfew is rung at 8 p.m.

North of the church are the old **Cloisters,** until recently the home of the incumbent, who is known as the Warden of Ruthin owing to the reinstitution by Dean Goodman of the wardenship in connection with **Christ's Hospital** which he refounded. Its buildings consist of twelve cottages at the east end of the church.

The Dean also founded the **Grammar School,** which originally occupied the buildings on the north side of the church, now used for church and community purposes. **Ruthin School**—a Public School for Boys—now occupies imposing buildings on a beautiful site on the Mold Road.

Llanrhydd, about a mile eastward, has the ancient church of *S. Mougan,* with many interesting features, especially its oak screen and a monument to John and Jane Thelwall (1586) and their ten sons and four daughters; those who predeceased their parents each carry a skull. The church has recently been restored. On the north side is *Plas Llanrhydd,* formerly the residence of the late Mr. Stanley J. Weyman, the novelist. **Pool Park,** a former residence of Lord Bagot and now a hospital, about 2 miles west of Ruthin, contains a stone seat called the **Queen's Chair** (originally near an earthwork called the *Queen's Court*) and a **Celtic Monolith,** bearing Ogham characters on its edges and a Latin inscription on one of its sides.

Llanfair Dyffryn Clwyd, two miles south, has a handsome Parish Church, supposed to have been built in 1403, with a Jesus Chapel built and endowed in 1619 by Rice Williams, a verger of Westminster Abbey.

HOLYWELL AND PANTASAPH

Holywell is the turning-point of a motor trip of which the outer portion runs near to the coast for most of the way, and the homeward half passes over pleasant hills a few miles inland.

The coast road passes **Mostyn Hall,** the seat of Lord Mostyn, in whose family it has been from time immemorial. The Hall is famous for the Welsh relics it contains. Elsewhere the route swings abruptly from labour to leisure—there are several busy collieries, and along by **Gronant** and **Talacre** are camping-grounds and bungalow towns.

The return route passes **Newmarket Trelawnyd,** a village noted for its **Gop,** or Cop, an artificial mound, or cairn, 350 feet in diameter at the base and 46 feet high. It is the largest tumulus in North Wales. In 1889 it was explored and many skeletons and fragments of pottery belonging to the neolithic or polished stone age were taken from a cave under the mound.

Offa's Dyke, which starts near Prestatyn, passes on the east side of Newmarket Trelawnyd.

HOLYWELL

Banks.—*Barclays, Midland, National Westminster.*

Car Park.—At rear of town hall (free).

Distances.—Chester, 16½; Rhyl, 14.

Early Closing Day.—Wednesday.

Golf.—*The Holywell Golf Club* has a 9-hole course on Penyball Mountain 800 feet above sea-level.

Hotels.—*King's Head; Bell and Antelope* High Street.

Market Day.—Friday.

Population.—8,566.

Holywell is an ancient town deriving its name and its importance from the **Well of St. Winefride.**

For 1300 years the well has been a centre of pilgrimage. Several kings of England are said to have visited the well, which was the most famous in Europe during the Middle Ages. Richard I made a pilgrimage in 1189 and Henry V in 1416. The last English king to visit the well was James II in 1687. From all parts of Britain pilgrims have travelled to St. Winefride's Well to seek favours—many sick having claimed to be cured.

The spring was once the largest in the country, the volume of water varying from 2,400 to 3,000 gallons a minute. Mining operations in 1917 caused the source to be tapped, however, and the flow is now considerably less. The water never freezes, but remains at a constant temperature of 50° fah.

According to legend, there lived in the neighbourhood in the seventh century a young girl named Winefride. She was loved by Caradoc, a local chieftain's son, but she had determined to devote her life to the service of the church, and so refused him. One day Caradoc attempted to force her consent. She fled from him and he, catching up with her, struck off her head with his sword. Where the head fell a large spring of water burst from the ground and at the same time the ground opened and engulfed Caradoc. St. Winefride's head was then restored by the intervention of St. Bueno, and the girl lived to become Abbess of Gwytherin.

The basin in which the spring rises is in a crypt under **St. Winefride's Chapel.** This chapel is one of the most perfect examples of late fifteenth-century Perpendicular architecture. It was erected by Margaret, Countess of Richmond and Derby and mother of Henry VII. It took the place of the earlier well chapel which was then falling down. In the ceiling of the well crypt and on the corbels of the chapel above, are carved the arms and emblems of the Lady Margaret and of her husband, the Earl of Derby.

On the steps of the well is a fine reddish moss (*byssus iolithus*) which appears like splodges of blood.

The principal feast of St. Winefride is on June 22nd, which commemorates her martyrdom, while a second feast each year on November 3rd celebrates the anniversary of her natural death.

A service is held at the well every weekday at 11.30 a.m. from Whitsun to end of September.

Behind St. Winefride's Well is the **Parish Church,** a plain Georgian structure containing the "Gloch Bach" (little bell) and other interesting items. **St. Winefride's Church,** the Roman Catholic Church, is in Well Street, while nearby is **St. Winefride's Convent.**

In New Road is St. Winefride's Catholic Primary School, in the grounds of which is a large bronze statue of the Sacred Heart. On the opposite side of the road is a large Hospice for pilgrims run by the Sisters of Charity of St. Paul.

A charming retreat is afforded by the **Strand Woods,** which extend from Strand Walk nearly to the railway station, where remains of **Wat's Dyke** are visible. At the end of the wood a footpath leads to the ruins of **Basingwerk Abbey,** originally built about 1131. The house was Cistercian, and was founded by Ranulph, 2nd Earl of Chester, for a community of monks already settled here, probably attracted to the neighbourhood by the well of St. Winefride.

The Community was dissolved in 1535, and for many years the Abbey lay in utter ruin and neglect. Recently, however, it has been commendably restored by the Department of the Environment.

About 3 miles south-east of the town, by the high road, is **Halkyn Castle,** formerly one of the seats of the Duke of Westminster. Near the entrance lodge is a beautiful church erected by the late Duke.

On the coast, about 4½ miles south-east of Holywell, is the ancient town of **Flint,** with the ruins of its historic castle. Flint Castle stands on a slightly elevated rock between the railway and the sea. It is a bare and square ruin consisting of four towers, and appears to have been built by Edward I about 1275. Two unfortunate kings are associated with its history—Edward II and Richard II. The former welcomed his banished favourite, Piers Gaveston, within its walls, and outside them Bolingbroke, if we may believe Shakespeare, offered his mock homage to the latter.

In a field near Whitford, 3½ miles north-west of Holywell, is the **Maen Achwynfan**—the Stone of Lamentations, one of the finest wheel crosses in the kingdom. It is probably an early Christian monument.

Westward of Holywell, at a distance of 2½ miles by road and 1½ miles through the fields, is—

Pantasaph

a small village containing numerous Roman Catholic institutions, which have clustered around a church built by a former Earl and Countess of Denbigh and opened in 1852. The buildings comprise a Franciscan Monastery, and Convent with a Convalescent and Child-Home. Francis Thompson, author of *The Hound of Heaven* and other famous poems, at one time lived in this village.

The **Church** contains some fine wood carving and stained glass, and a beautiful canopied tomb with the recumbent effigy of the Earl of Denbigh who died in 1892. At the rear of the monastery is a fir-clad hill, known as **Mount Calvary,** with a winding path containing the Stations of the Cross and leading to the summit, where are a gigantic cross and the Chapel of the Sepulchre. At the foot of the hill a disused quarry has been transformed into a representation of the Grotto of Lourdes.

Hawarden

Admission.—The main drives of the Park (entrance by village gate) are open to visitors daily from dawn to dusk. No dogs. Cars and picnics are not allowed.

The Old Castle is open Saturdays, Sundays and Bank Holidays, 2 p.m.–5.30 p.m. from Easter until the end of September. Entrance by Leopold Gate, admission fee. Parties wishing to visit the Old Castle at other times should apply to the Park Keeper at the Village Lodge.

Rather more than ten miles from Holywell on the Chester road is **Hawarden** (pronounced *Harden*), with a pleasant park, the picturesque remains of an old castle and a church which, though simple, has much of the dignity of a miniature cathedral. The views from the Castle and the churchyard are good and extensive.

Little remains of the Old Castle except part of the Banqueting Hall and the huge circular Keep, which gives an impression of great strength. The Chapel, which is well preserved, can be seen by climbing the steps in the Keep.

Hawarden Church stands north of the village street on an eminence overlooking the Dee estuary. It has a central tower surmounted by a short spire, a nave and two aisles and a chancel which does not geometrically fit in with the nave. The west window, by Burne-Jones is a memorial of W. E. Gladstone, who lived at Hawarden for over fifty years. Note also the effigies in white marble of Mr. and Mrs. Gladstone, lying side by side, with guardian angel.

The ecclesiastical status of the Parish, which is the only Peculiar in Wales, and which has enjoyed this distinction since pre-Reformation days, was challenged in 1953 but was confirmed and established by the High Court in 1957.

St. Deiniol's Residential Library is a national memorial to the "Grand Old Man". The Library is exceptionally well-equipped and is visited by Readers from all over the world. Residence is available for thirty. Students with some bona fide object wishing to apply for residence should apply to the Warden quoting personal reference.

Colwyn Bay

Access.—Colwyn Bay is midway between Chester and Holyhead on the L.M.R. Line. Colwyn Bay is only 5½ miles from Llandudno, with which it is also connected by bus, and the coastal steamers calling at Llandudno are therefore convenient.
Road Route.—See p. 8.

Banks.—*Midland*, Conwy Road; *National Westminster*, Abergele Road, Station Road and Conwy Road; *Lloyds*, Conwy Road; *Barclays*, Conwy Road, and at Rhos; *Williams and Glynn's*, Conwy Road; *Trustee Savings*, Penrhyn Road.

Bathing.—Safe and pleasant bathing. The beach is of firm, sloping sand. Open-air swimming pool at Rhos.

Bowls.—Public greens in Eirias Park. At the Constitutional Club, Coed Pella Road, is a crown green open to visitors, and there are good public greens at Old Colwyn, Rhos-on-Sea and Mochdre.

Buses to and from Llandudno, Old Colwyn and Abergele, Lysfaen, Rhyl, Conwy, etc. Runabouts traverse the 3-mile Promenade during summer.

Clubs.—*Constitutional* (billiards, tennis and bowling, and reading-rooms open to visitors), Coed Pella Road; various Sports Clubs. *Rotary Club:* Lunch on Mondays at Hotel Metropole, Penrhyn Road. *British Legion*, Coed Pella Road.

Distances.—Abergele, 6½; Aber Waterfalls, 15; Betws-y-Coed, 20; Caernarvon, 30; Conwy, 6; Llandudno, 5; Marble Church, 11; Penmaenmawr, 10; Rhuddlan, 12; Rhyl, 12; Trefriw, 15.

Early Closing Day.—Wednesday (except July–August).

Entertainments.—Summer shows in Pier Pavilion and at Prince of Wales Theatre. There are cinemas. Dancing at the Pier Pavilion and at other halls and the principal hotels. Miniature railway. Harlequin Puppet Theatre. Welsh Mountain Zoo.

Fishing is good from the Pier Head or from boats, pollock and codling being taken from May to September and bass and plaice from June to October. The freshwater angler will not need to be reminded of the North Wales lakes and streams. Full particulars can be obtained at the Information Bureau, Abergele Road.

Golf.—At old Colwyn and Rhos-on-Sea.

Hotels.—*Colwyn Bay*, Promenade; *Colbourn*, West Promenade; *Edelweiss*, Lawson Road; *Commodore*, Conwy Road; *Norfolk*, Princes Drive; *Green Lawns*; Bay View Road; *Queens*, Old Colwyn; and many others.

Information Bureau.—Abergele Road.

Library (public).—Woodland Road.

Newspapers.—*North Wales Weekly News; North Wales Gazette; Colwyn Bay Review; Colwyn Bay Pioneer.*

Places of Worship.—For times of services, see local announcements.
St. Paul's (Parish Church), Abergele Road; *St. David's* (Welsh); *St. Andrew's* (English); *Union* (English), Abergele Road; *Methodist* (English), *St. John's*, Conwy Road and Nant-y-Glyn, Abergele Road; *St. Joseph's Roman Catholic Church*, Conwy Road; *Presbyterian* (English), Conwy Road; *Baptist* (English), Prince's Drive; *(Welsh)*, Abergele Road; *Llandrillo Parish Church; St. John's*, Old Colwyn; *Bryn-y-Maen Parish Church* (English); *Society of Friends*, Erskine Road; *Christian Science Reading Room*, Woodland Road. Besides the above English Churches there are several Welsh Chapels.

Population.—Including Rhos and Old Colwyn, 25,470.

Post Office.—Prince's Drive. Open weekdays, 9 a.m.–5.30 p.m., Saturdays 9 a.m.–1 p.m. Sub-offices at Abergele Road (near the Dingle), and the west end of Conwy Road. Also at Rhos and Old Colwyn.

Putting and Miniature Golf.—In Eirias Park there is a putting green and an interesting miniature golf course of 9 short holes.

Road Routes.—Running through the town from east to west, is the Chester-Conwy road, joining the great Holyhead road a mile short of Bangor. The Llandudno road leaves this road on the western borders of Colwyn Bay (about ¾ mile from Station Road and just past the junction with Prince's Drive), and less than half a mile farther west the Llanrwst road runs off to the left. Eastward the main thoroughfare leads to Abergele and Rhyl, with a turning just short of Old Colwyn which forms the mountain route to Llanrwst.

Tennis.—Public courts in Eirias Park and at Old Colwyn and Rhos-on-Sea. There are also several clubs at which visitors are welcome.

Zoo.—*Mountain Zoo and Botanical Gardens,* Upper Colwyn Bay.

Colwyn Bay is a rebuke to those who maintain that a resort can develop rapidly only at the expense of its appearance. Eighty years ago its site was occupied by a single building, then the mansion of Lady Erskine, now the Pwllycrochan. Today the beautiful bay is bordered by an attractive town with a resident population of over 25,000, and which has absorbed its more venerable neighbours, Llandrillo-yn-Rhos and Old Colwyn. The place is fresh with the bloom of youth, yet there is nothing immature about it, while its sands are hardly excelled for bathing, paddling or digging.

On the landward side the town is nearly surrounded by well-wooded hills, and another pleasant feature are the dells, or "dingles," to give them their local name, which run down to the seaside, and usually contain a brawling streamlet and small cascades.

The **Climate,** except in the upper parts, is slightly relaxing in summer, but is remarkably mild in winter, so that the town is increasing in favour as a resort for invalids during the coldest months of the year. The place has a small rainfall (claimed to be the lowest on the Welsh coast), a splendid sunshine record, and almost complete immunity from fog.

The Bay

after which the town is named sweeps gracefully round from **Penmaen Head,** on the east, to **Rhos-on-Sea,** on the north-west, from which there is a slighter curve to Little Orme's Head, projecting farther north and protecting Colwyn Bay from the gales which occasionally sweep the Irish Sea. The shore, nearly four miles in length, is formed of sand, with a gradual slope; and as the tide rises and falls gently, bathing is both safe and pleasant, and boating may be enjoyed without risk. The **Promenade** borders the beach for three miles, from Old Colwyn on the east to the far end of Rhos-on-Sea westward. It is furnished with seats, shelters and kiosks, and at Rhos on Sea concerts are given by popular entertainers or bands, or by one of the male voice choirs for which Wales is noted.

On the **Pier,** near the centre of the Bay, is a Pavilion used for dancing and other entertainments.

Towards the east end of the Promenade is the **Dingle,** a feature reminiscent of the Hampshire chines. It is a delightful little tree-shaded valley through which a stream brawls its way to the sea, alongside a path which connects Abergele Road with the Promenade. Adjoining the Dingle on the east is—

Eirias Park

the town's principal recreation ground, covering over 80 acres. In addition to several playing fields, amenities at the Park include a fine model yacht pond, tennis courts, bowling and putting greens, a miniature golf course, boating lake and beautiful rock gardens. There is also a restaurant and cafeteria, and as the Park is laid out on high ground the sea-views are unobstructed and it forms a very pleasant retreat.

The main business thoroughfare runs parallel with the railway and a few hundred yards inland of it. Its eastward section is known as the Abergele Road; westward it becomes the Conwy Road, the change taking place at the top of Station Road, another busy shopping thoroughfare leading not only to the station but to Prince's Drive, where are the **Post Office** and other buildings.

On the south side of the main thoroughfare at this point is Woodland Road, with the **Public Library.** A few yards eastward of this, in Abergele Road, is **St. Paul's Church,** a plain structure of stone, with a massive tower.

The **Civic Centre** to the east of Eirias Park is the headquarters of the new Colwyn District Council, covering Colwyn Bay, Abergele and parts of the former local rural districts, Old Colwyn, Rhos, and Llysfaen, all described later, and also **Mochdre,** an area of industrial development, on the high road to Conwy, and **Bryn-y-Maen,** to which a pleasant walk can be taken either through the Nant-y-Glyn Valley, or *via* the Four Crosses.

Near the centre of the town are the pretty **Queens Gardens.**

and close by are the handsome buildings of Rydal School and St. John's Methodist Church, with a tall spire, the most conspicuous in the town. In the next block of buildings is the Roman Catholic Church of St. Joseph. Between the two churches just named is Pwllycrochan Avenue, continued northward to the Promenade by Marine Road and leading southward to the beautiful—

Pwllycrochan Woods

which form part of the background of the town and are one of its most attractive features. Having been purchased by the local authority, they are freely open to all. They cover an area of from 40 to 50 acres and contain numerous paths with comfortable seats so placed as to command charming views. Facing north, the woods are a favourite retreat on hot sunny days.

Along the lower side of the woods runs the Old Highway, part of the old Chester and Holyhead stage-coach road, running westward past the Four Crosses to Mochdre and Conwy. The Four Crosses is the meeting-place of four roads at the western end of the woods, and was the sign of an ancient inn which stood there. For a walk commanding excellent views go uphill from the Four Crosses and bear left, into Pen-y-Bryn Road, which runs high above the town. The road runs eastward for nearly a mile and then swings back, downhill, to the Old Highway (*see* our plan) not far from—

Nant-y-Glyn Valley

of which the Dingle is the northern portion. The Valley is entered from Nant-y-Glyn Road (opposite the Dingle). It is the most sheltered spot in the whole district. Being entirely screened from north and east winds, it has a temperature so genial that sub-tropical plants are cultivated in it, and flourish in the open all the year round. A walk of about two miles up the valley leads to Bryn-y-Maen, a pretty upland hamlet with a handsome church, known as the "Cathedral of the Hills," the tower of which commands one of the finest panoramic views in the district.

Two miles south-east from Colwyn Bay, and often visited on the return by those who have explored the Nant-y-Glyn Valley to its end, is—

Conwy Castle

View from the Great Orme

The Conwy Valley

Swallow Falls, Betws-y-Coed

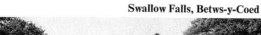

Llanelian

Llanelian Church stands 530 feet above sea-level. From its vicinity there is a good view, but the building is the main attraction. It is of the fifteenth century, and is said to have replaced one of much earlier date. The church has a spacious rood-loft, almost unique, and contains some very ancient paintings. At the east end is a modern carving of the Last Supper. In the churchyard are yew-trees of various ages. At the south-east corner is a quaint sundial, and by the south-east angle of the church is a tomb on which are coats of arms quartering the lion of Scotland, the leopards of England and the white heart of Richard II. It is supposed that he who was laid here to rest, one Thomas Holland, Esq., of Tierdan, who died in 1688, was a descendant of the first husband of Joan, "the fair maid of Kent," who became the wife of the Black Prince and the mother of Richard II.

No stone is left to mark the site of the **Cursing Well of St. Elian** which formerly brought great numbers of visitors, for it was destroyed by a rector to suppress the superstition it encouraged in his people. A tree overhangs the depression and is all that can be seen.

The well was greatly resorted to by persons from all parts of Britain. Even late in the nineteenth century it was visited by malicious people who desired to be avenged on their enemies. The name of the "devoted" person was written on paper, and a crooked pin was put through it. His or her initials were then written on a pebble, which was thrown into the well by the custodian, who, of course, had to be paid for the trouble. Then the enemy was supposed to be under a curse as long as the pebble remained in the water. To get it removed, the victim had to go to the well and pay a higher sum than that which was said to have been received for its immersion. The well was a terror throughout the Principality.

The Little Orme

is 3½ miles north-west of Colwyn Bay. It can be reached by buses which run between Colwyn Bay and Llandudno. The road route is along the Conwy Road as far as the Council School, and then to the right over the railway bridge, and past Llandrillo Church, 1½ miles from which, near the Little Orme, is the village of **Penrhynside**. A preferable route for walkers is along the shore or promenade past Rhos-on-Sea. The Little Orme affords magnificent views; but great care should be exercised, the seaward side being quite precipitous.

Between the Little Orme's Head and the village of Llanrhos are the Bodafon and Gloddaeth Hills, described in the excursions from Llandudno. The route from Colwyn Bay is by way of Llandrillo Church—the parish church of Rhos-on-Sea. Then, at a point where four roads meet, go to the left for a hundred yards, and at the cottage begin to ascend the **Bodafon Hills,** the summit of which will soon be reached.

Descending, and passing two or three cottages, the **Gloddaeth Hills** are reached at the site of an old mill, now used as a residence. The beautiful **Gloddaeth Woods** lie to the east of the house. By keeping a wall and the wood on the left, the visitor arrives at a point from which there is a delightful and extensive prospect.

Rhos-on-Sea

Access.—*See under* Colwyn Bay, p. 43.

Banks.—*Midland, National Westminster, Lloyds, Barclays.*

Buses to and from Llandudno and Colwyn Bay and Abergele.

Early Closing Day —Wednesday.

Golf.—The 18-hole course of the Rhos and Penrhyn Bay Club. Visitors can have rooms at the club-house. Sunday play.

Swimming Pool.—On Promenade.

Hotels.—*Rhos Abbey, Silver Howe, Meadowcroft,* all on Promenade; (*See also* Colwyn Bay).

Places of Worship.—*Llandrillo Parish Church* (English); *St. George's Church; United Reformed,* Colwyn Avenue; *Methodist* (English), Rhos Road.

Tennis.—Courts on the ground of the Colwyn Bay Cricket Club, and Rhos-on-Sea Tennis and Bowling Club.

Rhos-on-Sea, a suburb of Colwyn Bay, and under the same local government, is pleasantly situated on the western horn of the inlet from which the town takes its name. Wide streets and avenues have been laid out, and the fine Promenade and Marine Drive may be followed westward almost to the Little Orme or

eastward to the far end of Colwyn Bay. As the site projects into the sea, and is not crossed by the railway, the views over the bay on both sides, with the mountains in the background, are very charming.

The foreshore is rather stony, with good sand farther out, and many bathers prefer to swim in the Bay of Colwyn **Swimming Pool** and **Children's Paddling Pool** on the promenade.

A plaque on the roadside shows the site of the ancient Fish Weir, which consisted of a large number of stakes, so contrived that the fish which entered could not find their way out again. The water flows into the enclosure at every tide, and can escape only by a grating at one angle. Salmon, herring, mackerel, and other fish were caught, sometimes in large numbers.

The weir was first formed 700 years ago by the monks of the Cistercian Abbey at Conway, and confiscated at the Reformation. Before the weir fell into disuse the Vicar of the parish claimed and received a tithe of the fish caught. Those entrapped every tenth day were his, being hauled out by the sexton. In former times the proprietor insisted on the Vicar reading prayers at the weir three times during the fishing season, "as was customary on all sea-coasts in these parts when tithes of fish were paid."

The tithe paid to the Vicar used to be the due of the monastery.

The monks were accustomed to pray in the **Chapel of St. Trillo** for a good haul. This building covers a spring of water close to the shore, about a quarter of a mile westward of Rhos Abbey Hotel. It is a plain stone-roofed structure, 11 feet long by 8 feet wide, and with walls 2 feet thick. Services are held on the foreshore adjoining the diminutive building: H.C. Fridays, 8 a.m.

In the vicinity is Rhyd-y-Cerrig-Gwynion, where, according to tradition, Prince Madoc, son of Owen Gwynedd, embarked for the "New World" (Mexico) about 300 years before the time of Columbus.

The **Parish Church** (it is called Llandrillo Church, the Welsh name of the village being Llandrillo-yn-Rhos) is about three-quarters of a mile inland. It can be reached from the Promenade by Rhos Road, or from Marine Drive by Church Drive and Church Road. The building is mainly in the Perpendicular style, but its northern portion and the tower contain traces of Early English and Decorated work. The windows contain some very fine stained glass. On the north wall in the interior is a tombstone of the thirteenth or fourteenth century to

51

Ednyfed Fychan, Prime Minister to Llewelyn. The most noteworthy feature of the church is its massive square tower, with double-stepped battlements. The only other example of this in North Wales is at Llanbeblig. The lych-gate is dated 1677.

Westward of the church the 18-hole course of the **Rhos and Penrhyn Bay Golf Club** stretches toward the Little Orme.

A short distance from the church are the ivy-clad ruins of **Llys Euryn,** or **Ednyfed's Castle.** They are probably the remains of a fifteenth-century manor-house, which succeeded a castle inhabited in the thirteenth century by Ednyfed, whose tomb is in the Parish Church.

To the south of Llys Euryn is a grassy hill, called **Bryn Euryn,** in great favour with picnic parties. The summit (400 feet) shows traces of an ancient fortification and commands a wide view. At one's feet lies the whole length of the fertile Mochdre valley, and in the distance are the foothills of Snowdon. On the other side is the full sweep of the Bay from Penmaen Head to the Little Orme.

At the eastern end of Colwyn Bay is—

OLD COLWYN

Banks.—*Midland, National Westminster, Williams and Glynn's, Barclays.*

Bowling Green and Tennis Courts.—In Min-y-Don Park.

Buses to and from Colwyn Bay and Llandudno, Conwy, Llysfaen, Abergele, etc.

Golf.—9-hole course, open to visitors.

Places of Worship.—*St. Catherine's* (Parish Church, Welsh) English Services Sundays (except 2nd) and Saints' Days, 8 a.m.; *St. John's* (English); *United Reformed* (English); *Baptist* (English); *Methodist* (English); *Roman Catholic,* St. Augustine's Priory, Cliffe Road.

Old Colwyn, a village on the high road a little distance from the sea, is a pleasant, secluded resort, in favour with visitors who prefer a quiet place in which to spend a holiday. Indeed, its popularity has led to such developments that the adjectival prefix to the name is not only old but obsolete. As with Rhos-on-Sea, it is becoming difficult to say where Old Colwyn ends and Colwyn Bay begins—all three are for practical purposes one large town.

From its elevated site Old Colwyn commands a magnificent prospect, embracing the whole stretch of Colwyn Bay, Rhos-on-Sea, the Orme's Head, and several of the lofty heights of Caernarvonshire, whilst the hills at the back afford protection from east winds.

The principal public buildings in the village are **St. Catherine's Church,** a pretty edifice with a small tower, and **St. John's Church** for English services.

The shore is notable for its many kinds of marine life, and affords safe and pleasant bathing. Here is the eastern end of the fine promenade which skirts the Bay.

Behind the village is the **Fairy Glen,** a favourite resort of Old Colwyn's visitors. It is a picturesque, wooded dingle traversed by a stream which lower down accompanies the principal way down to the beach.

Also within a few minutes' walk of the centre of the village is a 9-hole **Golf Course,** laid out by James Braid. The course is excellently kept and commands glorious views.

A variety of pleasant walks may be taken among the neighbouring woods and hills. One of the most popular of these rambles is over the headland of **Penmaen-Rhos** to Llysfaen, a distance of a couple of miles. The road over the headland was much dreaded by travellers in olden days. It was narrow and unprotected, so that most travellers put their safety first by leading their horses over it. It was probably on Penmaen-Rhos that King Richard II was made prisoner, when on his way from Ireland to Flint Castle.

Llysfaen Hill, which rises 600 feet above the sea, is visited for the sake of the view. It was formerly one of the chain of semaphore stations from Holyhead to Liverpool, by means of which news of incoming vessels was conveyed. Note the grand view of the Great Orme, on which stood the next westward station.

Llysfaen Church (restored) is a good example of the two-aisled churches of this district. The present vestry was the original church. In the eleventh century there was added to it the portion which is now the north aisle. The remainder of the building belongs to the thirteenth century.

On the coast road is the village of **Llanddulas,** on the banks of the *Dulas*. Near at hand is a good beach of shingle and sand.

From Old Colwyn the coast road runs eastward through Llanddulas to Abergele and Pensarn, passing the long grey walls of—

Gwrych Castle

Open to the public daily (*fee*).

The Castle, was erected in 1815 on the historic pass of Jan-yr-Ogo in memory of the Lloyds of Gwrych. Later it became the home of the Earl and

Countess of Dundonald. It is now owned by Associated Pleasure Parks Ltd. Built on the site of an old fort, the front extends some 480 yards, and comprises 18 embattled towers, the principal one being 93 feet high. On each side of the Castle is a noble terrace about 420 yards in length. With its background of thickly wooded hills, Gwrych Castle is one of the most picturesque buildings in Wales.

The Castle contains many paintings, antiques and curios. Visitors are able to ascend the great Italian Marble Staircase with its fine wrought iron work.

From the Terrace Cafeteria is a magnificent view of the coastline. Additional attractions include a Miniature Railway, a Chamber of Horrors and various Exhibitions.

Outside the principal entrance there are tablets bearing some inscriptions relating to the "pass" at the foot of the cliff, along which lies, now as in olden days, the route between east and west.

They record the defeat of Harold, the "Last of the Saxons," by Gruffydd-ap-Llewelyn, Prince of North Wales; an attack upon Hugh Lupus, Earl of Chester, in the reign of William the Conqueror, by a band of Welshmen, of whom 1,100 were left dead upon the spot; the defeat of an English force in the reign of Henry II, by Owen Gwynedd, Prince of North Wales; and the capture of Richard II by the Earl of Northumberland, by whom he was placed in the power of the usurper, Henry, Duke of Lancaster.

A splendid view-point is the summit of **Cefn-yr-Ogof,** a hill containing (as the name denotes) several caverns. It has an elevation of 668 feet, and can be reached from the roadway skirting Gwrych Castle Park. The view includes St. Asaph, the Vale of Clwyd, Penmaenmawr Mountain, Carnedd Llewelyn, Penllithrig-y-Wrach, Tryfan, Moel Siabod, Anglesey and Puffin Island, and, in very clear weather, a sight of the Isle of Man and Liverpool.

Abergele

Banks.—*Barclays, Midland, National Westminster,* all in Market Street.
Early Closing Day.—Thursday.
Hotels.—*Bee,* Market Street; *Bull; Cambrian* (pension), Marine Road; *Yacht,* Marine Road; *Gwindy,* Market Street. *Harp,* Market Street; *Castle,* Water Street; *Hesketh Arms,* Bridge Street; *Penyboat,* Bridge Street.

Market Days.—Mondays and third Wednesdays of month.
Population.—12,560.
Post Office.—Market Street.
Places of Worship.—*St. Michael's (Parish) Church* (English)—8; *Abergele Methodist,* (English)—8; *Roman Catholic, St. Teresa's*—9.30. Several Welsh Chapels.

A pleasant market town, Abergele is about a mile from the sea, five miles westward of Rhyl and six miles eastward of Colwyn Bay. Between the two places there is an extensive stretch of sand providing safe bathing. Its suburb, **Pensarn,** is close to the sea and the railway station.

There is a good golf course on which there is Sunday play. Buses and coaches run to various places in the vicinity.

Abergele Church is of eighth-century foundation, the present building dating from the fifteenth century, with extensive nineteenth-century restorations. On the screen separating the nave from the chancel the date 1511 is carved. Another screen at the west end cuts off a portion wherein a school was held in the sixteenth century. The pillars are in places curiously indented, probably by archers, who used them as grindstones for their arrows or by workmen sharpening their tools.

Other objects of interest in the interior are a thirteenth-century stone cross in the floor within the Communion rails, "probably the coffin lid of an Abbott"; remnants of early glass in the vestry window; a wooden safe made of a single log of oak; and the Communion plate, which includes a chalice dated 1601.

A few yards past the Castle Hotel, at the head of Dundonald Avenue, is a passage leading to a footpath through Abergele churchyard. In the short length of wall on the right, on entering the burial-ground, is a modern tablet inscribed, "Here lieth a man who had his dwelling 3 miles to the north." The words were taken from an adjacent stone that had become illegible. Unless some mistake has been made, the inscription tends to prove that the sea has considerably encroached upon the land, for a spot three miles to the north of the grave is now two miles out at sea.

Less than a mile south-west from Abergele is **Castell Cawr,** the ancient British hill fort, standing on the highest point of the line of hills recently afforested above Tan-y-Gopa. It affords a fine view of the Vale of Clwyd. From the Junior School in the Colwyn Bay road, a field-path leads to a lane under the hill. By turning to the left on reaching the lane, one is led past a disused quarry to the remains of the ancient entrenchments.

From a field near to **Tower Hill,** crowned with an ancient watch-tower, there is a good view of Rhuddlan Marsh. The path to it is alongside the miniature river *Gele*.

Southward is **Moelfre Isaf,** which can be reached by a pleasant walk of 3½ miles. The best route is to the right of Tower Hill through Plas Uchaf Woods. Another way is along the St. Asaph Road for 1½ miles and then to the right. The summit is 1,038 feet above sea-level, and affords a delightful view of Snowdonia. The most conspicuous peak is Moel Siabod; to the right of that is Snowdon. The descent may be made to a road on the south, and the village of Llanfair-Talhaiarn reached in about an hour.

Abergele to St. George and Bodelwyddan

St. George is a small village, 2½ miles to the south-east of Abergele, and the site, tradition says, of the great conflict between St. George and the Dragon. In bygone days those who told the story sought to convince their hearers of its truth by pointing to the marks of the horse's hoofs on the coping stone of the church-yard wall.

According to another tradition, Oliver Cromwell was once at neighbouring **Kinmel Hall.** The original building was destroyed by fire in 1841. In 1936 the present building was converted into the famous "Rheuma Spa." It was requisitioned as a hospital during the war, and is now a girls' school.

Above the village is a wooded height locally known as **Fort Dinorben.** Upon it are the remains of extensive ancient British fortifications among which exhaustive excavations have been carried out.

Two miles from St. George is—

Bodelwyddan Marble Church

(Open daily.)

The elegant spire, 202 feet high, forms a landmark for miles around. The church is three miles south-west of Rhuddlan, and six miles by the direct road from Rhyl. It is a magnificent edifice, erected in 1856–60, at a cost defrayed by the Dowager Lady Willoughby de Broke, as a memorial of her husband. The church is dedicated to St. Margaret.

The material of the main portion of the fabric is hard limestone, quarried in the locality and rough or dressed according to position. It has much the same appearance as marble, and is apparently as unsullied as when fresh from the hands of the workers. The interior of the Nave is faced with Talacre cream-coloured stone, and in no part of the building is there any plastering. The nave piers have clustered shafts of Belgian red marble, while the capitals, richly carved with the passion flower and oak and ivy leaves, are in native stones, except the abacus, which is of Belgian red marble. There are also shafts of this marble in the spandrils above the piers. Each of the corbels on which these shafts rest is foliated, and exhibits a coronet with one of the letters of the name of Lord Willoughby de Broke.

The details in the Chancel are richer than those of the nave. Ogee crocketed canopies, rising from shafts and corbels, and projecting to form niches, run along the three sides. Alabaster, varied in tint, is used for the backs of the niches at the sides, Languedoc marble for shafts, and picked white alabaster for the capitals and corbels, the bases being Purbeck marble. The canopies here are of Caen stone, while those of the reredos are of alabaster. The chancel ceiling is formed into square panels by moulded ribs, with rosettes and bosses at the intersections. The roof principals are supported by beautiful "Griotte" marble.

The pavement of the church is composed of Irish black and rouge-royal marble polished, and Portland stone rubbed. The steps to the sanctuary, the chancel vestry, and the private entrance to the chancel are of polished Sicilian marble.

The **Font** is a block of Carrara marble that has been carved into the form of two girls holding a shell.

Bodelwyddan is within a few miles of **Rhuddlan, St. Asaph, Denbigh** and other places in the Vale of Rhuddlan (*see* p. 25–42). Motorists desirous of varying the return may either go by Rhuddlan to Rhyl and so back to Abergele by the coast road; or by turning up the Vale of Rhuddlan, by St. Asaph, to Denbigh, they can make a much longer return by way of the lonely but good moorland road from Denbigh to Pentrefoelas, whence one quickly drops down to Betws-y-Coed, and regains Colwyn Bay by Llanrwst and Glan Conwy.

ABERGELE TO LLANRWST

This is a pretty if in no way remarkable road, running for many miles through pleasant hills and agricultural land and with a surprising scarcity of villages. (*N.B.*—check petrol).

Llanfair-Talhaiarn is a small, straggling village, five miles nearly due south of Abergele, in a picturesque situation on the *Elwy*, a tributary of the Clwyd. The main road to it from Abergele ascends to a height of about 600 feet and then dips down to the bed of the River Elwy, which offers sport to anglers. Welshmen regard Llanfair-Talhaiarn with great interest, as the churchyard contains the grave of the Welsh bard Talhaiarn, whose memory is as fondly cherished by his countrymen as that of Burns is by Scotsmen. In the church are valuable pewter vessels, and a place of immersion, so that people can be baptized by being completely immersed.

Permits for fishing in a 1-mile stretch of water can be obtained from the *Black Lion Hotel*, or the Rhyl Anglers' Association.

The Bryn-y-Pin Pass

The Bryn-y-Pin Pass forms part of a popular motor tour through this locality. The sides of the rugged mountains are beautifully wooded, magnificent views are obtained, and the effects of a great landslip add further interest. The Pass is 7½ miles long. At the northern end is the *Cross Foxes* (once an inn), concerning which much interest has been aroused by coach proprietors and others associating it with Sir H. M. Stanley, but though it was at one time the home of his mother, the great traveller himself never lived in it.

Five miles south-west of Llanfair-Talhaiarn the Llanrwst road reaches the old town of **Llangerniew,** beyond which the road ascends to a point over a thousand feet above sea-level, passing on the way the pleasant residence called **Hafodunos** ("built in the night," or "a one night's rest"), now used as a Girls' School, and going through an avenue of *Araucaria imbricata*—"Monkey Puzzle" trees. The summit of the road commands beautiful views of mountain, vale and sea, and is the site of an old-fashioned Welsh inn, a solitary building, bearing on its signboard, as does also the *Holland Arms Hotel* in Llangerniew, the following quaint invitation—

> "As you venture here to pass this dreary mountain o'er
> Pray do take a refreshing glass of 'Cwrw da'[1] or porter:
> But if you wish to call for more, or like to have a ration,
> Coch-yr-Wden,[2] I have in store hanging o'er the kitchen floor
> Just ready for a luncheon."

Cwrw da, good beer.   [2] *Coch-yr-Wden,* hung venison.

The final two miles to Llanrwst are of great beauty owing to the fine view over the Conwy valley to the distant mountains; but motorists should heed the various warnings regarding gradients and turns.

DENBIGH TO PENTREFOELAS

The mountain road from Denbigh to Pentrefoelas (A543—17 miles) reaches a height of 1,523 feet, and passes over the hills known as **Mynydd Hiraethog,** a featureless group extending across Denbighshire from the Conwy to the Clwyd and forming an irregular platform of wild moorland from which there are magnificent views of Snowdonia. The highest point of the group, $3\frac{1}{2}$ miles north-east of Pentrefoelas, is 1,742 feet above the sea. From the road the Birkenhead and Rhyl reservoirs are well seen.

At **Pentrefoelas** the Holyhead road is joined and the scenery rapidly improves.

The way through **Betws-y-Coed** will be best understood by reference to the map on p. 106, but here we may remind motorists that unless the river is crossed the village is not seen. Those who do cross the bridge may pass through the village and should then cross the Llugwy by the old Pont-y-Pair. The road down the western side of the Conwy valley is followed as far as **Llanrwst,** where the charming old bridge carries one back to the eastern side. Thence the way is plain to the cross-roads at Glan Conwy, where take the right-hand road.

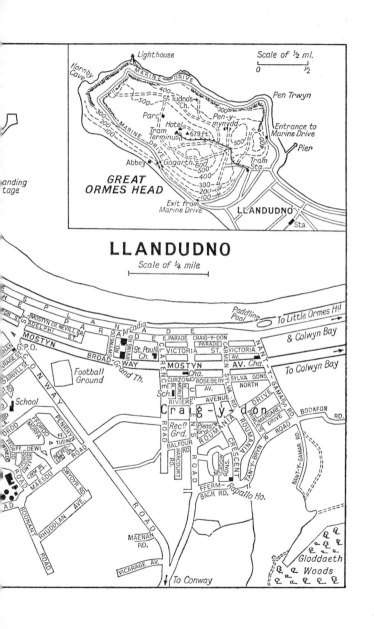

GREAT ORMES HEAD

Lighthouse

Hornby Cave

MARINE DRIVE

400

St Tudno's Ch.

500

Pen-y-mynydd

Pen Trwyn

Entrance to Marine Drive

300

Parc

Hotel

Tram Terminus

▲679 Ft.

500

400

Pier

MARINE DRIVE

300

200

100

Abbey

Gogarth

600

500

400

300

200

100

Tram Sta.

Exit from Marine Drive

LLANDUDNO

Sta.

Scale of ½ ml.

0   ½

LLANDUDNO

Scale of ¼ mile

anding tage

Paddling Pool

To Little Ormes Hd

& Colwyn Bay

THE   PLAS

Arcadia

DEGANWY RD.

CLARENCE RD.

E.PARADE

CRAIG-Y-DON PARADE

VICTORIA   ST.

VICTORIA AV.

To Colwyn Bay

MOSTYN CR. NEVILL GR.

ADELPHI ST.

G.P.O.

MOSTYN

BROAD   WAY

IRVING RD.

GWYNEDD RD.

St Paul's Ch.

CARMEN

SYLVA AV. Cha.

CONWAY

ARGYLL ST.

GARAGE ST.

Football Ground

Grand Th.

MOSTYN

Cha.

CURZON RD.

MORLEY

ROSEBERY AV.

SYLVA GDNS.

NORTH

GAMARI RD.

Sch.

RIVIERE

AVENUE

GLODDAETH AV.

MARGARET

DRIVE

BODAFON RD.

School

FFORDD MOIRA

PENRHYN

FF. TUDNO

BELVEDERE ROAD

Craig-y-don

Rec.n Grd.

Pleas.e Grd.

ROUMANIA ROAD

ROAD

CRESCENT

ROUMANIA

TAN-Y-BRYN

ROAD

NANT-Y-GAMAR RD.

FFORDD DEWI

CEFN FFOR

CADNANT

MAESDU

RHUDDLAN AVE.

BODNANT ROAD

BALFOUR ROAD

HARCOURT RD.

SNOWDON AV.

MOSTYN

FFERM-BACH RD.

Rapallo Ho.

MAENAN RD.

VICARAGE AV.

↓ To Conway

Gloddaeth Woods

Llandudno

Access.—(1) By the Chester and Holyhead line. (Passengers who are not in a through carriage change at Llandudno Junction.) Frequent through express trains—4 hours from London (Euston), 3 from Birmingham (New Street), 3 from Manchester (Exchange), 3 from Liverpool (Lime Street). Passengers from stations on the Western Region and North-Eastern Region lines change to the London Midland Region at Chester. (2) **By Road**—During the season coaches link Llandudno with the Midlands, London and the North. (3) By steamer from Liverpool (*see* p. 8).

Angling.—Excellent from Great Orme Rocks, and boats. Sea Angling Festivals are held in April and September. Salmon and trout in nearby rivers and mountain lakes.

Banks.—*Midland, Lloyds, National Westminster, Barclays, Williams and Glyn's, Trustee Savings,* all in Mostyn Street.

Bathing.—Bathing in the sea is quite safe. Indoor Swimming Pool, Mostyn Broadway.

Bowls.—Crown greens on the Sports Ground, The Oval, Gloddaeth Avenue, and at Craig-y-don.

Buses.—To and from Deganwy, Llandudno Junction, Conwy, Llanfairfechan, etc.; and up the Conway valley to Llanrwst and Betws-y-Coed. Eastward to Colwyn Bay Rhyl, etc. Great Orme bus service from the Town Hall, Lloyd Street, to St. Tudno's Church. Bus station and enquiry office, Clonmel Street.

Cinemas.—*Astra, Savoy.*

Coach Trips.—Tours available to all well-known beauty spots.

Concerts and Music.—Pier orchestra at the Pierhead Pavilion mornings and evenings. Town Band at the Promenade Bandstand each evening. Sunday concerts also at Pier Pavilion. Symphony orchestras, recitals and celebrity concerts.

Cricket.—The Oval cricket ground off Gloddaeth Avenue is one of the finest in North Wales. Fixtures are arranged by the *Llandudno Cricket Club.*

Dancing.—At the Café Royal and Winter Garden Ballrooms, and at many of the hotels.

Early Closing Day.—Wednesday.

Golf.—There are three 18-hole courses—*The Maesdu,* the *North Wales Links* and the residential *Rhos and Penrhyn Bay Club.* These are all within easy reach. The links of the *Caernarvonshire Golf Club,* on Conway Morfa, are also available. *See* under Deganwy, p. 83. *Rhos and Penrhyn Golf Club* (*see* p. 50). *Miniature Golf* near Arcadia in centre of bay and at The Happy Valley.

Distances.—Aber, 13; Abergele, 13; Bangor, 20; Beaumaris, 25; Bethesda, 23½; Betws-y-Coed, 19; Capel Curig, 24; Caernarvon, 27; Conwy, 4; Denbigh, 28½; Dolwyddelen, 24; Gloddaeth, 2; Liverpool, 67; Llanberis, 36; Llandulas, 11; Llandrilloyn-Rhos, 4; Llanfairfechan, 11; Llangelynin, 8; Llanrhos, 1½; Llanrwst, 14½; London, 227; Mochdre and Pabo, 5½; Menai Bridge, 20; Penmaenmawr, 8½; Penrhynside, 2½; Pen-y-Gwryd, 29; Pontypant, 23; Rhuddlan, 20½; Rhyl, 17; Ruthin, 35; Snowdon, 36; St. Asaph, 19; Trefriw, 15½.

Hotels.—*St. George's,* on Sea Front; *Imperial,* on Sea Front; *Marine,* on Sea Front; *Hydro,* Nevill Crescent; *Empire,* Church Walks; *Grand,* North Prom; *Gogarth Abbey,* West Shore; *North-Western,* Vaughan Street; *Queen's,* Promenade; *Royal,* Church Walks; *Clarence,* Gloddaeth Street; *Esplanade,* Promenade; *Warwick* (private), Church Walks; *Dorchester* (private), Promenade; and many others.

Information Centres.—Chapel Street; Promenade near Pier.

Library.—Public Library in Mostyn Street. Open weekdays. Lending and Reference Libraries, 10–7; Reading Room, 9–8.

Museum and Art Gallery.—Rapallo House, off Queens Road.

Newspapers.—*Llandudno Advertiser, North Wales Weely News* (Thurs.), *Herald of Wales* (Fri.). Evening Papers: *Liverpool Echo* and *Evening Express, Manchester Evening News* and *Chronicle.*

Parking Places.—The seaward side of the Parade, between South Parade, and Nant-y-Gamar Road, Craig-y-don, in North Parade, overlooking the Pier, in Gloddaeth Street, Lloyd Street, Back Madoc Street, and elsewhere in the town.

Places of Worship, with hours of service on Sundays.—**The Church in Wales.** The Parish Church of *St. George,* Church Walks—10 and 6.30; H.C. at 8.30 p.m.; *Church of Our Saviour,* Great Ormes Road, 8, 11 and 6.30; *Holy Trinity,* Trinity Square, 8, 11 and 6.30; *St. Tudno's Church,* on the Great Orme, Whitsun to Sept., 11 a.m. Open-air services in fine weather; *St. Paul's,* Craig-y-don, 8, 11 and 6.30; *St. Hilary's* and *St. Cystenin's* are the parish churches of Llanrhos and Llangwstenin. *United Reformed* (Welsh), Deganwy Avenue, 10.30 and 6; *(English) Christ Church,* Abbey Road, 11 and 6.30. **Baptist.** *(Welsh) Horeb,* Cromlech Road, Great Orme, 10.30 and 6; *Tabernacle,* Mostyn Street, 10 and 6; *(English)* at Rehoboth 11.15 and 6.45. **Methodist.** *(Welsh) Ebenezer,* Lloyd Street, 10 and 6; *(English) St. David's,* Mostyn Avenue; *St. John's,* Mostyn Street, both 11 and 6.30. **Presbyterian.** *(Welsh) Bethania,* Nant-y-Gamar Road, Craig-y-don; *Hyfryde,* St. Beuno's Road, Great Orme; *Rehoboth,* Trinity Avenue; *Sello,* Arvon Avenue, all 10.30 and 6. *(English)* Chapel Street, 11 and 6.30. **Roman Catholic.** Our Lady, Star of the Sea, Lloyd Street, 8, 9.30, 11 and 6.30; and, in summer, 7 a.m. **Jewish.** The Synagogue, Church Walks. **Christian Science.** First Church of Christ Scientist, Clarence Road, Craig-y-don, 11 and 6.30. **Christodelphians.** Mostyn Broadway, 10 and 6.30.

Police Station.—Oxford Road. Tel.: 76149.

Population.—About 19,000.

Post Office.—Vaughan Street, close to Station, Sub-offices in Gloddaeth Street, Queen's Road, Alexandra Road, and in Great Orme's Road, West Shore and Craig-y-don.

Putting and Miniature Golf.—In Happy Valley, Haulfre Gardens, on the Promenade and on the Great Orme.

Riding.—On the sands and surrounding countryside. Mounts may be hired locally.

Rotary Club.—Hydro Hotel, Promenade.

Sailing.—In North Bay; also with *Llandudno Sailing Club,* centred in Mostyn Broadway.

Schools and Colleges.—*Ysgol John Bright,* Oxford Road and Trinity Avenue; *Craig-y-don School,* Morley Road; *Dyffryn Road School; Great Orme School,* Llwynon Road; *Llandudno Junior and Infants,* Lloyd Street; *St. George's School,* Church Walks; *St. Beuno's School,* Great Orme; *St. David's College for Boys,* Gloddaeth Hall; *Ysgol Morfa Rhianedd Welsh School; Stella Maris Catholic School; Ysgol Gogarth School for Physically Handicapped Children; Lorete Middle School* (co-educational).

Steamer Trips to Isle of Man and to Liverpool. Also from Conwy Quay, motor launch up the Conwy River to Trefriw (*see* p. 95).

Swimming.—2 heated pools of varying depth. Sun bathing area, spectator area and a café.

Tennis.—Hard courts at Queen's Road Recreation Ground, hard and grass courts at the Oval.

Theatres.—Excellent summer shows at the Pier Pavilion, and at Arcadia. Open-air entertainment in Happy Valley, and stage plays at the Grand Theatre.

Youth Centre.—There is a thriving centre at the corner of Trinity Avenue and Caroline Road.

Llandudno, the most widely-known resort on the coast of North Wales, is situated on a narrow peninsula projecting into the Irish Sea, and terminating in the bold headland known as the Great Orme. Its principal sea-front borders the beautiful bay which sweeps eastward from the Great Orme to the Little Orme, but Llandudno is fortunate in the possession of another "front" which commands magnificent views across Conwy Bay to the Snowdonian mountains. In Llandudno Bay the water never goes far out, but Conwy Bay at low tide exhibits a considerable expanse of sand. The beach of the former is usually the more crowded; the sands of the West Shore (the more purely residential quarter) are ideal for children. When the wind blows from the west, there is shelter in Llandudno Bay; while the Ormes protect Conwy Bay to the north and east.

The name of the town is formed of two words, *Llan* and *Tudno*, the former signifying a consecrated enclosure, or church, the latter being the name of the saint to whom the old Parish Church was dedicated. St. Tudno was a saint of the Celtic Church and belonged to that period of the British Church famous for missionary zeal. He was the son of a chieftain of considerable power and wealth, who lived early in the sixth century, and was sometimes called *Seithenyn Feddw*—Seithenyn the Drunken—associated with the legendary drowned city of Cardigan Bay. St. Tudno founded his cell where St. Tudno's Church now stands.

In the middle of the nineteenth century Llandudno consisted only of a few scattered cottages and two small inns, but it was then on the eve of its wonderful development. Recognizing the possibilities of the site as a health and pleasure resort, the owner, the Hon. E. M. L. Mostyn, M.P., caused it to be planned on the lines of a first-class watering-place, and in 1849 plots to the number of 176 were offered for sale by auction. Then began that orderly piling up of bricks and mortar which has resulted in a town containing such an array of residences, blocks of buildings, hotels, boarding-houses, shops, etc., as cannot be surpassed in the Principality.

The town has grown rapidly, covering the plain between the two bays, and extending up the headlands. Eastward, it is now almost linked with Colwyn Bay. There are no shops or vendors on the promenade. Llandudno can accommodate 60,000 visitors, and as a holiday resort it becomes more popular every year. Usually the weather on this coast is mild in December, and those hotels which remain open make a special effort to provide seasonable entertainment for their guests.

There are also concerts and dancing, and Llandudno is fortunate in possessing two excellent amateur companies, The Llandudno Amateur Operatic Society and The Llandudno Musical Players.

During the summer and Christmas seasons, many hotels cater especially for children, providing play-rooms and nursery meals. Pets are welcomed at many hotels and there are Boarding Kennels nearby, at Llandudno Junction.

The geographical position of Llandudno makes it pre-eminently the centre for North Wales steamer passenger traffic, as well as a capital starting-point from which to make excursions

by road or rail into Snowdonia, to explore the beauties of the River Conwy, or to visit the many places of interest along the coast. Its situation, climate, and magnificent beach—the ease with which it can be reached, and the unceasing efforts of the local authorities to promote the health, comfort, and enjoyment of visitors, fully account for the popularity Llandudno has achieved both as a holiday resort and a conference centre.

Llandudno, the Ideal Seaside Resort

There is ample accommodation for visitors, and even at the height of the season the wide, tree-lined streets never appear overcrowded. Whichever way one looks the surrounding mountains form a picturesque and impressive background to the gay scene.

There are no slums in Llandudno. The future of the town has been carefully thought out, and it has been planned accordingly. It is due to this planning, and to Llandudno's exceptional advantage in being situated between two such beautiful bays, and almost surrounded by mountains, that the air here is always fresh and pure.

A walk along the Promenade in the evening is an experience to be remembered with pleasure. Then, Llandudno Bay becomes a fairy sea, the promenade a blaze of light, and the Great Orme, rising beyond the town, lending a delightful air of mystery, as one by one, scattered lights appear in the windows of dwellings, set upon its steep slopes.

Climate. In respect of climate, Llandudno is one of the most favoured health resorts of Great Britain, being admirably adapted to be both a summer and a winter resort. For the three winter months, the temperature is shown to be practically the same as that of Torquay, Weymouth and Ventnor, the greatest difference occurring in the comparison with Ventnor. On the other hand, its summer temperature is rather more than two degrees lower than that of Brighton and of Ventnor, nearly two lower than that of Weymouth, and four-fifths of a degree lower than that of Torquay. In other words, while it is cooler at Llandudno in summer than at some of the most favoured wateringplaces in the South of England, it is warmer in winter.

Each succeeding winter finds Llandudno sheltering an increased number of those who seek a pleasant retreat during the coldest months of the year. The plants and shrubs which remain in the open gardens throughout the winter months bear testimony to the mildness of the weather. They include camellias, carnations, fuchsias, geraniums, hydrangeas, japonica, myrtle, pansies, roses, verbenas, veronicas and many others.

The presence of the sea, which surrounds three-fourths of the town, is one cause of this exceptional climate, and the shelter from the north winds given by the Great Orme is certainly a contributing factor.

Llandudno also possesses that "moderately dry air which is best adapted to the physical constitution of mankind generally." The inland mountain ranges intercept the vapour-laden winds that blow from the tropics, and rob them of their moisture before they reach the coast, and the rain that Llandudno does receive is quickly absorbed, for the subsoil, composed chiefly of gravel and sand, is extremely porous.

Statistics compiled by the meteorologist to the Llandudno Council, show that the average annual registration of bright sunshine is 1,601 hours. The average rainfall during a long period has been less than 30 inches. Llandudno receives but half an inch more than Ventnor and only a quarter of an inch more than Brighton.

A glance at the map will show that as—

A Motoring Centre

Llandudno is almost unrivalled in North Wales. The moors of

Denbigh and the mountains of Snowdonia are as accessible as lovely Betws-y-Coed or the rugged coast of Anglesey. Of note is the run over the Mynydd Hiraethog from Denbigh to Pentre-foelas—a link in a fine circular run described on page 59. Another good cross-country route is the road from Abergele to Llanrwst (*see* pp. 58–59).

For an evening run it would be difficult to improve upon the round of the Great Orme by the Marine Drive. The Drive is narrow in places and has one or two sharp elbows, and one-way traffic is in operation: all vehicles enter the Drive at the Happy Valley gateway and leave at the gate near Gogarth Abbey ruins and the West Shore. At sunset the scene from near the Lighthouse is superb.

Road Exits from the town: *Mostyn Broadway*, the left-hand road at the North-Western Hotel, at the eastern end of busy Mostyn Street; and *Conway Road*, the right-hand road at that point. Mostyn Broadway leaves Llandudno eastward (the sea-front can be followed as far as Craig-y-don), running to Rhos, Colwyn Bay, etc. Conway Road leads to Deganwy, and near Llandudno Junction joins the roads to Betws-y-Coed *via* Llanrwst and to Bangor *via* the new Conwy bridge. A third exit, especially convenient for those starting for the West Shore, is by way of Bryniau Road, starting from near the western end of Gloddaeth Avenue (*see* our plan). This road joins the Conway Road at Deganwy.

Sea-Fishing

Good fishing is to be had all the year round from boats and rocks. From the end of May to September, plaice, sole, and mackerel are plentiful. Whiting, cod, skate, dabs, and occasionally bream are also caught. August and September are the best months for bass and conger. Various competitions are held during the season and Llandudno Sea Anglers' Association holds a sea angling festival in September.

The Flora of the District

is remarkably different from that of adjacent areas. Indeed, the plants which constitute the Llandudno flora surpass in number and variety of species those in any other area of equal extent. Some of the plants in the neighbourhood are very rare; one, the *Cotoneaster vulgaris*, is found nowhere else in the British Isles than on the Great Ormes Head.

A feature of the flora of the Great Orme is the comparatively large number of plants formerly in repute for medicinal purposes. Their presence may be due to their having been cultivated in the gardens of Gogarth Abbey.

Many will be interested also in the large collection of rock and alpine plants at the upper end of the Happy Valley, *see* p. 75.

The Fern Flora of the district is relatively poor in comparison with the flowering plants. One of its members is the Sea Spleenwort, which may be found on the seaward cliffs.

Wild Birds

Bird lovers will find much to interest them at Llandudno. Here, over 100 species of wild bird may be seen, many of them in sufficient numbers to make study of their habits easy and fascinating.

Geological Note

The principal rock in the vicinity of Llandudno is *Carboniferous Limestone*, either exposed or covered with a thin coating of derived soil. It occurs in the Great Ormes Head, the Little Ormes Head, a ridge that runs from the latter towards the estuary on the Conwy, and a second ridge running parallel to the first. Between the ridges is *Millstone Grit*. The limestone also occurs in the high ground beyond Colwyn Bay, in the ridges of Clwyd beyond Rhyl, in Puffin Island, and in places along the Menai Strait. Elsewhere in the district the rocks are of the Silurian period.

Owing to tidal action there has been considerable lowering of the beach at Llandudno in recent times. As a result of this, forest remains have been exposed, which may be seen at Craig-y-don, and at West Shore. These trees were probably growing as late as the tenth century. On the West Shore, stag's horns have been found, in the black peat underlying the sand dunes. In the eighteenth century, fields lay between Gogarth Abbey and the sea. The legend of a great inundation of the fertile valley lying between Pen-y-Gogarth (Great Ormes Head) and Priestholm (Puffin Island) is, however, without foundation in fact. The sea had covered all this plain before the historic era, and certainly long before the sixth century, when, according to tradition, the disaster is supposed to have occurred.

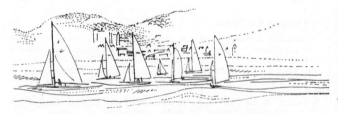

In and About Llandudno

Llandudno has been laid out with fine wide streets. The general direction of one set is parallel to the line of Llandudno Bay, and these are connected by another set crossing them at right angles.

The Sea-Front is bordered by a splendid **Promenade,** 90 feet wide and over 1½ miles long. Here is no monotonously straight "sea wall," but a spacious pavement which as it curves round the Bay provides continually changing views not only of the headlands on either hand or of the Pier, or the boats and the bathing, but of the Promenade itself and its ever-interesting crowd. There is an Information Centre near the Pier.

On the left rises the grey and green mass of the Great Orme, its steep sides scaled by roads and dotted with houses. At the foot of the Orme is the group of white-painted buildings from which the Pier stands out to sea, and from which the wide Promenade sweeps round in a splendid curve to the Little Orme, away to the right. Southward the grey of the Little Orme changes to red-brown at the quarries beyond Craig-y-don, and thence our eyes are carried back along the rim of the bay by the long line of hotels and boarding-houses. In passing, it may be said that the frontages of many of these deserve notice, though Llandudno would be the first to disclaim any architectural fame.

About midway along the Promenade a balcony-like **Bandstand** projects over the sands.

The North Shore

is composed of firm smooth sand, fringed with shingle, so that it is both an admirable playground for children, and a pleasant place to bathe.

Strong swimmers may bathe from below the Marine Drive, near the Pigeon's Cave, but caution must be observed, as this is not the safest of bathing places.

In the season, special attractions are arranged for the benefit of visitors.

With the children, sand castle competitions, and donkey riding over the sands, are always popular. In addition, at the Little Orme end of the promenade, there is a modern paddling pool with facilities for canoeing and the hire of paddle boats. Another popular attraction with children is a Punch and Judy Show.

Towards the western end of the Promenade stands the fine **War Memorial** and a tree-shaded green—the latter a pleasant place to sit and to enjoy the Bay, the hills beyond Craig-y-don, and the lovely outline of the Little Orme.

At the western end of the bay is—

The Pier

Admission.—Day or weekly tickets issued. A landing fee is chargeable at the pierhead. Concerts (small charge) morning and evening.

The Pier, nearly half a mile long, enables steamer passengers to land or embark at any state of the tide, and also provides a good view of Llandudno and its mountainous background. The Pier is in two portions: one extending from the end of the Promenade and in front of the Pavilion and the Grand Hotel and the other continuing thence to sea. There are two entrances, one at the Promenade, and one near the entrance to the Marine Drive. On the Pier are kiosks for the sale of fruit, sweets, newspapers, books, views, and other articles. An unofficial attraction are the gulls, wonderfully tame and with inexhaustible appetites.

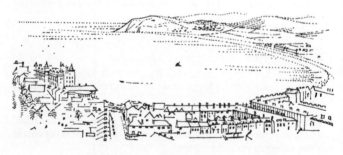

The **Pavilion,** near the upper end of the Parade, is entered either from the Pier or from the North Parade. The main hall is used for concerts, plays, recitals, etc. It is built of stone, iron and glass, and is capable of seating 2,000 persons. The orchestral and other concerts have more than local fame. The Pier Pavilion has also, in recent years, housed many of the large National Conferences which have been held at Llandudno and famous people in the political world have addressed meetings from this stage.

Every morning and evening during the season, at Easter, and from Whitsun to October, the Pier Co.'s orchestra performs at the Pier Head Pavilion. During the evenings excellent summer shows are given in the Pier Pavilion.

The view inland from the Pier is very pleasant. The most prominent of the mountains that are seen rising in the distance is Foel Fras, at the head of the Aber Glen. To the left of this is Tal-y-Fan, in the rear of the Conwy mountains, and still more to the left is Pen-Llithrig-y-Wrach, some three miles short of Capel Curig.

Llandudno is well provided with facilities for—

Indoor Amusement

In addition to the Pier Pavilions there is **Arcadia,** where entertainments are given from Easter until the end of October. Close by is the **Grand Theatre,** with resident company. Dancing may be enjoyed at the **Winter Garden** Ballroom, Gloddaeth Street, the Café Royal and at many of the hotels. The Astra Cinema is next to the Winter Garden and the Palladium (bingo) is also in Gloddaeth Street. The Savoy Cinema is in Mostyn Street.

In Fferm Bach Road, Craig-y-don, is—

Rapallo House

Open.—Weekdays (except Saturday), 10–12.45, 2–5 (April and September to November until 4 p.m. Closed from December to March). Admission free.

for some time the residence of the late Mr. F. E. Chardon. On his death in 1926 he directed that the house should be arranged as a museum or picture gallery. There are some interesting pictures and a number of articles on loan from the National Museum of Wales (to which Rapallo House is affiliated). The collection is displayed in a building which was formerly Mr. Chardon's charmingly situated residence. In an outhouse is a replica of an old Welsh kitchen and in the armoury are Roman exhibits from Conovium.

Mostyn Street

is Llandudno's principal thoroughfare. Starting at the Vaughan Street end and following it towards the Great Orme, we come immediately to **Holy Trinity Church,** in the Transition style.

Next, on the right, is **St. John's English Methodist Church.** Then almost immediately on the left is the Renaissance building of the **Public Library.** A circular hall gives access to the lending department, junior library, reference room, newspaper and magazine rooms. On the first floor is a lecture room occupying the whole front of the building.

Passing on, we come to the break caused by **Lloyd Street,** which runs inland from the sea-front towards the cricket and tennis grounds and the bowling-green, and contains various public buildings. A few yards inland from Mostyn Street is the **Town Hall,** an English Renaissance building, with a Public Hall accommodating over 800 persons. The principal apartment on the first floor is the **Council Chamber,** a beautiful hall in which marble and walnut have been largely employed. Committee rooms and the Town Clerk's and other offices are also on the first floor. At the George Street corner of the Town Hall is an Information Bureau.

Just beyond the Town Hall and in similar style, is the **Welsh Methodist Chapel.** A little farther along, on the other side, is the **Catholic Church of Our Lady, Star of the Sea.** The **Lifeboat House** is equidistant from Llandudno Bay and the West Shore.

Gloddaeth Street and its continuation, **Gloddaeth Avenue,** together form a thoroughfare of which the town is rightly proud. It runs in a straight line from the shore of Llandudno Bay to the West Parade, on the shore of Conway Bay. On the eastern side of Gloddaeth Street are the **Astra Cinema** and **Palladium** (bingo) and the **Winter Gardens.** At the corner of Chapel Street is the **English Presbyterian Church,** and on the opposite corner the **Welsh Presbyterian Chapel.**

Entered from Gloddaeth Street is—

The Sports Ground

the principal feature of which is the **Cricket Ground,** where important county and other matches are played. There are tennis courts, hard and grass, and bowling and putting greens, open to the public. During the winter months, the cricket ground is used by the Llandudno Hockey Club and each Easter they promote a Hockey Festival which attracts teams from all parts of the British Isles and, on many occasions, from the Continent.

Mostyn Street goes north-westward of Gloddaeth Street, past the Welsh Baptist Chapel, at the corner of Llewelyn Street, to Church Walks, from which a further climb leads to—

The Haulfre Gardens

which are laid out in terraces on the steep side of the Great Orme, the terraces being connected by woodland paths and the whole place forming a charming retreat and a fine view-point. Teas and refreshments are served at the house; there is a small aviary and an aquarium of tropical fish, and in the upper part of the Gardens is a miniature golf course. The paths through the Gardens form an attractive approach to the Great Ormes Head.

In Church Walks is the lower station of—

The Great Orme Railway

First tram up, 10 a.m.; time of last down is varied to meet current requirements.

The railway is worked by cables of plough steel with a hemp core, tested to a point much in excess of the working strain. Half-way up is the power-house, containing the engines which work the drums on which the cables are wound or from which they are uncoiled as the cars are hauled up or let down the

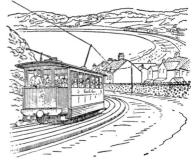

headland. The brakes are extremely powerful, and include emergency brakes in addition to those in ordinary use. Over 200,000 persons use the Tramway every year. The total length of the line is about 1½ miles. Near the upper terminus is a quarry, known as the **Bishop's** or **Fossil Quarry,** from the great number of beautiful fossils it contains. From the summit of the Orme a splendid view is gained in clear weather.

A little beyond the railway station, but on the opposite side of Church Walks, is **St. George's Church,** which has superseded St. Tudno's as the Parish Church.

For the Great Orme *see* p. 78.

By Church Walks and the upper end of **Abbey Road,** or along Gloddaeth Street and Gloddaeth Avenue, one may pass from the vicinity of the Pier to—

The West Shore, or Conwy Bay

The stranger who first makes acquaintance with the spot when the tide is up must wonder why the town turned its back, as it were, upon such a scene. A little later the reason is obvious. The water retires to a much greater distance here than in the other bay, leaving a large expanse of sand interspersed with pools of water. But even so, there are many popular seaside resorts that would suffer by comparison, and it is a magnificent playground for children. The West Shore has the advantage of splendid views across to Conwy and the mountains beyond. It is not surprising, therefore, that this part of the town has in recent years changed from a straggling suburb to a busy community with well-built and attractive houses.

Between the ends of Abbey Road and Gloddaeth Avenue is a a **Model Yacht Pond.** Overlooking the pond is a statue commemorating the fact that "on this very shore" Lewis Carroll (the Rev. C. H. Dodgson), the creator of *Alice in Wonderland,* used to amuse his child friends. The neighbouring *Gogarth Abbey Hotel* boasts of having been actually "the birthplace of *Alice.*" Lewis Carroll is commemorated by the alabaster font in the **Church of Our Saviour,** a short way from the Pond.

Southward from the Pond is the gorse-covered warren that extends to Deganwy and contains the fine **Golf Links** of the North Wales Club and also the Maesdu course (both 18 holes). Northward looms the Great Orme, with the Marine Drive clinging to its sides as it climbs up and round to the extreme point. Close to the entrance to the Drive is the commencement of the footpath known as the **Invalids' Walk,** which skirts the slope of the Headland and commands fine views of the town and the plain beyond, as well as of the heights of the Snowdonian range.

Now let us pass from Llandudno's streets and shores to neighbouring spots that contribute in no small degree to the popularity of the town as a holiday resort. Proceeding behind the Pier Pavilion, we take a footpath that goes off on the left, and in a few minutes reach—

The Happy Valley

a pleasure-ground nestling in a hollow of the Great Orme and presented to the town by Lord Mostyn, the Lord of the Manor. The Valley is extremely attractive with its grassy slopes and grand sea and mountain views in all directions. It is plentifully supplied with seats and is laid out with lawns, rockeries, shrubs and flowers.

During the season entertainment is provided and there is a café and an attractive illuminated garden.

In the upper part of the Valley is an extensive **Rock Garden,** where thrive well over 300 varieties of Alpine and rock plants from such distant spots as the Pyrenees, Sardinia, and the Himalayas. The eminence beyond, known as **Pen-y-Dinas,** is easily accessible and commands a magnificent view of the town and its shores. It is also of much historical interest, as it is believed to be the site of a British fortress. There are the remains of an encircling wall of great thickness and a large number of circular cavities, about 12 feet in diameter, edged with stones. In the Happy Valley and the adjacent slopes Llandudno possesses one of the most attractive public pleasure-grounds in Britain.

A novel amenity is of the **Llandudno Cabin Lift,** which conveys passengers from the Happy Valley to the summit of the Great Orme, a distance of just over a mile, in nine minutes. It is operated by a monocable.

The Marine Drive

Small toll for motor traffic.

This fine roadway almost encircles the Great Orme, one end lying near the foot of the Happy Valley and behind the Pier Pavilion and the Grand Hotel; the other being on the West Shore. Owing to the narrowness of the road, vehicular traffic proceeds in one direction only, entering the Drive at the east gate, near the Pier.

The Drive was completed in 1879, at a cost of £14,000, and was owned by a private company until 1897, when it was purchased by the Urban District Council, which in 1910 abolished the toll for pedestrians. The number of foot-passengers who made use of the Drive during the previous year was upwards of 80,000, so that in making it free to foot-passengers the Council relinquished a sum equal to nearly a penny in the £ on the rates. At each end is a toll-house. The distance between them is 4¼ miles, and the total circuit of the Head measures nearly 6 miles.

The road was formed by cutting away the precipitous limestone rock. It is well protected by a wide parapet. At some points the passenger is high above the sea, and looks sheer down into the glittering water; at others he descends and passes under overhanging cliffs. These variations of altitude add greatly to the scenic beauty of the Drive.

For the sake of the view of Conwy town and bay and their mountainous background, it is advisable to start from the Pier end of the Drive (those in cars, as already explained, have no choice of direction). Setting out in this direction we rapidly climb to Pen Trwyn, a good view-point, from which the Clwydian mountains and the coast in the vicinity of Rhyl are well seen. Continuing our course, we come to a path that leads up to *Pink Farm*, and a little farther (a mile from the toll-house) is a road to St. Tudno's Church, situated but a short distance above.

About half-way round the Orme is the castellated **Great Ormes Head Lighthouse** (only open to visitors who have an order of admission from the Mersey Docks and Harbour Board, Liverpool). It is a solidly built structure crowning a steep precipice at a height of over 300 feet. It is a group-flashing light (four flashes every 30 seconds) of 13,000 candle-power on the white sector and 5,000 on the red sector. The beams are visible on the sea for a distance of 24 miles, and, under suitable atmospheric conditions, are clearly discernible from Snaefell, in the Isle of Man, 54 miles away. The beacon is situated at the point of the Head, and in the cliff below is the **Llech,** or **Hiding Cave,** one of several caverns in the face of the promontory.

The hiding cave is called in Welsh "Parlwr Llech." Llech means a slab or rock, and "the rock-parlour" is certainly an apt name for this cave, which is 8 feet high and 7 feet across, and furnished with a stone bench and the remains of a stone table. The age of the cave is not known. It was probably used as a summer-house by long-ago members of the Mostyn family. It is also known as the Monk's Cave and is thought to have been a place of retreat for the monks of Gogarth Abbey. There are many reminders of these men of prayer to be found on the Orme. The Evergreen Path which runs up the side of the mountain is believed by many to be the path the monks trod on their many journeys between Saint Tudno's church and the Abbey.

From the western side of the Great Orme the view is magnificent. Anglesey, Puffin Island, the Menai Strait, the Snowdonian mountains, the River Conwy, Conwy Castle and Bridge, etc., form a grand panorama. At sunset the scene is particularly fine, the mountains and valleys seeming to change form as well as colour in the failing light.

From this point the Drive runs down to the Conwy shore toll-gate, shortly before reaching which the scanty ruins of **Gogarth Abbey** are passed. They are situated in the grounds of British Rail's Old Abbey Holiday Home, and consist chiefly of the remains of a chimney stack, fragments of walls, and some traces of foundations. The building is supposed to have been at one time the residence of the Bishops of Bangor, but it was already in ruins when visited by Leland, the historian and topographer, in the reign of Henry VIII.

Outside the west gate of the Drive stands the *Gogarth Abbey Hotel*, on the site of what was the residence of Dean Liddell. It is said that here "Lewis Carroll" wrote *Alice in Wonderland*; and we can readily believe that the Walrus and the Carpenter in *Alice Through the Looking Glass* "wept like anything to see such quantities of sand" where are now the Golf Links. (*See also* p. 74).

St. Tudno's Church can be approached by way of the Marine Drive, from which there is a steep but good road to it a few yards past the stone "1 mile from the lodge" (the road continues past the church to the summit of the Orme). The Church can also be approached by a path from the Happy Valley, or by following the road running up from Church Walks or the path through Haulfre Gardens.

St. Tudno's Church

Open from 9.30 a.m. to sunset daily. Sunday services (Whitsun to September 30) 11 a.m.

St. Tudno's was formerly the parish church of Llandudno, and in bygone days was the only place of worship in the neighbourhood. During the summer months divine service is held in the churchyard when the weather is suitable, every Sunday morning.

The Church is of considerable interest. It is said to stand on the site of the cell of St. Tudno, who lived in the sixth century. The west end of the north wall is thought to be a portion of a church erected in the eleventh or twelfth century, but the rest of the old work belongs to the fifteenth century. In 1839 the roof was stripped off by a storm, the building being so badly damaged that no attempt was made to repair it, but, instead, St. George's Church was erected in Church Walks, a site more accessible to the towns-people. St Tudno's lay neglected until 1855, when it was restored. Subsequent restorations were carried out in 1906–7 and 1957–8.

The building is oblong, with a gable turret for one bell, a low, arched entrance on the west, and a porch on the north. On the south side is an open-air pulpit and reading-desk. The interior measurement of the church is 67 feet by 16¾. The chief objects of interest in the interior are a Norman circular font and two thirteenth-century tombstones on the south wall. A portion of the old rood-screen, carved with vine pattern, is fixed to the West wall and on the wallplate north of the altar is carved a long dragon.

There still remain a few words to be said respecting—

The Great Orme

which at one time was an island. The changing of the course of the Conwy River, which occurred about the year 500, resulted in its being joined, as at present, to the mainland. This change probably took place over a long period. The Great Orme consists of alternate beds of chert and limestone, uniformly dipping from every side to the centre, where a deposit of copper ore is embedded.

Above St. Tudno's Church there are three deserted mines, namely, Ty Gwyn, the Old Mine and the New Mine, and less than a hundred years ago ore to the value of a quarter of a million sterling was raised annually. The discovery of stone hammers and bone augers in ancient workings is held to indicate that the ore was obtained by the Britons prior to the Roman invasion, as the Roman tools were of iron or bronze.

The cliffs are very abrupt, and hollowed by the action of the sea into various caverns, in whose secure recesses multitudes of gulls, cormorants, herons, razorbills, ravens and rock-pigeons make their nests. Many of these caves are quite inaccessible, but some may be examined from the sea. The most curious is the Hiding Cave, situated at the point of the promontory. A short distance southward is the **Hornby Cave,** named after a brig that was wrecked off the Point on New Year's Day, 1824, with the loss of all the crew except one, who chanced to be upon the bowsprit when the vessel struck the Great Orme, and was flung by the concussion upon a narrow ledge of rock, from which he succeeded in climbing to the top of the precipice. Eastward of the Hiding Cave is the **Gulf Cave,** or Ogof Hafnant. Some considerable distance farther eastward is **Ogof Colomennod** (the Pigeon's Cave), accessible at low water, and a little way farther east is the **Dutchman's Cave.**

A short distance westward of the Pigeons' Cave is the **Steward's Bench,** a flat stone ledge covered at high water to a depth of about two feet. Tradition says that any steward of the Mostyn estates convicted of wronging a tenant was placed upon the ledge and was compelled to remain there during two tides.

Above the Happy Valley is the eminence called **Pen-y-Dinas,** to which reference has already been made. Near to this is the Rocking Stone, sometimes called Crud Tudno (**Tudno's Cradle**).

Just above the tramline half-way station is a **cromlech.** This is popularly supposed to have been used as an altar for Druidical rites. It is probably part of a circular burial place erected in the Bronze Age and goes by the name of Llety-y-Filiast.

Near the upper terminus of the tramline is the **Bishop's Quarry,** a treasure-house for geologists, being filled with beautiful fossils.

The highest point of the Great Orme is 679 feet above sea-level. In clear weather can be seen: Puffin Island, Anglesey, the Isle of Man, the Cumberland Hills, the line of the Irish Coast, and Elidir Fawr.

Little Ormes Head

The Little Orme, at the eastern extremity of Llandudno Bay, although less imposing than the larger headland, has features of much interest. It is about 200 feet lower than the Great Orme, being only 463 feet above the level of the sea, but the views from the summit are extensive and delightful, and the cliffs are much finer than those of the loftier headland, some having a sheer height of 300 feet. Like its more famous neighbour across the bay, the Little Orme is composed of limestone, in which a number of caverns have been formed by the waves. The best known are the **Eglwys Wen** (White Church), **Porth Dyniewyd** (the gate of the young steer), and **Ogof Cythreuliaid** (The Cave of the demons). The last-named is large enough to allow a boat to be rowed into it at high tide, but it is inadvisable to make the attempt unless accompanied by an experienced boatman.

The low rocks near the cliffs are a rich hunting-ground for naturalists and others. Mussels, whelks, limpets, starfish and innumerable other creatures abound, as do also beautiful sea-weeds.

The walk round the headland is easy and pleasant, and can be accomplished in about an hour and a half. Follow the road along the shore until it ascends between the Little Orme and Mynydd Pentre

(pentre = village), and there take the path leading to the headland. For the sake of the view the complete circuit should be made, but the greatest care should be exercised, because the cliffs are precipitous and fatal accidents have occurred.

For an easy means of ascent the road that goes eastward from the Parade to the Craigside Hydro should be followed. Just after passing the Hydro, take a path that will be seen leading up the slope. By following it and keeping to the left, the summit is soon reached, and then the beautiful view of mountain and sea more than compensates for the toil of the climb.

The prospect from the cairn on the summit includes Moel Fammau, the highest point of the Clwydian range, with the tower of St. Asaph Cathedral and the lofty white spire of Bodelwyddan Church in front of it. Then to the right are Penmaenmawr and the Isle of Anglesey. Nearer are the Gloddaeth Woods, with Conwy Castle behind them; and in the rear of that are Penllithrig-y-Wrach to the left, and Foel Fras and Carnedd Llewelyn to the right. On a clear day there may be seen far away in the south the peak of Arenig-fawr, near Bala.

About 90 feet from the summit is a small cave called *Ty-yn-y-graig*—"the house in the rock"—which, tradition says, was used as a priests' hiding place at the time of the Reformation. Overlooking the sea, the cave provided a safe retreat. When discovered in 1587 the cave contained weapons and food, an altar and a printing press. The occupants are said to have escaped. These probably included William Davies, a missionary priest later martyred at Beaumaris, and his friend and companion Robert Pugh of Penrhyn.

Pleasant Walks from Llandudno

1. **To Gloddaeth,** about 2½ miles. Of the many pleasant walks in the immediate neighbourhood of Llandudno that which lies through the woods of Gloddaeth is one of the most delightful. Although there is no timber of unusual size, the trees generally have a remarkable aspect of antiquity.

Either afoot or by bus follow the Conwy Road (the thoroughfare left of the Post Office) as far as the Church of Llanrhos (1½ miles), and then turn to the left by a footpath across the fields.

Parts of the **Church of Llanrhos** (Eglwys Rhos) belong to the thirteenth century, but it is reputed that there was a church on this site in the time of Maelgwyn, King of Gwynedd, in the sixth century. Tradition asserts that he died in this church, to which he had come in the hope of escaping the "yellow pestilence." Some authorities think that the sickness from which the king fled occurred after one of the many great battles in which his armies were engaged, and was caused because the bodies of the slain could not be buried. Whatever the truth of these old tales, the graveyard is to-day a most peaceful spot, overlooking Gloddaeth Woods. Note the stone porch, and the steps of the church by the lychgate. From these worshippers used to mount their horses in bygone days. It is the burial place of the Mostyn family.

Inside the church is an inscribed stone dating from the sixth century. It was removed to the church in 1906, from Tyddyn Holland. The inscription apparently reads, "Sanct Anus Sacer . . . s." It was reported that John Bright on one occasion borrowed a basin of water from a neighbouring cottage and cleaned the inscription.

Gloddaeth Hall (now a boys' school) is one of the old residences of the Mostyns. Part dates from before 1550. On the dais of the great hall are the arms of Queen Elizabeth I and the Earl of Leicester. Over the fireplace in the reception hall is the family motto, "Heb Dduw, heb ddim, Duw a digon," of which the English is "Without God, without all; God and plenty." In the centre of the hall are the Tudor arms and the words, "God save our Queene Elizabeth, send her long reign, 1584."

2. **"My Grandmother's Chair."** A seat formed of two flat stones a few hundred yards to the north of Gloddaeth Woods. Follow the shore road until Nant-y-Gamar Road is reached. Continue along this road to gate at end. Beyond gate approach wall bordering the wood and keeping wall and wood on left a farmhouse is seen below. Turn right past farmhouse and the stones will be found on the slope of the hill. On a clear day, the view from this point is very beautiful.

To reach the seat from Gloddaeth Woods, make for an old tower, on the hill, bear to left, around wood until the farmhouse is seen below. Then turn right as above.

3. **To Bodysgallen,** one of the residences of the Mostyn family. It is pleasantly situated on a hill near Llanrhos and is now an hotel. The

first builder is said to have been Caswallon, Prince of North Wales, in the fifth century. The shortest route from Llandudno, 2½ miles, is along the Conwy Road as far as the second turning on the left past Eglwys Rhos. Southward of Bodysgallen is **Marll Hall**, said to be the scene of Wilkie Collins's *Haunted House*.

4. To Ffridd, or Quarry Hill. This is easily accessible, and though only 350 feet in height commands one of the finest views in the neighbourhood. Proceed through the wood at Bodysgallen, pass through the upper gate, and turn to the right for a short distance. Then take the first turn to the left (by a lane leading to the village of Pydew). From here a gate gives access to the green slope by which, in about three minutes, the top of the hill is gained.

5. To Penrhyn Old Hall. This was for several centuries the seat of the family of Pugh. It is now used as a club and café and is open to the public. It stands to the right of the bus route between the Little Orme and Llandrillo, and is reached from the road along an avenue of poplars, and these trees of charm and dignity are a fitting compliment to a fine old house.

6. A charming **Circular Walk** is along Conwy Road to **Llanrhos,** thence past the lane leading to Bodysgallen (referred to already), up Tywyn Hill to Marl Lane on the left. Follow the lane, bearing always to the left, through the village of **Glanwydden** to the foot of Penrhyn Hill, and thence back along the main road running at the foot of the Little Orme. Distance, about 6 miles.

Deganwy

Access. By the Chester and Holyhead line to Llandudno Junction, thence to Deganwy station on the branch line to Llandudno. By *bus* from neighbouring towns.

Amusements.—Bathing, boating, yachting, sea and river fishing, golfing, mountaineering; excursions by rail, steamer, or coach.

Banks.—*National Westminster, Midland.*

Bathing.—On a sandy beach.

Boating and Yachting.—These are among the principal attractions of the place. Various craft are available for hire. There are two clubs: North Wales Cruising Club and the Conwy Yacht Club.

Bus Services.—To Llandudno, Colwyn Bay, Llanrhos, Conwy, Llandudno Junction, Llanrwst, Trefriw, etc.

Fishing.—Salmon, sea-trout, and brown trout, in the *Conwy.* Other waters for fly-fishing are within easy reach of Deganwy.

There is good fishing for bass within the river, and outside the harbour and round Gt. Orme's Head there is good fishing for plaice, skate and codling. From July to October mackerel visit the bay. There is an unlimited supply of mussels and soft crabs for bait.

Golf.—The *Caernarvonshire Golf Club* has its course on the Morfa, on the opposite side of the river. Also available are the *North Wales Golf Club* on the Warren and the *Maesdu* links.

Hotels.—*Bryn Cregin, Castle.*

Places of Worship, with hours of English services on Sundays.— *All Saints' Church*—8, 11 and 6.30; *Bethel Methodist Chapel*—11 a.m.; *English Presbyterian*, Victoria Drive, Llandudno Junction—11 and 6.30; *Roman Catholic*, Conwy—8.30, 10 and 8 p.m.

Post Office.—Near station.

Deganwy stands on the east side of the estuary of the River Conwy.

"Sunny" Deganwy, as it is called, faces south and south-west, and in that respect alone it would be acknowledged to have a most favourable aspect; but part has the further advantage of being on sloping ground inclined at right angles to the sun's rays all the winter, a position which ensures for it during the cold season all the solar warmth possible.

Like most of the watering-places of North Wales, Deganwy suffers through the railway hugging the coast. Happily there has been left sufficient space between the line and the beach for a row of houses and a promenade.

There is, moreover, good bathing from a sandy beach, sensibly developed by the local authority.

Magnificent views are to be obtained from the fine **Marine Crescent** and still wider from—

The Vardre

which rises immediately behind the village, and has upon its flat top two great masses of igneous rock, crowned by the remains of the once famous **Castle of Deganwy,** or Din-gonwy, "the Fortress on the Conwy."

The way to the summit is up York Road and across **Gannock Park.** Having traversed a sunken path, along which the latter part of the route runs, we are free to roam over the twin hills, through the courtesy of Lord Mostyn, their owner. So we go to the foot of the second rock, and then turning left, to the hollow between the two hummocks, ascend the ancient approach to the Castle, and cross the earthworks which defended its courtyard. In the courtyard we turn left again, and ascending the steep pathway up the southern face of the larger hill, are led to the site of the Keep. From it there is a glorious prospect.

Deganwy Castle. The first Castle of Deganwy is said to have been built by Maelgwn Gwynedd, King of Britain and the Outer Isles, early in the sixth century. It and the town were destroyed by lightning in 810. The castle was rebuilt by a Norman, Hugh Lupus, Earl of Chester, and was demolished by Llewelyn the Great. Once more it was restored by an Earl of Chester, and was finally destroyed by Llewelyn ap Gruffydd in the year 1262. There are a few remains.

An army which King John led into Wales in 1211 encamped here, and was reduced to such distress that horse flesh was gladly eaten. In the end the King was obliged to retreat. Shortly afterwards, Deganwy Castle, and all the other castles held by the English between Conwy and the Dee, fell into the possession of Llewelyn, who, it will be remembered, had married John's daughter Joan.

Walks from Deganwy

Along the Warren to the Black Rocks, a group of seaweed-covered boulders in the direction of the Orme.

To the hill-tops of **Pydew and Pabo,** starting by the footpath below the Church, going through the Marl Park Estate, or across the fields to Marl Old Hall, and thence by the Nun's Steps.

To **Little Orme's Head,** across the Vardre to the village and ancient Church of Llanrhos, then through the Gloddaeth Woods to Pen-rhynside, and so to the Head.

To **Conwy Mountain,** a mile across the Morfa (bus to Conwy).

Visitors to Deganwy can join the excursions arranged by several of the Llandudno coach companies, whose vehicles "pick up" in the village. For Road Routes, *see* pp. 8–10. Situated on the Llandudno branch line, a few minutes' run from Llandudno Junction, Deganwy is within easy access of all the popular places served by the railway. Many an enjoyable sea-trip can be had from Llandudno by the steamers of the Isle of Man Steam Packet Company.

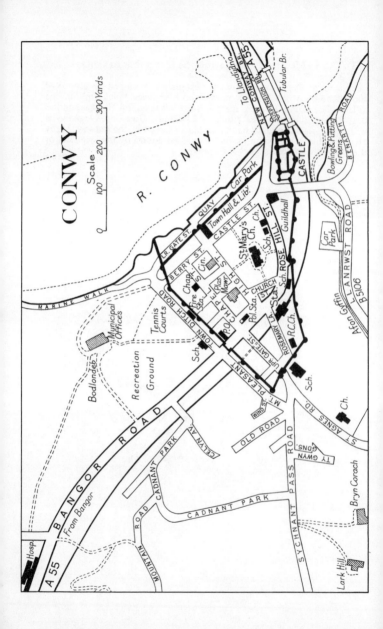

Conwy

Access.—By the Chester and Holyhead line (London Midland Region). From London, Conwy can be reached in 5 hours, from Birmingham in 4, Manchester and Liverpool in 2¼. Connection with the Western Region Line at Chester.

Road Route.—from Chester, *via* Holywell, Rhuddlan and Colwyn Bay; from Shrewsbury *via* Llangollen, Corwen, Betws-y-Coed, and Trefriw (*see* pp. 8–10).

Amusements.—Boating, yachting, fishing, bathing, mountain-walking, golfing (*see* below), tennis, bowls, cricket.

Banks.—*Barclays*, High Street; *Midland*, Lancaster Square; *National Westminster*, Castle Street; *Williams and Glyn's*, Lancaster Square.

Bathing on Conwy Morfa; good sandy beach.

Boating.—At the quay are rowing and sailing boats as well as motor-launches, while the bay is a favourite anchorage for yachts, which have good berths on the west side of the river. The holding ground is good, and the site is sheltered from the prevailing westerly winds. A hard, shingly beach, running steep down to dead low-water springs, makes landing particularly clean. Ample fishing facilities.

Bowling Green on south side of Castle.

Bus Services.—Conwy is well served by buses running east and west and also up the Conwy Valley.

Camping and Caravanning.—There is a municipally owned and controlled caravan and camping site at Morfa Conwy. All facilities laid on, including shop and store. Open from 1st April to 30th September. There are several private sites both seasonal and residential.

Cinema.—*Palace* in High Street.

Early Closing Day.—Wednesday.

Golf.—The Caernarvonshire Golf Course is on Conwy Morfa, 1 mile on Bangor road, Visitors are welcome. This championship course is one of 18-holes of typical seaside character. Sunday play. Fully licensed clubhouse with catering.

Hotels.—*Castle*, High Street; *Park Hall*,

coastal road; *White House*, coastal road; *Erskine*, Rosehill Street; *Bridge*, Rosehill Street; see also Deganwy.

Library.—Reference and Lending Library in Town Hall. Open Mon. to Thurs. 9–6. Friday 9–7. Saturdays 9–5.

Markets and Fairs.—Two fairs are held in the course of the year. The September fair is noted for the sale of honey and beeswax in Vicarage car park, Rosehill Street. Seed Fair in March.

Newspapers.—*Weekly News*, Thursday; *The Pioneer*, Friday.

Parking Places.—Castle Square, Porth Bach, Mount Pleasant, Morfa Bach.

Places of Worship, with hours of Sunday services.—*St. Mary's* (the Parish Church)—English, 8 (Holy Communion); 11.15, Matins and Sermon (H.C. 1st Sunday); *St. Agnes'*.—6.30, English Evensong and Sermon; *St. John's*, English Methodist—11 and 6.30; Tabernacle, Welsh Methodist, Baptist, Carmel Calvinistic Methodist, Sion United Reformed—all at 10 and 6; *St. Michael's* (*Roman Catholic*)—8.30, 10 and 8 p.m.; *St. Benedict's*, Gyffin—8, 11 (English), 6 (Welsh).

Population.—12,152.

Post Office.—Bangor Road, near North Gate.

River Trips.—During the season motor-launches ply to and from Trefriw, according to tide. The round trip takes about 3¼ hours. *See* announcements and the description of the journey on pp. 95–8.

Road Routes.—The Chester-Bangor road comes into Conwy by the new bridge (opened December 1958), passes to the right of the Guildhall (facing) and by Rose Hill Street and past the Square it ascends to the northern gate, just above the Post Office.

For *Trefriw* turn sharp left beside the Castle and to right at foot of hill, or from Square follow Bangor Road for 100 yards and then turn left for Upper Gate. At fork beyond Gate keep left for Trefriw; right for Sychnant Pass (1 in 7¼ descent) and Penmaenmawr.

Tennis.—Public courts at Civic Centre Bodlondeb.

Conwy is a popular tourist centre, and in the holiday season is a lively little place, a large proportion of the visitors to the coast of North Wales being drawn to the town by its many historical buildings.

The old town is closely packed between its walls on a slope on the left bank of the river from which it takes its name, an Anglicized form of the two British words *cyn*, first or chief, and *wy*, water. It is seen to the greatest advantage when approached by road from Llandudno Junction, less than a mile to the east. The road passes over the new bridge, (opened 13th December, 1958) superseding the Telford suspension bridge. The work was carried out by Sir William Arrol & Co. Ltd. of Glasgow, builders of the Forth Bridge, and took almost four years to complete. The bridge has a single span of 310 feet carried on four steel arch ribs. The total width between parapets is 31 ft. 6 ins. providing for a single 22 ft. carriageway, a 7 ft. 6 in. footpath on the northern side, and a 2 ft. reserved strip on the south side.

The **Telford Suspension Bridge** alongside dates from 1826 and in its turn replaced an ancient and dangerous ferry. Its span, between the centres of the towers, measures 327 feet and is 18 feet above high water.

There are two other bridges over this part of the river, both being tubular viaducts constructed for the railway by Robert Stephenson, the first of their kind.

Overlooking the bridges is—

Conwy Castle

Admission.—Charge. Open March, weekdays 9.30–5.30, Sundays 2–5.30; April, weekdays 9.30–5.30, Sundays 9.30–5.30; May–September, weekdays and Sundays, 9.30–7; October, weekdays 9.30–5.30, Sundays 2–5.30; November–February, weekdays, 9.30–4, Sundays, 2–4. The castle is in the care of the Department of the Environment, and is floodlit during the summer.

The Castle was begun in 1283 for Edward I. It is of oblong form, and extends along the verge of a precipitous rock, washed on two sides by the river. The other sides front the town. The walls are at least 15 feet thick, and are flanked by eight vast circular embattled towers, four of which retain their original turrets. The Castle had two entry points. One, by a narrow flight of steps cut out of the rock, formed a communication between the fortress and the river. This is now destroyed, but the position may be seen from the eastern terrace, close to the Tubular Bridges. The main entrance was at the north-west end by way

of a ramp and over a drawbridge. The entrance is now by a zigzag path, but the drawbridge remains.

The interior of the fortress consists of two wards. On the south side (i.e. to the right) of that which the visitor first enters is the **Great Hall.** Its length is 125 feet, breadth 38 feet and height about 30 feet. It has lost its roof, which was supported by eight arches, of which the one rebuilt serves to indicate the former beauty of the Hall. Gone, too, is the floor, under which were extensive cellars. At one end and on two sides are the fireplaces. The hall was lighted by six narrow windows on the side towards the river, three larger and more ornamental ones that looked into the inner court and another at the east end. Beyond the well is the entrance to the Inner Ward, originally defended by a drawbridge. The rooms on the south side are known as the **King's Hall** and the **King's Chamber** and the south-east tower as the **King's Tower.** On the first floor of the north-east tower is a beautiful little oratory of the thirteenth century.

Beautiful views of the town and of the surrounding country are obtained from a small grassy platform known as the **East Barbican,** beyond the eastern towers, and from the battlements, reached by steps leading from the main courtyard and near the entrance to the Great Hall and cellars. The north-western tower should be ascended for the remarkable views.

The History of the Castle is full of interest. On the final destruction of Deganwy Castle by Llewelyn in 1262 preparations were made by England for the complete subjugation of Wales. Snowdonia was Llewelyn's stronghold, and Conwy the key to the eastern portion. Edward I made Conwy his headquarters, and began the erection of the Castle in 1283 after the defeat of Llewelyn. In 1290, Edward, having pushed ahead of his army with only a small following, was shut up within the castle by a large Welsh force from the hills, who had observed the swollen state of the river. Its subsidence enabled the English to rescue him from a position of great peril and privation.

In 1399 Richard II threw himself into Conwy, then considered impregnable, but finding it unprovisioned was compelled to treat with his foes. Travelling under a safe-conduct to meet Bolingbroke, he was led into an ambush a few miles from the Castle, and delivered as a prisoner.

The fortress played a prominent part in all the disturbances of subsequent years. In 1646 it was garrisoned for the King, but was taken, after a siege of three months, by the Parliamentary army. Charles II granted it to the Earl of Conway, by whom it was dismantled. Under the pretence of the requirements of His Majesty's service, the Earl ordered all the iron, timber and lead to be taken down and shipped to Ireland for sale. The local gentry vainly opposed the design, and the noble pile was reduced nearly to its present condition. The Earl, however, did not profit by his vandalism, for the vessel conveying the material to Ireland was wrecked and its contents were swallowed by the sea. It will be remembered that reference is made to Conwy Castle in Gray's poem "The Bard".

Opposite the Castle entrance is Castle Street, leading to the Town Hall (used for meetings and library) and **Porth Isaf** (the Lower Gate), on the right, passing through which we have a good view of the Harbour and its craft. To the left of the gate, along the quay, is the **Smallest House in Great Britain** (admission fee), a claim few will dispute. Open daily, Easter to October.

Re-entering the town by Porth Isaf we have before us **Aberconway,** a picturesque house dating from 1300, now held by the National Trust and open to visitors. There are some interesting antiques.

Pass up High Street and on the right will be found "the Great

Mansion," an ancient house called—

Plas Mawr

Admission.—Charge. Open daily, April to September 10–5.30, October to March 10–4.30.

Plas Mawr was built by Robert Wynne, of Gwydyr, in the reign of Elizabeth I, and is a typical example of the domestic architecture of that period. It is now the head-quarters of the **Royal Cambrian Academy of Art,** which has restored to Plas Mawr something of the appearance it presented in its early days. Exhibitions of paintings and sculpture are held throughout the year. The building is in two parts. One faces High Street and is entered through a portico decorated with the royal arms and Greek and Latin inscriptions signifying "bear and forbear." On the house also were the initials "I.H.S.; X.P.S.," with the date 1585.

The house contains a beautiful **Banqueting Hall,** a fine wainscoted apartment with fixed seats. The fretwork ceiling, the mouldings and crests over the fireplace, the original oak fender, and the large banqueting table, are among the objects that attract attention. Leaving this room by the doorway leading to the tower staircase, turn to the right and enter the **Small Kitchen,** containing a huge fireplace, a stone oven, and an old-fashioned bread safe suspended from the ceiling. A doorway opposite that by which we entered gives access to the **Still Room,** used by those in attendance at the side gate near by. Beyond the Small Kitchen is **Queen Elizabeth's Sitting-room,** in which attention is claimed by the letters E.R. and the royal arms above the fireplace, the richly decorated ceiling and walls, and the old oak panelled door with its original wooden latch.

Opposite this apartment is the **Great Kitchen,** which contains a fireplace about 9 feet 6 inches wide, 5 feet deep, and nearly 6 feet high. (It is worth stepping out into the courtyard for the sake of the view of the house.) On leaving this kitchen we turn to the right and ascend the first flight of a spiral staircase. Turning to the left we enter the **Wynne Room,** where portions of the arms, the boar and the bear and ragged staff, may be seen on the walls and ceilings. Beyond is the **Victoria Room,** a modern picture gallery approached through what was a wall cupboard. Opposite the Wynne Room is **Queen Elizabeth's Bedroom,** the ceiling decorated with heraldic devices.

Next to this chamber is the **Reception Room,** with seats similar to those in the Banqueting Hall, two of the original tables, and a fine geometrical ceiling. We leave this room from the side opposite the door by which we entered, and pass under a secret hiding-place formed in the thickness of the wall. Then we ascend a short flight of steps on the left, and, again keeping to the left, arrive at the **Lantern Room,** so named from an old lantern window in the far right-handed corner. This room has the distinction of being the haunted room of the house.

It is a curious fact that there are 365 windows and 52 doors in the house, and 52 steps from the bottom to the top of the tower, thus associating the windows, doors, and stairs with the days and weeks of the year. Whether this is due to accident or design is not known.

St. Mary's Church

Mainly of the Decorated period, Conwy's parish church was originally part of a Cistercian Abbey founded in 1186, of which few remains exist. The original Cistercian church seems to have comprised the present chancel, nave and aisles. The transept is fourteenth-century. In the north porch, by which entrance is usually made, is a nameless *cross fleuris* found with skeletons and believed to date from the Wars of the Roses or earlier.

Not far from the vestry door is another nameless *cross fleuris* marking the tomb of those hapless lovers, David and Morfa, for an account of whom readers are referred to Owen Rhoscomyl's *Battlement and Tower.*

The edifice contains finely carved stalls, a beautiful rood-screen of the fifteenth century, and an interesting font in which Archbishop John Williams was baptized. (*See below.*) Near the south door is a fine marble bust to the memory of the sculptor, John Gibson, R.A. (1790–1866), a native of Conwy. In a recess in the south wall is a stone figure of the mother of John Williams, Archbishop of York in the reign of Charles I. Near the screen is the tombstone of "Nicholas Hookes, of Conway, Gent., who was the forty-first child of his father, William Hookes, by Alice, his wife, and who was himself the father of twenty-seven children; he died on the 20th March, 1637." In the south wall of the chancel is a stone bearing a rudely cut cross and "Y.Z. 1066." Its history is unknown. In the parish museum are some good specimens of old lace and an ancient processional cross (restored).

The West Front is interesting; the tower, built in stages in the fourteenth, fifteenth and sixteenth centuries, was restored in 1953.

In the churchyard, near the south porch, is a sundial of 1761. East of it, with the remnant of its stone protected by an iron screen, is a grave *said* to be that associated with Wordsworth's "We are Seven."

The *Castle Hotel* occupies the site of some of the buildings of the Abbey (a statue of the founder, Prince Llewelyn, stands in Lancaster Square).

The Walls

surrounding Conwy cannot fail to interest the visitor. Their circuit measures a mile and a quarter, and somewhat resembles the form of a Welsh harp. Believed to be contemporary with the castle (1282–3) they are best seen from the castle. In some places 12 feet thick they are fortified by battlements and twenty-one semicircular towers. There were three principal gates, the Upper Gate (Porth Uchaf) at the entry of the Trefriw and Sychnant Pass roads, the Mill Gate, in Rosehill Street, and the Lower Gate (Porth Isaf) sometimes called Water Gate. The Castle Gate and Wing Gate are of later date. From the top of the walls, to which the public now have access, there are some fine views. The entrance to the walls is in Derry Street. Open daily in summer. *Charge.*

The saltwater Mill (Felin Heli) was situated near where the *Conwy* is joined by the *Afon Gyffin*.

WALKS FROM CONWY

Conwy is an excellent starting place for a number of walks, having easy access to the hills and mountains behind and being well placed for the utilization of train, bus and boat services.

Among the walks which should on no account be missed is the climb to the summit of **Conwy Mountain.** It starts from the Penmaenmawr road, crossing the railway by a foot-bridge opposite the old gasworks, then following a green track to the summit, about 800 feet above the sea, on which is *Castell caer Lleon*, the remains of an ancient British fortress. The walk can be continued to the Sychnant Pass and Penmaenmawr. An alternative route is by the Upper Gate (reached from the Square by Rosemary Lane) and the Sychnant Pass road, from which the mountain may be reached by obvious pathways across the fields.

Another is the **Marine Walk,** which extends round the fir-clad knoll of Bonc Hill and the mansion of Bodlondeb. It can easily be accomplished in half an hour, and is especially delightful when the tide is up. It affords the best view of the Castle.

Other recommended walks are:—

By Benarth Wood. A walk of 2½ miles. Turn down the Trefriw and Betws-y-Coed road, by the castle. With castle on the left, cross the *Gyffin* stream, and the bowling green on left. A public path across fields to the left leads past a farmhouse, and along the fringe of **Benarth Woods** (*private*). For the return turn right through Gyffin or continue for three-quarters of a mile to Baclaw Farm, and there turn to the right for Conwy.

To Llangelynin Old Church (3 miles). Leaving Conwy by the Upper Gate (reached from the Square by Rosemary Lane or Uppergate Street), take the left-hand road and in about half a mile disregard the turn (the Betws-y-Coed road) which dips down to the left. Pass through the hamlet of Hendre (*Hendre* = winter quarters) and in half a mile go behind the hill-side hamlet of Groesffordd. Disregard lanes right and left and with a chapel on right make towards Pen-y-Dinas, the lower shoulder of Tal-y-Fan. As the road rounds this little eminence the old church comes into view. It is of great age, and most impressive in its simplicity and environment.

Return routes, eastward by a descent to the valley, northward by footpath to Rô Wen.

To the Sychnant Pass and Dwygyfylchi. Leave by the Upper Gate and follow the right-hand road to the romantic Sychnant Pass (2 miles), from which there is a descent into the village of Dwygyfylchi (2¼ miles), and the approach to the Fairy Glen described in the Penmaenmawr section. The return can be made *via* Penmaenbach, making a circular excursion of 5 miles; over Conwy Mountain, making a walk of 4½ miles, or cross the hill from the top of Fairy Glen.

Penmaenbach is the prominent headland cutting Conwy off from Penmaenmawr. It is a fine view-point, easily ascended from Conwy mountain.

Rô Wen is the turning-point of a pleasant little walk which leaves Conwy by the Upper Gate. Take the left-hand road and in about half a mile turn steeply down to left to Gyffin. Cross the bridge and immediately turn right. The road then meanders happily through pretty country to the hamlet of Rô Wen. From Rô Wen a Roman road runs westward to Aber and Llanfairfechan.

A mile east of Rô Wen, a few hundred yards east of the Conwy-Betws-y-Coed road, is the old church of **Caerhûn**, which stands in the corner of the Roman fort of *Conovium*. The church is usually locked, however.

To Penmaenmawr. A good upland walk. As described above to Sychnant Pass, at top of which take a path southward over hills to the *top* of the Fairy Glen, beyond which a gate with signpost will be seen on skyline westward. From the gate are paths to the Jubilee Walk, Green Gorge, etc. (*see* pp. 127–8).

UP THE CONWY RIVER

During the season motor-launches ply between Conwy and Trefriw. The round trip takes 3½ hours.

The **Conwy River** has its source in Llyn Conwy, a small lake in the mountainous district where the counties of Merioneth, Denbigh and Caernarvon met. It receives the waters of the rivers Machno, Cletwr, Lledr, and Llugwy, and some other smaller mountain streams. Through nearly its whole course it follows the line of the old boundary between the former counties of Denbigh and Caernarvon. Its extreme length is about 30 miles. It is navigable for about 14 miles, and is tidal for about 12. Midway in its beautiful valley is the town of Llanrwst. From the village of Trefriw, a little below Llanrwst, to its outlet, one mile below the town of Conwy, it is a large river navigable by small vessels.

Throughout the trip, from the beginning until quite the end, there is something to interest and attract, new vistas of romantic scenery being revealed at every turn of the ever-winding river.

Further descriptions of certain places mentioned here will be readily found with the aid of the Index.

Opposite Deganwy is **Conwy Morfa,** a sea-plain, much used as a camping-ground, and well-known to golfers as the site of the Caernarvonshire Club links. On the farther side of the plain is **Conwy Mountain,** rising to a height of some 800 feet, terminating seaward in bold Penmaenbach. On the left, above **Deganwy,** is the peculiarly-shaped **Vardre,** a hill on which are the remains of **Deganwy Castle.** As the boat proceeds, we get a fine view of

Conwy Castle and the bridges, while the wood-covered rock of Bodlondeb, on the right, also adds to the beauty of the scene.

Before the construction of the **Suspension Bridge** in 1826, the only means of communication between the banks of the river at this point was a ferry. For the new bridge *see* p. 88.

Having passed under the bridges, we have, on the right, the well-wooded hill of **Benarth;** and looking back when the boat has proceeded some distance, we get one of the best views of Conwy Castle and town lying at the foot of the surrounding hills.

After the boat has rounded Benarth we come to **Cymrhyd Point** on the right, and **Glan Conwy** on the left, between which in olden times was a ford across the river. Having rounded the point, we have before us a magnificent panorama of distant mountains, and quickly are abreast of a little farm, on the right, known as *Tyddyn Cynal.*

By the side of a hedge running up from the opposite bank of the stream may be seen a **Cromlech,** consisting of five upright stones supporting a block 12 feet long, 8 feet broad and 4 feet thick, and weighing about 20 tons. Behind are two upright stones, each about 9 feet high, and some 6 feet apart. A short distance farther on the same side is *Meddiant Farm,* the residence for some years of Hugh Hughes, celebrated as a painter and wood engraver in the first half of the nineteenth century, and especially famed for his *Beauties of Cambria,* published in 1823.

Immediately afterwards we are abreast of the old house of *Hendrewaelod,* also on the left. About a mile farther we have, on the same side, *Bodnant Hall,* standing in its beautiful grounds.

Bodnant Gardens.—Bodnant Gardens (National Trust) consisting of over 60 acres of fine grounds are four miles south of Conwy on the east bank of the river. They are open to the public from Easter to October, Monday to Saturday 10–5, Sunday 1–5. Charge. The entrance gate and car-park are on the Eglwysbach Road.

At **Tal-y-Cafn,** we pass under the bridge which some years ago replaced the large old-fashioned ferry-boat by which horses, carts, cattle and sheep, as well as human beings, were conveyed from one bank to the other, and which itself is now free of toll. Beyond the bridge some rocks called the *Arrows* are passed, and then we may see on the right, in the midst of gigantic yew-trees, the old **Church of Caerhûn**, erected in one corner of the Roman fortress known as Conovium. From this point, the great half-circle of mountains on the right, towering range above range to the rounded summit of Carnedd Llewelyn (3,484 feet), offers a grand spectacle, especially towards sundown.

Two miles farther, and some little distance from the river, we have, on the right, the villages of **Tal-y-Bont** and **Llanbedr**, the summer quarters of many artists. Then we come to an extensive plain, on which some say Llewelyn encamped in 1282 on the eve of a battle with Edward I, the site of the conflict being between this spot and Cymryd Point. After long-continued rain the river formerly overflowed its banks, the tract being covered with water to a depth of several feet. On the hills to the right are the **Falls of Porthlwyd** and **Dolgarrog**, and at this point we observe the entrance to the Canal leading to the hydro-electric generating station, whose machinery is run by turbines actuated by water coming down to the works in the pipe line which can be seen on the face of the hill. Dolgarrog narrowly escaped extinction in 1925, when the pent-up waters of Llyn Eigiau burst their dam and swept unrestrained down into the Conwy Valley. Far away in the recesses of the mountains are the lakes from which Llandudno, Conwy and Colwyn Bay draw their water.

The *Dolgarrog Hydro-Electric Power Works* are of interest to many on account of the extent to which the water resources of the locality have been utilized. These works in their original form were constructed for the smelting of aluminium ore, but were given over in later years to public electricity supply. The works are now owned and operated by the Central Electricity Generating Board and utilize a total catchment area of some 39 square miles on the slopes of the hill-range centred on Carnedd Llewellyn. The principal storage lake is Llyn Cowlyd, augmented by water from Ffynnon Llugwy and Llyn Eigiau, with surplus water out of Llyn Dulyn along with the lower level water catchment collected in Coedty Reservoir. Llynoedd Cowlyd and Dulyn are the water supply reservoirs for the Conwy Valley Water Board and for the Llandudno district respectively. Llyn Cowlyd, enlarged by the construction of a dam nearly 40 years ago, has a storage capacity of 330 million cubic feet; Llyn Llugwy 40 million cubic feet, and Llyn Eigiau also 40 million cubic feet.

The Board also operates the Maentwrog Hydro-Electric Power Station at Maentwrog, near Ffestiniog. The storage reservoir for this station is Trawsfynydd Lake, which is a purely artificial reservoir constructed about 1927. It has a capacity of 1,150 million cubic feet with a total water catchment area of about 35 square miles. Cwm Dyli Power Station, near Beddgelert, is also operated by the Board. The storage reservoir is Llyn Llydaw.

97

On the opposite side, a wooded hill called **Porth Hywel Goch** (the gate of Red Howel) rises almost from the river bank. According to tradition, a giant who lived in this locality was accustomed to stand with one foot on the summit of this hill, and the other on the hills above Dolgarrog whilst he washed himself in the stream flowing between.

The river narrows very rapidly as we get near **Trefriw**, nestling at the foot of wooded hills (*see* p. 103).

Among the forms of life which add interest to the voyage are sheldrakes, cormorants, herons, and many rare birds.

YOUR HELP IS REQUESTED

A GREAT part of the success of this series is due, as we gratefully acknowledge, to the enthusiastic co-operation of readers. Changes take place, both in town and country, with such rapidity that it is difficult, even for the most alert and painstaking staff, to keep pace with them all, and the correspondents who so kindly take the trouble to inform us of alterations that come under their notice in using the books, render a real service not only to us but to their fellow-readers. We confidently appeal for further help of this kind.

THE EDITOR

WARD LOCK LIMITED
116 BAKER STREET,
LONDON, W.1.

Llanrwst

Access.—By rail *via* Chester, Llandudno Junction and the Vale of Conwy.
By bus running between Llanrwst, Trefriw, Conwy and Llandudno Junction.
Road Routes.—see pp. 8–10.

Banks.—*Midland, National Westminster, Barclays.*

Buses to Trefriw, Conwy and Llandudno, starting from Ancaster Square. Also frequent services to Abergele and to Betws, Penmachno and Cwm.

Car Parks.—Plas-y-Dre, Station Road; Watling Street; by Council Offices; and at Recreation Ground. Free parking.

Distances.—Capel Curig (via Betws-y-Coed), 10; Trefriw, 1 from Station by new road, 3½ by old road; Conwy, 12; Llandudno, 16.

Early Closing Day.—Thursday.

Fair.—Wednesday following the first Tuesday in each month.

Fishing.—Excellent trout and salmon fishing in the water of the Conwy Fishing Association and Crafnant Lake. For particulars apply Mr. D. C. Roberts, 30 Llwyn Brith, Llanrwst: *see also* Fishing note under Betws-y-Coed, p. 107.

Hotels.—*Eagles; Pen-y-Bont; Corn-u-copia; Victoria.* Furnished chalets are available at Glan-y-Borth. Apply Snowdonia National Park Centre, Llanrwst.

Information Centre.—Snowdonia National Park Centre, "Glan-y-Borth", Llanrwst.

Licensing Hours.—11–3, 5.30–10.30.

Market Day.—Tuesday except fair weeks.

Places of Worship.—*St. Grwst*—8, 11 and 6; *Roman Catholic*, Llanddoget Road*—11 alternate; *Presbyterian; Baptist; Wesleyan; Welsh Methodist; Welsh United Reformed.*

Population.—2,850.

Post Office.—Station Road.

Reading Room and Library.—Scotland Street.

Recreation.—Putting and bowling greens, and other games are played in the Recreation Grounds in Gwydir Park. Cinema. Concerts and other entertainments are given in the Church House. Community Centre.

Llanrwst is a market-town in a rich agricultural district. It is a capital centre for anglers and for visitors who delight in grand scenery. It is situated near the centre of the Conwy Valley, amidst lofty hills, rich meadows and lovely woods. The air is clear, dry and bracing, and the winters are usually mild.

About half a mile from the station is **Ancaster Square**, used as a market-place. From a corner of the Square, by the **Eagles** Hotel, a short thoroughfare leads to the **Parish Church** dedicated to the sixth-century saint St. Grwst.

A church was probably built here in the twelfth century and tradition has it that Rhun, a son of Nefydd Hardd, founder of the fifteen tribes of North Wales gave land for it to expiate the murder of Prince Idwal, son of Owain Gwynedd, by order of his foster father Nefydd to whom he had been entrusted. This building was burned by the armies of the Earl of Pembroke during the Wars of the Roses. Most of the present building dates from 1670. There is a magnificent carved rood-loft probably brought from Maenan Abbey (which formerly stood some two miles north of the town) at the Dissolution.

Adjoining the church is the—

Gwydir Chapel

(Key from verger at the churchyard entrance.)

a mausoleum erected by Sir Richard Wynn of Gwydir in 1634, on the instructions left in the will of his famous father, Sir John Wynn. It is an elaborate Gothic building and retains many of its original fittings. Tradition associates the name of Inigo Jones with the design. The ceiling is of heavy finely carved oak, probably from Maenan Abbey. Some of the Wynns are commemorated by marble monuments, and others by portrait brasses. Of the latter the most admirable is that of Dame Sarah Wynn, daughter of the old chevalier, Sir Thomas Myddelton. Several interesting objects within the building have been brought to it for preservation. Chief of these, perhaps, is the stone chest of Llewelyn-ap-Iowerth—Llewelyn the Great—Prince of Wales from 1194 to 1240 and a son-in-law of King John. He was buried in an abbey which he founded at Conwy. On the dissolution of that monastery in the reign of Edward I, his coffin was removed to Maenan Abbey, from which it was taken to its present resting-place. There is a stone effigy of Hywel Coetmor (1390) a descendant of David, Prince of Wales. It was from his family that the Gwydir Manor was bought by the first of the Wynns to settle in the district. Of interest is a spur reputed to have belonged to the Rob Roy of Wales—Dafydd-ab-Siencyn—who had his haunt in the rock known as the Falcon's Rock overlooking the town. There is also the unique Portable Bell, of bronze, with the date 1635, but this refers to a time of repair, as the bells are known to be of earlier origin. Originally cattle bells, they were adapted for ecclesiastical use.

At the entrance to the churchyard are almshouses, known as **Jesus Hospital.** They were founded by Sir John Wynn in 1610.

Returning to the Square and thence passing along Bridge Street, we come to—

Llanrwst Bridge

which bears date 1636 and is said to have been designed partly, if not entirely, by Inigo Jones. It is protected as an Ancient Monument. It rises to a sharp point in the centre.

Adjoining the west side of the bridge is **Tu Hwnt I'r Bont,** a fifteenth-century stone cottage (*teas*), once used as a court house. It is now National Trust property, the Pilgrim Trust having subscribed towards its restoration. Its low-beamed interior contains some old Welsh furniture and relics of the past. Welsh pottery, woollens and books can be bought here.

Running south-westward from the bridge is a straight road, which, at the end of half a mile, brings us to the highway between Conwy and Betws-y-Coed. Along this, some 200 yards to the left, is the entrance to **Gwydir Castle,** formerly the seat of the Wynn family, restored after fire damage. The castle and grounds (note the peacocks) are open Easter to October, daily except Saturdays, *charge.*

101

Opposite the Castle entrance a steep path leads through the woods to *Gwydir Uchaf*, where the Gwydir family once had a summer residence; it is now the district office of the Forestry Commission. Here is a remarkable little Episcopal Chapel, now in the care of the Department of the Environment. It is approached by a flight of steps. Over the door is the inscription "1673 S.R.W.B." The exterior is plain. A special feature of the interior is the decorated ceiling. The seats are carved oak chairs of ancient date.

From the west end of the Chapel a path leads to a road. By turning to the right on this and proceeding a short distance, a lovely view of the Vale of Llanrwst is obtained. At the end of a quarter of a mile the road joins the Llyn-y-Parc route between Llanrwst and Betws-y-Coed (*see* below). The junction is opposite the Nant Cottage.

Llanrwst to Betws-y-Coed *via* Llyn-y-Parc

(About 6 miles.) This is an exceedingly beautiful walk, and for a considerable distance lies through a wood, the loss of which farther on is amply recompensed by wonderful prospects of distant Snowdonia. Cross the old bridge and on reaching the Betws-y-Coed-Trefriw road cross over this taking the lane straight ahead.

a) The road on the right runs along the side of the valley, above the main road, which it joins near the quarries south of Trefriw village.
(*b*) The well-made road ahead leads up over the hills to Ty Hyll Bridge, a mile above the Swallow Falls on the Capel Curig road (*see* p. 103).
c) The track on the left is that which works up through plantations to Llyn-y-Parc, and then continues to Betws-y-Coed, as described on p. 114. As an alternative route to Betws-y-Coed, however, the path by Pen-yr-Allt is strongly to be recommended, though rather longer than that descending from the dam.

Llanrwst to Trefriw

1. **By the High Road.** (2½ miles.) This passes over the old bridge, and half a mile beyond turns to the right and continues straight into Trefriw. A more agreeable alternative, scarcely any longer, is by the road (*a*), passing Nant Cottage mentioned below, keeping to the right at the fork.

2. **Past Llanrhychwyn Church.** (About 5 miles.) Proceed as above, and at Nant Cottage take road (*a*) to the right. It at once crosses a stream just above a small fall, called the *Grey Mare's Tail*. Proceed along this road for about ¾ mile until a small hamlet of four or five houses is reached, then take the road to the left, passing through a farm gate, and the church can then be seen on the right-hand slope partly obscured by yew trees.

Llewelyn's Old Church, as it is called, is one of the oldest churches in the Principality, and is a unique specimen of primitive ecclesiastical architecture. It is about 40 feet long internally, and consists of two aisles, of which the northern is the older, and a bell turret. Proof of its antiquity is given by the arrangement of the roof timbers, by the extreme thickness of the walls and by the entrance door, which is hinged on wooden pivots. The font is said to belong to the eighth century. On the lych-gate is the puzzling inscription: IT. ID. OT. 1462. WO. The church owes its popular name to the tradition that it was used by Llewelyn the Great, who had a residence in Trefriw, until, at the request of his wife, who objected to the toilsome journey, he erected one in the village. The Trefriw building, if it ever existed, has gone.

On resuming the journey to Trefriw, pass into the lane at the west end of the church, and follow that to the right for about a quarter of a mile, and then take a track on the left. This goes to the left of a hill called *Clunllom*, the summit of which (slightly off the track) has an elevation of 938 feet, and commands a grand view. Thence a path leads first round the southern extremity of a wood and then through the wood into a road which soon enters Trefriw.

3. *Via* the **Old Church and the Lakes.** (About 6½ miles.) Proceed to the church as above. The route thence is described in the reverse direction under Trefriw.

The mountain road (*b*) provides the opening to three good walks of two or three hours each from Nant Cottage. For a mile or more it rises past woods, and small farms and deserted mines, and then suddenly reaches open moorland and presents one of the best views of Moel Siabod.

Soon after the descent begins, and just past an abandoned mine, a lane on the right leads to Llyn Geirionydd, at its upper end (straight on leads, as already stated, to the Capel Curig road at Ty Hyll Bridge).

Those who go to Geirionydd should follow the road alongside the lake; at the far end of which go up to the right for Llewelyn's Old Church and Trefriw, or down to the left for Llyn Crafnant and Trefriw; or from the head of Geirionydd there is a way over the hills to the head of Crafnant—a preferable route, since Crafnant is the more interesting lake.

Trefriw

Access.—(1) By rail, via Llandudno Junction to Llanrwst and Trefriw Station.
(2) By motor-coach or bus.
(3) By motor-launch from Conwy in summer.
For *Road Routes* see pp. 8–10.

Early Closing Day.—Thursday.
Fishing in Lakes Crafnant (apply at Cynlwyd by the lake) and Cowlyd and several rivers (Licences from Gwynedd River Authority).
Hotels.—*Belle Vue, Ye Olde Shippe Inn, Fairy Falls.*

Trefriw (pronounced *Trev-rewe*) is a large village, pleasantly situated under the tree-clad hills on the western side of the Conwy River. Through it runs the high road between Conwy and Betws-y-Coed, 11 miles from the former, 4¾ from the latter.

It is in the midst of romantic scenery and is a favourite resort of those requiring quiet quarters within easy reach of upland walks and yet in touch with busier centres such as Llandudno. Pleasant boating may be had on the Conwy and the village is also a good motoring centre.

The pretty little **Fairy Falls** are on the stream coming down from Llyn Crafnant, two and a half miles distant.

The **Chalybeate Wells,** about a mile from the village, yield the richest sulphur-iron waters in the world.

One of the most enjoyable walks in the neighbourhood is that to—

Llyn Crafnant

which lies to the south-west of Trefriw, in a most beautiful spot in the midst of the mountains. The route leaves Trefriw village by the lane beside the Glanrafon flats and is unmistakable if it is remembered to keep right at the fork about half a mile above the village (*i.e.* to follow the north side of the stream). The lake is about a mile long, nearly half a mile wide, and 600 feet above sea-level. To increase its utility to the village the level of the water has been artificially raised. Towards the far end is a cottage where refreshments may be obtained, boats are on hire and fishing facilities are available. Cars can be taken to this point.

The continuation to—

Llyn Geirionydd

however, is for walkers only. There are two routes; one starting behind the tea-house just mentioned, the other beginning at a gate below the falls at the lower end of the lake. The path first leads to the left of a slate quarry, then across another track, and finally over the slopes. Geirionydd Lake is inferior in beauty to Llyn Crafnant. It is said to have been the ornamental water in front of the reputed residence of Taliesin, the first and greatest of Welsh poets. He lived in the sixth century, and, if tradition may be believed, was, when a babe, accidentally discovered in a coracle on the mud-bank of the Dovey estuary. At the foot of the lake is a monument to the bard.

Misled by the cross on the monument, the ordnance surveyors marked the spot on their maps as Bedd Taliesin—Taliesin's Grave—but tradition places the grave in a tumulus above the estuary of the Dovey, a good 40 miles away.

To reach **Llanrhychwyn Church** from Llyn Geirionydd, take the road running up the hillside to the left of a spectator standing by Taliesin's monument and facing the water. After a short distance, the route bears round to the right and after an up and down course enters a narrow lane opposite a swing gate guarding the path to the Church which is seen on the far side of the field. (Key is kept at cottage down lane to left.) For description of the old building, *see* p. 103.

The return to Trefriw is made by descending the lane to a cross-roads, where turn left. By this last route the distance from church to village is 1¼ miles.

Porthlwyd Falls are three miles north of Trefriw. The west side of the valley is hideous with the works and cottages in connection with the aluminium works formerly at the foot of the falls, while the lower portion of the Porthlwyd stream runs through such a scene of confusion as is rarely encountered outside countries subject to the avalanche. This confused area of boulders and the debris of woods and houses was the work of water liberated from Llyn Eigiau by the bursting of a dam in 1925. There are important hydro-electric undertakings near the foot (*see* p. 97).

Trefriw to Capel Curig by Llyn Cowlyd

(*About 10 m., 3–4 hours.*)

Leave Trefriw up the steep hill a few yards north of the bridge opposite the Fairy Falls Hotel, and very soon fork right on the road signposted to the cemetery. About ten minutes after pass through a gate when shortly afterwards the road forks. Take the left fork, up the hill. We get views of Llyn Crafnant and Llyn Geirionydd on the left during the ascent. After passing the long and almost level ridge of Cefn Cyfarwydd (1,407 feet), a tiresomely boggy one, you see two farms, *Brwynog-isaf* and *Brwynog-uchaf,* "Lower and Upper Brwynog," by which the path goes, crossing the stream by a bridge at the bottom of the valley. During the descent a corner of Llyn Cowlyd comes into view, with Pen Llithrig towering beyond it. From the stream the path leads past two cottages, *Carregwen* and *Cwm Cowlyd,* about ¾ mile apart, and then bears down to the lake, with which it runs parallel, about 100 feet above the water.

From Cwm Cowlyd the ascent of **Pen Llithrig-y-Wrach** ("The top of the Hog's Slide," 2,621 feet) may be made. Turn up west for the ridge, which is rather boggy, and follow it to the top. Descend by a steep grass slope—quite easy, but a stiff *ascent*—to about the middle of the lake.

Llyn Cowlyd is over 1½ miles long by ¼ mile wide and 1,165 feet above the sea. Its east side is a steep green slope, with a crest of dark rock, *Creigiau Gleision.* The west side is not so steep, and the path is distinct. It supplies water to Conwy, Deganwy, Rhos, Colwyn Bay, Old Colwyn, and Llysfaen, the surplus water going to the Dolgarrog works.

At the south end of the lake the path leads over a spur on Pen Llithrig, and high up along the side of the corrie. It then skirts a patch of boggy ground, turns left to the cairn on the top of the *col* (1,366 feet; Tryfan's three humps and Glyders in view) at an angle of a wire fence, which it skirts for ten minutes, after which, for another ten, it passes over a bog to a gate, beyond which the descent to *Tal-y-Waen* farmhouse takes four minutes. The Bangor road is soon afterwards entered ¾-mile from Capel Curig.

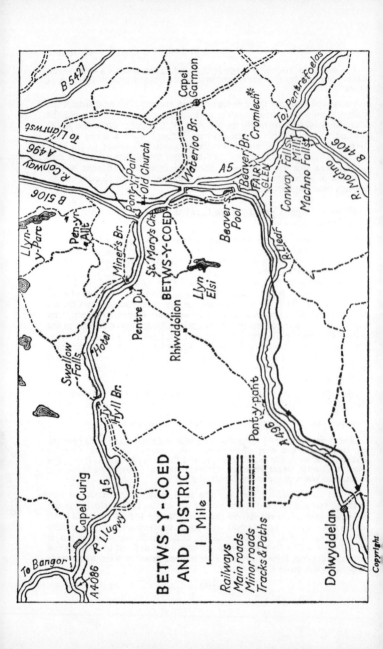

BETWS-Y-COED
AND DISTRICT

1 Mile

Railways
Main roads
Minor roads
Tracks & Paths

Copyright

Betws-y-Coed

Access.—(*Rail*) By L.M.R. *via* Chester, Llandudno Junction and the Vale of Conwy. By bus from Corwen (22 miles) *via* Cerrig-y-Drudion. (*See also* pp. 8–10.)

Bank.—*Midland.*

Buses to Penmachno and Cwm and to Llanrwst and Abergele; also to Cerrig-y-Drudion and Ruthin; and to Capel Curig. Bethesda, and Bangor.

Distances.—Beddgelert, 18; Bethesda, 14; Capel Curig, 5½; Caernarvon, 24; Conwy Falls, 3; Dolwyddelen Castle, 7; Fairy Glen, 1½; Llanberis, 16; Miners' Bridge, 1; Nant Ffrancon, 10; Pandy Mill, 3½; Penmachno, 4½; Pen-y-Gwryd, 10; Pontypant Bridge, 4; Swallow Waterfalls, 2½.

Early Closing Day.—Thursday.

Entertainments.—Concerts, and other entertainments.

Fishing.—Excellent fishing for trout and salmon in the waters of the Conwy Fishing Association and the Betws-y-Coed Anglers' Club.

Several classes of tickets are issued by both the Association and the Club to visitors for salmon and trout fishing, charges vary with the water to be fished.

Fishing on the Elsi Lake (30 acres), which has been well stocked by the Conwy Fishing Association with Loch Leven trout, *charge.*

Ticket-holders must also possess a rod licence issued by the Gwynedd River Authority.

Tickets and licences: Conwy Fishing Association waters—Gwydyr Hotel Betws-y-Coed, Tel: 217; Club waters—Tan Lan Café, Betws-y-Coed, Tel: 232.

Hotels.—*Gwydyr; Royal Oak; Waterloo; Glan Aber; Craig-y-Dderwen.*

Places of Worship.—*St. Mary's Church*—8.30, 11.15 and 8; *United Reformed* and *Calvinistic Methodist Chapels* (English and Welsh); *Roman Catholic* Coed-y-Pair, 9.30.

Population.—726.

Road Routes.—The Holyhead road comes down from Capel Curig and past the Swallow Falls, forms the main street of Betws-y-Coed, crosses the Conwy by the iron Waterloo Bridge and at once begins to climb towards the moors in the direction of Cerrig-y-Drudion.

At the top of the village, the old stone Pont-y-Pair bears the road running down the *west* side of the Conwy Valley to Trefriw and Conwy.

Beyond the Waterloo Bridge the road to the left leads down the *east* side of the Conwy Valley to Llanrwst, Llandudno Junction, Colwyn Bay, etc.

The road forking to the right as the Cerrig-y-Drudion road begins to climb after crossing the Waterloo Bridge, leads to Beaver Pool, Dolwyddelen, the Lledr Valley and Ffestiniog.

One other road is worth noting: the by-road which branches from the main road just short of the elbow leading to the Waterloo Bridge, and runs round to Beaver Pool and the Ffestiniog road. It is more hilly than the more usual route, but affords good views of the surrounding hills and some charming peeps of the river and the Beaver Pool.

Betws-y-Coed is charmingly situated among tree-clad hills at the point where the Llugwy valley meets the wider, softer valley of the Conwy. It claims with justification to be "the Beauty-spot of Wales." During the season it is besieged by visitors, for although the village consists almost entirely of hotels and apartment houses, "Betws-y-Coed" to the world at large includes also the far-famed Swallow Falls and the romantic glen of the Conwy.

The name means "the Chapel (or the Sanctuary) in the Wood," and woods and water are its characteristics, despite the heavy toll of war-time foresters on neighbouring hill-sides. To some extent Betws suffers from its reputation as a show-place, for it deserves far longer than the few hours usually devoted to it. As a centre for walks or motoring it is splendid; there is first-class fishing and accommodation to suit all tastes and purses.

The site is low, 80 feet above sea-level, but it is healthy. The climate is very mild, and the temperature equable. The rainfall is somewhat heavy, but as the soil is light and porous, the water is quickly carried off, so that the air is kept free from fogs. The water supply and drainage are excellent.

The village has long been a favourite haunt of anglers and artists. David Cox visited it for many years, and in the entrance hall of the Royal Oak Hotel is the signboard he painted in 1847. It is now under glass and valued at a very high price.

The Old Church

one of the oldest in Wales, is now used only for weddings and funerals. To reach it, turn to the left over the railway about 50 yards south of the Post Office. It contains the recumbent effigy of Gryffydd ap Dafydd Goch, a grandson of the last Llewelyn's brother David. He lived in the Lledr Valley, in the fourteenth century. For the old building, which is dedicated to St. Michael, there has been substituted **St. Mary's Church,** on the main road.

Towards the northern end of the village is the picturesque—

Pont-y-Pair

"the Bridge of the Cauldron." It is sometimes attributed to Inigo Jones, the great architect of the first half of the seventeenth century, but tradition says it was designed and partly built by a native mason named Howel, who died about 1470, before the work was finished. The bridge is a favourite subject with artists and photographers, and always makes a pretty picture. Jagged rocks here form the bed of the river, causing a miniature cataract. Just above the bridge is **Fir Island,** and on the left bank (the north side) are flat rocks much used as seats by visitors. Above Fir

Island is the **Still Pool,** alongside which is a path that may be followed to the Miners' Bridge and the Swallow Falls.

At the opposite end of the village is the graceful **Waterloo Bridge.** *Y Bont Haiarn* ("the Iron Bridge"), the Welsh have always called it. As the inscription on the bridge testifies, it was built in the year in which the battle of Waterloo was fought, and to that circumstance owes its English name. From the bridge the view up and down the valley is extremely picturesque.

SHORT WALKS AND EXCURSIONS

Note.—Visitors with only a few hours to spare should bear in mind that the two principal sights of Betws-y-Coed lie respectively some two miles west and two miles south-east of the village. Buses and coaches usually take the Swallow Falls *en route*, as they lie beside the Capel Curig road, but properly to appreciate the Conwy Falls and the Fairy Glen transport should be taken to the entrance to the Falls (on the Pentrefoelas road) and the village, or at least the Beaver Bridge, regained on foot. If there is time, it is well worth the extra distance to visit Pandy, the conveyance being taken as far as the mills off the Penmachno road.

At the station cars, coaches and other transport await the arrival of most trains.

TO THE MINERS' BRIDGE AND SWALLOW FALLS

These lie near the right-hand side of the road to Capel Curig (respectively 1 and 2½ miles north-west of the village).

Walkers may approach the falls by a more beautiful route than that available for vehicles, though the route is rather dangerous. Cross Pont-y-Pair Bridge, immediately turn to the left and go straight on for about a couple of miles. Some little way after emerging from the woods, the lane turns up to some cottages on the right. The path to the Swallow Falls keeps ahead, across a little stream. Beyond this, it turns down to the left and enters another wood by a ladder stile. On reaching a foot-bridge turn left over the stream and shortly the Swallow Falls will be seen, far below on the left.

By taking the left-hand branch where the path forks it is possible to make a cautious way down to a point commanding a fine full-length view of the fall, though the view is rather of a foaming torrent than the graceful fall seen from the more popular viewpoint on the other side of the river. It is not possible to cross the river at this point, and the path must be followed westward through wood and meadow for about ¾ mile to a stone bridge called **Ty Hyll Bridge.** "Ty Hyll" means "Ugly house." The building from which the bridge gets its peculiar name is a cottage whose walls are formed of huge boulders uncemented by mortar. It will be seen on the right just as one emerges into the Holy-head road.

The Miners' Bridge

is a wooden structure, placed like a ladder, the lower end resting on one bank of the stream, the upper end on the rocks on the opposite side. It was originally erected to enable the miners of

Pentre Du, the village on the left, to pass to and from the mines on the opposite hills, where formerly about 500 hands were employed.

From the bridge a path climbs steeply up the north bank to the route already mentioned. This can be followed back to Betws-y-Coed or leftward to Ty Hyll, as above.

The main road contin-ues to climb beside the Llugwy for another mile, with beautiful glimpses of the stream dashing over its rocky bed. Two and a half miles from Betws-y-Coed are—

The Swallow Falls

Admission.—Charge.
Car Park at entrance to Falls.
Restaurant, facing Falls.

Here the Llugwy, hurrying down from the mountains beyond Capel Curig to mingle its waters with those of the Conwy, and reinforced by countless torrents, hurls itself into a chasm some 60 feet wide. Jagged rocks break the stream into three large falls, and these again are subdivided and broken by jutting crags, which disperse the waters and dash them in all directions.

Borrow's description of the Falls still holds good:

"The Fall of the Swallow is not a majestic single fall, but a succession of small ones. First there are a number of little foaming torrents, bursting through rocks about twenty yards above the promontory on which I stood. Then come two beautiful rolls of white water, dashing into a pool a little way above the promontory; then there is a swirl of water round its corner into a pool below on its right, black as death and seemingly of great depth; then a rush through a very narrow outlet into another pool, from which the water clamours away down the glen. Such is the Rhaiadr y Wennol, or Swallow Fall; called so from the rapidity with which the waters rush and skip along."

The period allowed to coach parties is all too short. One could spend many hours in this beautiful nook, with its wonderful combination of woods and stream.

There is an old tradition that, as a penance for his oppression of the people, the spirit of Sir John Wynn, of Gwydyr, was doomed to remain in the depths of the pool under the fall, there to be purged and purified. Sir John was M.P. for the county of Caernarvon in 1596 and one of the Council of the Marches of Wales.

TO PANDY MILL AND FALLS, CONWY FALLS AND THE FAIRY GLEN

In addition to the special vehicles running from Betws-y-Coed there are the buses to Penmachno and Cerrig-y-Drudion.

We have inverted the usual order in which these three places are mentioned because—although the **Fairy Glen** is nearest to Betws-y-Coed and the most popular of the trio—the best way to see this part of the Conwy Valley is to walk *down*.

At least 3 hours should be allowed if Pandy is to be included; 2 hours should suffice for the Conwy Fall and return to Betws *via* Fairy Glen if transport is taken to the Conwy Falls.

The Fairy Glen

can be reached directly from Betws-y-Coed by crossing the Waterloo Bridge and taking the river-side road immediately beyond it on the right, or (a prettier route) by turning up a narrow lane on the right a little short of the railway bridge. The two roads are of about the same length. They reunite on the east side of **Beaver Bridge,** at the Beaver's Pool, about a mile from the village. From the east end of the bridge a lane leads to the Glen, a truly enchanting spot. Rocks and trees tower high above the stream, which here rushes tumultuously over the rocks; there forms a placid pool reflecting and heightening the beauties of the lovely scene.

Pandy Mill and Falls

are reached by turning off the main Corwen highway by the
Penmachno road, about 2 miles from the Waterloo Bridge. This
leads high above the Conwy River, and, at the end of half a mile,
to a lane on the right, beside a mill. Just below the point where
this lane crosses the Machno is an ancient semicircular bridge,
probably of Roman origin.

Penmachno, a small village two miles farther south-west, contains the
gravestone of Carausius (a relic of ancient British Christianity), and in the
Church is a memorial window to Bishop Morgan, the translator of the
Bible into Welsh, his birthplace being *Ty Mawr*, in this parish.

A delightful 8-mile walk may be had by visiting the Fairy Glen, then on
by the old lane to Conwy Falls and by road and lane to Pandy. From
Pandy Mill a rough path runs through a charming wood along the west side
of the stream to the old **Lledr Bridge** connected with the Dolwyddelan road.
After crossing the Lledr, turn to the right, and you soon arrive at the
Beaver Bridge, from which it is but a mile to Betws-y-Coed. The round may
be shortened by crossing the Lledr by a bridge about a mile east of the old
bridge, just above the confluence of the Lledr and the Conwy.

A few hundred yards beyond the "Roman" bridge the lane
arrives at the farm where is kept the key (*fee*) of the path leading
to the **Falls of the Machno.** In a neighbourhood famed for falls,
Pandy is one of the best worth seeing. It is small, but perfect, and
the glen below is equally charming.

From Pandy return to the Holyhead-Corwen road, at the
junction with which is the entrance to—

The Conwy Falls

Admission, charge. *Hotel* (private) and car park.

Here the Conwy, rushing wildly down to the sea after receiv-
ing the waters of the Machno, is turned in its course by the
unyielding cliffs and split into two streams by an immense
boulder. Between the two falls is the old salmon ladder. The
actual falls have not the grace of the little fall at Pandy, but the
setting of greenery and rocks is beautiful. From the entrance
to the Falls return to the main road. A few yards to the left at a
lay-by take a stile in stone wall. Take path parallel to main road
and then follow lane to the entrance to the Fairy Glen (*see* p. 111).
The walk of about a mile, first through woods and then along a
grassy open lane with magnificent views up the Lledr Valley, is

one of the prettiest of the easy walks around Betws. On the way a cottage is passed where refreshments may be obtained.

TO CAPEL GARMON CROMLECH

The Cromlech is a very good specimen and the three miles' walk to it opens up most charming views. The road crosses the Waterloo Bridge, goes to the left for about 300 yards and then branches up on the right. (This lane is steep and in parts rough, and motorists will probably prefer to take the lane turning back a mile or so nearer Llanrwst.) Walkers can cut off a corner by going a few yards to the right after crossing the Bridge and ascending some steps to a footpath which leads into the above road. At the junction turn to the right. Three-quarters of a mile farther turn to the right for **Capel Garmon.** Two-thirds of a mile beyond the village, pass through a gate on the right to a cart-track that leads past Tyn-y-Coed Farm to the **Cromlech.** The latter is in a fenced enclosure, and the notice-boards are seen ahead as the track rounds the corner above the farm, whence a field path is followed.

Although locally referred to as "the Cromlech" the monument is more correctly described as burial chambers of the long barrow type in use at the beginning of the Bronze Age, and in fact pottery dating from that time (1800 B.C.) was found in the entrance passage in 1925. Until the middle of last century the monument appears to have been intact, but since then all but one of the roofing slabs have been removed and at one time the chamber formed a stable. The site is now an Ancient Monument and as such well cared for by the Department of the Environment.

Apart from its archaeological interest (which is considerable) the spot is well worth visiting on account of the magnificent views westward.

From the Cromlech there is a path to the Corwen and Pentre-foelas road, by which the return can be made. The circular walk will be about 5 miles; it may be varied or extended by way of the path from Pandy along the west side of the Lledr or the lane above the Conwy Falls and Fairy Glen.

LLYN ELSI

Llyn Elsi, a small lake up among the hills, two miles to the south-west of Betws-y-Coed, is a pleasant spot for a picnic. The lake is the main source of water supply of Betws.

From the vicinity of the lake the mountain panorama is very fine,

113

Moel Siabod (due west) predominating. To the right are Tryfan and the Glyders, while Arenig Fawr reigns supreme in the south. Snowdon is behind Moel Siabod.

The best route from Betws to the lake is by the "Jubilee" Path starting from the Capel Curig road about half a mile from the Post Office, against a house known as Mount View. The way is clear and there are seats. At the fork beyond the fourth seat bear left, cross a wall by steps and thence make for a cairn and flagstaff and so to the monument erected in 1914 by the Earl of Ancaster.

Another route starts by the lane running up beside the (modern) Parish Church. The way is unmistakable, but steep in places.

TO LLYN-Y-PARC

Llyn-y-Parc, or Park Lake, lies up in the hills to the north of Betws-y-Coed, about $\frac{1}{2}$ to $\frac{3}{4}$ of an hour's easy walk from the village. One can return the same way; return by Pen-yr-Allt, or continue alongside the lake to the main road beside Gwydyr Castle, Llanrwst.

From Betws-y-Coed cross Pont-y-Pair and turn sharp to the left, through car park. At the top of the first rise turn right up the road between two houses. In about 200 yards the road forks. Take the right-hand (descending) road and follow it for about a quarter mile, until at the top of a rise, a path is seen on the left, leading up through the woods. Hence the way hugs the hillside and eventually comes to a ravine which is forlorn with the debris of an old mine. Here the path goes steeply up to the left and at the top a short strip of green path brings us to the end of the lake.

For Trefriw keep along the lake side and thence follow the track down to Nant Cottage at an important crossing of ways (*see* p. 103): but for the return to Betws *via* Pen-yr-Allt cross the dam and go over the ladder stile ahead. Ascend beside the wall, disregard tracks running right and left and just over top of rise pass through gap in wall. For the next few hundred yards there are splendid mountain views; then the path descends. Keep to left on meeting another path and on reaching Pen-yr-Allt Farm pass through gate and then turn to right down cart track. The track is followed down through the woods to the road on the north side of the river. Turn to the left here and in less than half a mile you are back at Pont-y-Pair. The walk down from Park Lake takes about an hour.

THE VALLEY OF THE LLEDR

This valley is extremely picturesque, particularly the portion between Betws-y-Coed and beautiful **Pont-y-Pant**. Beyond that point the scenery becomes more open, and at Roman Bridge takes on an aspect of moorland which is only lost when the slag heaps of Blaenau Ffestiniog are reached. The Lledr Valley is highly interesting both to the geologist and the botanist.

About 1½ miles beyond Pont-y-Pant is the village of—

Dolwyddelan

at one time busily engaged in the now declined slate-quarrying industry. A mile beyond the village, overlooking the road to Ffestiniog, are the remains of a **Castle**, in which Llewelyn the Great is said to have been born. He reigned from 1194 to 1240. The last Prince Llewelyn was his grandson. The ruins are cared for by the Department of the Environment. (*Admission charge. Apply at the Farmhouse below the Castle.* Official Guide Pamphlet.)

Dolwyddelan has a curious ancient **Church** as well as a modern church. The former was founded early in the sixteenth century by Meredydd ap Ifan, the ancestor of the Wynns of Gwydyr and of the Wynns of Wynnstay, who is commemorated by a brass inside the church.

A short way beyond the Castle, where the road crosses the river, there is a good distant view of Snowdon over the lower parts of Moel Siabod.

The archaeologist attracted by the name of *Roman Bridge* station may be warned that there is neither bridge nor foundation to substantiate the railway company's enterprise. Another local name arousing strange reflections is **Crimea.** Beyond Roman Bridge the road rises, to fall on reaching **Blaenau Ffestiniog,** one of the great slate-quarrying centres of Wales. (*See the Red Guide to the Southern Section of North Wales.*)

Motorists wishing to make a circular tour can continue through Ffestiniog to Maentwrog and Penrhyndeudraeth, whence roads run northward to Beddgelert and so either to Caernarvon or Capel Curig.

Capel Curig and Excursions

Capel Curig

Access by bus from Betws-y-Coed (5½ miles) or from Bangor (15 miles).
Road Routes.—See pp. 8–10.
Fishing.—All the neighbouring lakes provide excellent fishing, though some are private or held by clubs. See local announcements. Cobden's Hotel has 1½ miles of Llugwy fishing. (*See also under* Betws-y-Coed and Bangor, pp. 107 and 141).
Hotels.—*Cobden's*; *Bryn-Tyrch*; *Tyn-y-Coed.*
Licensing Hours.—11–3, 6–10.30.

Capel Curig, beautifully situated on the Shrewsbury and Holyhead road, is one of the oldest tourist resorts in the Principality. The village is about 600 feet above sea-level, and has a bracing air. It is a capital resort for anglers, for, besides the lakes close at hand, there are other good fishing waters not far away, and it is much frequented by climbers and walkers, since it is one of the handiest centres for Tryfan, the Glyders and Snowdon. The church is dedicated to St. Curig, a British recluse; hence the name of the village.

There are first-class hotels, several good boarding houses, and accommodation can also usually be found, in one or other of the cottages. The village is strung along the Holyhead road for nearly two miles at the point where the Beddgelert and Llanberis road strikes off westward. Buses pass through it on their way to or from Betws-y-Coed or Bangor.

From Capel Curig the Holyhead road rises steadily until it reaches an altitude of 1,000 feet as it passes between the mighty **Tryfan** (3,010 feet) and **Llyn Ogwen**, the latter famed for trout and eels. From the western end, at Benglog, the road begins the long gradual descent of **Nant Ffrancon**, "the Vale of Beavers." But to be properly appreciated the pass should be *ascended* (*see* p. 151).

116

TRYFAN

(3,010 feet) is a really noble mountain and one beloved of climbers. It is no place for the inexpert, however. In shape it resembles a pyramid, and, bristling as it does with fantastic and pinnacled rockwork, it affords unlimited scope for the hardy cragsman. The Eastern Traverse is the goal of many parties of expert climbers. On the summit are two stones known to climbers as *Adam and Eve*; they are clearly visible from the high-road and look like a couple of statues.

To ascend Tryfan from Ogwen Lake, take the path to *Llyn Idwal* (*see* below). Where this bends sharply to the right, leave it and strike across boggy ground to the stream which flows from *Llyn Bochlwyd*. Follow a steep narrow track by its side to the lake above. Thence make for *Bwlch Tryfan* (the narrow pass between Tryfan and Glyder Fach), and just before reaching its top, bear up the steep, rugged slopes to the left (there is a slight track) and the rocky summit will be gained after a stiff scramble.

TO LLYN IDWAL AND THE DEVIL'S KITCHEN

To Benglog, at the head of Nant Ffrancon, as described on p. 116 (*bus service*).

It should be understood that walking in this neighbourhood is often terribly rough, and frequently would be more accurately referred to as "climbing." It is inadvisable for an inexperienced person to set out without a companion, particularly in bad or doubtful weather.

Take the path striking up beside Ogwen Cottage and its neighbouring *Youth Hostel*, and in about a quarter of a mile turn sharp to the right, over swampy ground. The point to make for is a gate in a fence which is at the foot of **Llyn Idwal**, at an elevation of 1,200 feet in a hollow ground out by a glacier. On the western side are four moraines, arranged in long symmetrical mounds, one within another. Few scenes of the same dimensions in Wales are more stern and wild than those around this lake. In some places the rocks are perpendicular, and stand like a defiant wall around the pool. It is one of the many spots in the Principality with which a dark tradition is linked. A young prince whose name was Idwal (whence the name of the tarn) was here drowned by his foster-father, and it was long believed that, in consequence of the fell deed, no bird would fly over the lake.

Beyond Llyn Idwal the rocky heights of Y Garn on the right and Glyder Fawr on the left descend so steeply as apparently to bar further progress. Looking up the Cwm, however, we may note, a little to the right of its far corner (W. side), a narrow rift in the rocky wall—a small "V" on the cliff-top. This is Twll-du (literally the "black hole"), and to reach it from the end of the lake the climb is a very steep and rough one, first up the ridge of a moraine, and then over rough debris, which descends almost to the water's edge. The height of Llyn Idwal above sea-level is about 1,200 feet; of the "Kitchen" (the bottom of the chasm) 1,700 feet, and the top of the chasm 2,000 feet.

Twll-du (the **Devil's Kitchen**) is only a few yards wide, and the perpendicular rocks which form its walls are from 200 to 300 feet high. It is quite impassable, the small stream which threads it leaping from rock to rock in the wildest fashion.

Most tourists will be content to admire the chasm from below, but for stout walkers a very steep and somewhat loose path strikes up across the face of the rock to the left of the Kitchen. The path is indistinct in places, therefore keep close to the precipitous cliffs. The path becomes less steep, and near the summit bends to the right. When the ridge is reached, a walk of three minutes takes you to the top of the chasm, a little beyond which is the small lake, *Llyn-y-Cŵn*. Shortly beyond this the view opens out westward over Snowdon and Llanberis. To the left the ground rises steeply to the summit of **Glyder Fawr** (3,279 feet) For *descent* to Pen-y-Gwryd, *see* below.

The Glyders

The tongue of land enclosed by the Holyhead and Beddgelert roads, and upon the tip of which Capel Curig may be said to stand, rises steeply westward to Glyder Fach (3,262 feet) and Glyder Fawr (3,279 feet). The word Glyder has a significance similar to the "clitter" of Dartmoor, and the aptness of the name will not be disputed by any who have passed from the Fach to the Fawr. The twin summits of the Glyders provide the roughest going in Wales.

From Capel Curig direct to Glyder Fach (2–2½ *hours*). For this ascent you may either follow the ridge (Cefn-y-Capel) all the way, striking up it directly from the Post Office, or (shorter and better) you may take the Pen-y-Gwryd road for about 1½ miles, passing the two lakes, and then turn up the fell by the farmhouse of *Dyffryn Mymbyr*; whence, after crossing a wall, you will come to a long smooth ascent over grass to the part of the ridge which overlooks **Gallt yr Ogof**. Hence Tryfan comes into prominent view. A stretch of level swampy ground, containing a few tarns, is crossed, beyond which, passing another northward spur, you look down into the desolate **Cwm Tryfan**. Glyder Fach is now directly in front. A series of cairns marks the way from the edge of the swampy ground nearly to the summit.

Pen-y-Gwryd (or **Gorphwysfa**) **to Glyder Fawr** (1½–2 *hours*). Go for a good 200 yards along the Capel Curig road from Pen-y-Gwryd; then pass through an opening near a shed and go north-westwards with the little height of *Moel-Berfedd* between you and the road on your left and the stream issuing from *Llyn-cwm-Ffynnon* some distance on the right. Cross this stream as it issues from the north-east end of the lake, and make straight ahead for the ridge which leads up to the Glyder Fawr. Hereabouts the ground is thickly strewn with moraine debris. The way to the ridge is steep but easily found, and when once you are on the ridge you have only to bear away slightly to the right till you reach the top of the mountain.

From Ogwen Lake.—This has already been described in connection with the Devil's Kitchen excursion.

To **Glyder Fach** the way lies along the summit plateau of Glyder Fawr in an east-north-easterly direction till it narrows at the slight depression between the two mountains. Hence the direction is almost due east, over an extraordinary jumble of rocks and stones, to negotiate which care is required. The summit of *Glyder Fach* itself is composed of huge blocks of rock, the surmounting of which is not easy.

Descent to Pen-y-Gwryd presents no difficulty. Those making their way down from Glyder Fawr to Pen-y-Gwryd should proceed cautiously on account of the numerous masses of rock over and between which it is necessary to pass. In clear weather these are merely awkward; but in mist or darkness they are *dangerous*, especially to strangers, since a fall from one of these boulders might easily result in a broken leg, or worse. The hotel is seen below, but the point to aim at is a little way down the road on the Capel Curig side of the hotel.

It should be borne in mind that the Glyders are extremely precipitous on their northern sides and that almost everywhere the going is arduous.

Descent by Devil's Kitchen. Except to those who know the way, this is emphatically a dangerous route, owing to the difficulty of hitting off the top of the path down the face of the rocks to the Kitchen Door.

Y Garn and the Elidyrs

A capital expedition may be taken over these heights from the head of Nant Ffrancon to Llanberis. The first part of the route is that to the top of the *Devil's Kitchen* (*see* p. 118). From this point strike up the side of **Y Garn** (3,104 feet) in a north-westerly direction till the summit is reached. Thence the way lies due north to **Foel Goch**, fine views being obtained on the way of the wild scenery at the head of Nant Ffrancon. From Foel Goch a steep descent along the ridge takes us to the head of a little green valley on our left, and bending round this till we face due west, a track will be struck which leads along the narrow rocky ridge of **Bwlch-y-Brecan**. No mistake can be made now, for the fine, craggy summit of **Elidyr Fawr** (3,029 feet) rises straight in front of us. The descent to Llanberis takes us in a westerly direction over the summit of **Elidyr Fach** (2,564 feet), and then on between quarries to a road. Follow this till the main road is gained, by which the Llanberis Lakes are reached.

Moel Siabod

(2,860 feet) is easily ascended from Capel Curig by crossing Pont Cyfyng at the lower end of the village. Take the second by-road right, beyond the bridge, and ascend a stony farm track that rises above the woods. Pass two small farmhouses, and leave the track for a straight grassy road. Half-a-mile on go through a wire fence, and along a shallow grassy hollow to the skyline. At the top, turn left for about a mile of ridge walking, then for a last few hundred yards over grass to the summit.

Standing a little apart from the group, this peak gives a grand view of the mountains of Snowdonia, with their lakes and hollows, and of the Irish Sea, with the bays of Caernarvon and Cardigan. Guides can be engaged at local hotels.

The Carnedds

These lie north-west of Capel Curig, in the angle made by the Bangor road. Compared with Tryfan and the Glyders, they are not thrilling to ascend, but those who appreciate tramping over good turf will enjoy them, and the views are very good.

Carnedd Dafydd (3,426 feet) is the nearer to Llyn Ogwen and can be reached by an obvious route leaving the main road near the 36th milestone from Holyhead. Follow the farm track at first, but just before reaching the house bear off to left and climb Craig Llugwy. From Carnedd Dafydd to **Carnedd Llewellyn** (3,484 feet) the way is rough and those who diverge from the direct path miss the best views.

A better ascent leaves the main road 2½ miles from Capel Curig Post Office, strikes up to Tal-y-Braich cottages and then climbs the ridge called "Braich." From the top of **Pen Helig** (2,731 feet) follow a path winding down among rocks and out on to a narrow grassy ridge reminiscent of Striding Edge on Helvellyn. Onward the way to the summit of Llewellyn is undeniably rough, but the scenery is fine.

TO LLYN CRAFNANT AND TREFRIW

Take the path from the north side of the Church at Capel Curig. After crossing a small stream follow the right-hand fork, which leads across boggy ground between two craggy bluffs. After winding round the base of the crags on the left, the path turns left across a bog, and a stream is crossed by a wooden bridge. The path is now unmistakable up to the top of the col. From this point alternative routes are available. (*a*) Take a narrow track on the right, which runs along a little ridge, from which the views are very lovely. Soon a descent is made by a little hollow and a wall is reached on the left, which must be crossed in a short distance, and the track followed through the wood along the side of the steep slope, till another wall is reached. Cross this and a good path is gained which leads down to the road by the head of the lake. (*b*) An unmistakable path winds down to the valley, and after passing through two iron gates, joins the road which begins there.

BY LLYN COWLYD TO TREFRIW

From *Plas-y-Brenin* follow the Bangor road for a mile and just beyond a brook ascend by footpath to *Tal-y-waen Farmhouse,* behind and above which is a cart-track which leads to Llyn Cowlyd. Cross a brook, ascend to a gate, turn to right (*i.e.* N.) over bog to a wire fence, which is skirted as far as a cairn at an angle of the fence at the top of the *col* before the lake. Thence follow path over spurs of Pen Llithrig, above a corrie and the end of the lake, continuing along (about 100 feet) above the lake. For the rest of the way *see* the description of the reverse route, p. 105.

Other routes to Trefriw and Llanrwst begin at Ty Hyll Cottage (*see* p. 109), the lane climbing through woods to the abandoned mine mentioned on p. 103 and so to Nant Cottage.

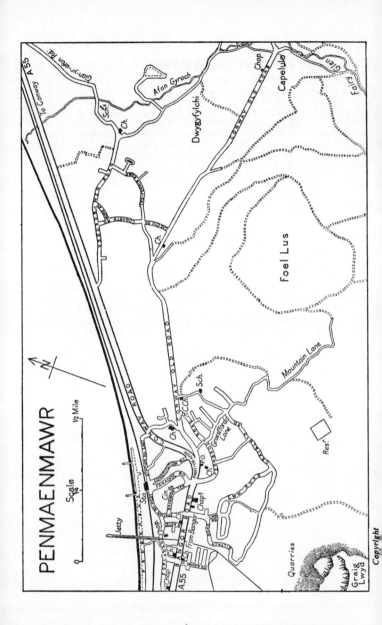

PENMAENMAWR

Scale

0 — ¼ — ½ Mile

To Conway A 55

Glan-yr-afon Rd.

Afon Gyrach

Sch.

Ch.

Dwygyfylchi

Chap.

Capelulo

Fairy Glen

OLD CONWAY ROAD

Ch.

Sch.

Foel Lus

Mountain Lane

Resr.

Ch.

Sch.

Greenfield Lane

P.O.

Ch.

Chaps.

Jetty

A 55

Chap.

BANGOR

From Bangor

Quarries

Graig Lwyd

Copyright

Penmaenmawr

Access.—By the L.M.R. main line. From London in 4 hours; Birmingham, 4; Leeds, 4¼; Manchester, 2¼; Liverpool, 2¼; Holyhead, 1¼.
Road route from Chester (50¾ m.). *See* p. 8.

Amusements.—Boating, bathing, and mountain-walking. Golf, bowls. The Young Men's Institute, containing four billiard tables, is open to visitors.

Banks.—*National Westminster, Midland* and *Lloyds.*

Bathing.—Perfectly safe. The beach is of firm sand and slopes gradually. Chalets fitted with electric points, etc., on the promenade.

Beach.—A fringe of shingle, succeeded by a good stretch of fine sand.

Bowls.—Green near Railway Station. Also at Dwygyfylchi.

Buses *via* Conwy and Deganwy to Llandudno, also to Llanfairfechan, Aber, Bangor and Caernarvon. There is also an ample service to Dwygyfylchi, Golf Links, Fairy Glen and Sychnant Pass. At Conwy connection is made with the Llandudno-Llanrwst buses, and there are also buses to Colwyn Bay, etc.

Car Parks.—Car parks near beach and shopping centre.

Distances.—Bangor, 11; Betws-y-Coed 21; Birmingham, 125; Caernarvon, 18; Chester, 51; Colwyn Bay, 8; Conwy, 5; Llanfairfechan, 2; Llandudno, 9; Liverpool, 65; London, 231; Manchester, 90.

Early Closing Day.—Wednesday.

Golf.—A 9-hole course in a valley at the back of the town, below the road to Dwygyfylchi, 10 minutes' walk from the centre of the town. Buses run to and from the links. It is well drained and is dry all the year round. The hazards are natural and varied. There is a well-equipped club-house.

Hotels.—*Puffin,* Conwy Road; *Plas Arvon,* Ysguborwen Road; *Mountain View,* Pant-yr-Afon; *Fairy Glen,* Dwygyfylchi.

Places of Worship, with hours of services on Sundays.—*St. Seiriol's*—8, 11 and 6; *St. Gwynin's* (at Dwygyfylchi)—8, 10.30 and 6; *St. David's* (Welsh)—10 and 6; *Roman Catholic* (Our Lady of the Rosary), Conwy Old Road—8, 10.30 and 6; *United Reformed, Methodist,* and *Presbyterian* Churches —at 11 and 6; *Baptist*—11.

Population.—4,000.

Post Office.—Close to junction of Conwy Road and Conwy Old Road. Also at Penmaenan and Capelulo.

Road Routes.—The Chester-Caernarvon road forms the main thoroughfare of Penmaenmawr and leads eastward to Conwy, etc.; westward to Llanfairfechan, Bangor, etc. For motorists almost the only deviation worth noting in the village is the old Conwy road, cutting up between the Mountain View Hotel and the Post Office, and running *via* Dwygyfylchi and the Sychnant Pass (1 in 7¼ ascent) to Conwy.

Penmaenmawr is one of the pleasant, quiet seaside resorts of North Wales. It stands at the mouth of a beautiful valley noted for its fertility, and bounded by lofty hills terminating in headlands known respectively as Penmaenmawr and Penmaenbach: the great and little headlands. From the larger and nearer of the two the town takes its name. It is a majestic rock 1,300 feet high, rising almost perpendicularly from the sea, and forming the

northern termination of the Snowdon range. Unfortunately this headland is composed of stone having a commercial value. and consequently its sides are scarred by quarries.

Penmaenmawr offers an almost unique combination of sea, woodland and mountain and is every summer the resort of numerous walking parties and of family folk who appreciate the opportunity of varying the delights of the sands by an occasional moorland tramp or an easy stroll to a picturesque valley. It is also a favourite spot for campers, both those who carry or provide their own equipment and those who join large parties and live in marquees.

As in the case of most of the resorts along this part of the Welsh coast, the railway runs between the sea and the village, but by reason of the elevation of the site of Penmaenmawr the line does not block the view, which is charmingly varied and extensive. On the north is the sea, with Puffin Island and the north of Anglesey to the west; on the north-east the rugged rocks of Penmaenbach and Great Orme's Head. On the south-east the hill of Y Foel Llys with its many paths and its carpet of heather and bilberry plants; on the east the Fairy Glen and the Sychnant Pass, while between the two hills is a beautiful valley.

Its sheltered position gives the spot a genial climate, as is attested by the myrtles, gigantic fuchsia-bushes and other shrubs and flowers that abound. Yet the air in summer is bracing and invigorating.

The centre of the town is linked with the railway station and the sea-front by Paradise Road, at the head of which a bronze bust of W. E. Gladstone recalls that statesman's association with "dear old Penmaenmawr," as he called it.

The beach is an expanse of clean, firm sand, with a fringe of pebbles. It is bordered by an asphalted **Promenade,** a mile long, well supplied with seats and shelters. Near the centre are rows of attractive chalets for bathing, etc. As the tide never recedes very far, safe bathing may be enjoyed at all hours of the day, and the bay is equally favourable for boating. Paddling pool.

The site of the bay was once a tract of fertile land dotted with dwellings, and there is a legend which tells how one of the inhabitants was a maid of high degree who loved and was beloved by the son of a house at feud with hers, but a bard foretold that the two families would never be united until eels came of their own accord to her father's cellar, so that there seemed no possibility of the lovers ever marrying. But one day there was a sudden inrush of the sea over the smiling land, and only with great difficulty did the maiden escape to higher ground. Some say that she alone was saved; others that some of her relatives escaped also.

A bold projecting spur midway in the vale bears the name of Trwyn-yr-Wylfa, meaning "a good look-out point." At very low tide it is possible to step from a boat on to the ruins of the ancient mansion, known as *Llys Helig*. In 1909 squared stones were raised from the spot. The site of the remains is a favourite haunt of conger-eel fishers.

The railway pierces right through Penmaenmawr and Penmaenbach mountains by means of tunnels. Until the 1930's the high road to Bangor and Holyhead wriggled round the headlands with a minimum of spare room; but the increase of traffic made it necessary to tunnel through the headlands. When the wind hurls in from the sea the passage westward is an experience to be remembered.

Walks from Penmaenmawr

1. The Fairy Glen

The Fairy Glen is situated at the apex of the triangular valley of which the Penmaenmawr-Conwy road forms the base.

It is reached by the road leaving the village near the Post Office and passing through the hamlet of **Dwygyfylchi,** a name signifying "the place of the twin semicircles," and giving an accurate description of the parish, the conformation of which corresponds exactly to two semicircles side by side.

Cars and vehicles are left here. (It is inadvisable to take a car up the lane, which is very narrow, while if there is another car at the end it may be impossible to turn.) The narrow lane between the hotels runs in among hills for about half a mile to the entrance to the glen.

The lower part of the glen, with its solemn pines and quietly murmuring stream, will remind many Southern visitors of a Hampshire chine; but the upper portion is more characteristic of Welsh scenery and has a pretty display of rocks, pools and falls.

It is a delightful retreat on a hot day. (Tea and refreshments can be obtained at lower entrance.)

From the upper gate we step out on to grass and bracken-covered moorland surrounded by mountain peaks. A short way ahead (westward) will be seen a gate with a sign-post directing to the Green Gorge, the Jubilee Walk, etc; the path following the wall leading down from the gate descends to the lane close to the lower entrance to the Fairy Glen. From the upper end of the glen there is an excellent walk towards Conwy, through bracken and heather. The Sychnant Pass will be reached in a short distance.

2. The Sychnant Pass

Sychnant Pass may be reached by the road leaving the village near the Post Office and passing through the hamlet of Dwygyfylchi. The steep ascent of the Pass begins by the Fairy Glen Hotel. The road rises about 300 feet in a mile, and the *descent* (1 in 7½) requires caution from motorists, as there are sharp elbows where the narrow road runs between unyielding cliffs of rock and a steep open precipice—awkward points at which to suffer a collision.

The scenery is impressive, the bareness of the rocky flanks of the pass contrasting vividly with the luxurious green slopes above the Fairy Glen. On the right, near the top, is a cliff in the vicinity of which a fine echo can be awakened. Almost opposite this rock is the beginning of a path which crosses the head of the valley and leads over Conwy Mountain into the town of Conwy; walkers bound for Conwy should take this in preference to the high road.

3. **The Jubilee Walk.** This is a promenade cut across the breast of **Y Foel Llys** (the Bilberry Hill), rising 1,181 feet high, at the back of the village, from which the view is grand and extensive. The visitor who frequents the hills will soon discover that there are several routes by which this pleasant walk can be reached. We will briefly indicate three:—

(*a*) The most direct route is by the lane leading to the Green Gorge (*see* No. 4). Two stone pillars mark the beginning of the path from this direction, and will be a sufficient guide as soon as they are in sight.

(*b*) The opposite end of the walk can be reached by following the old (the upper) Conwy road for some three-quarters of a mile. Here the road forks, and leaving it you follow a mountain road to the right, and are led to a point from which the upper entrance to the Fairy Glen can be plainly seen away on the left. Continuing to ascend a grassy path you will before long see the Jubilee Walk on the right.

(*c*) This end of the walk can also be gained by following a winding path that starts from the vicinity of the lower entrance to the Fairy Glen or that from the gate near the upper end of the Glen (*see* p. 126).

4. The Green Gorge. Pass at the back of the Mountain View Hotel, and almost immediately turn up Groesffordd Lane (the first on the right). It is very long and in parts steep. At the upper end is a gate, through which pass, and the Green Gorge is straight before you.

5. The Druids' Circle. This is on the moorland at the back of the village. It is about 1,200 feet above sea-level, and consists of a dozen stones, some 6 feet high, intermixed with smaller stones. The nearest way (1½ miles) is by Gilfach Road, in which turn to the left by Cwm Road. In a hundred yards or so a path crosses the field on the right to Graiglwyd Road, in which turn to the left for about 100 yards to a road leading to Graiglwyd Farm, through the precincts of which you pass. The way is then unmistakable, sign-posts giving a clear indication of it.

The Circle can also be reached *via* the Green Gorge by following the cart-track from that to the right, or by following the second route to the Jubilee Walk, and then, instead of turning to the right for the walk, continuing along the green road, and, so passing by the back of Foel Llys.

A short distance west of the Circle is a smaller collection of stones. In 1921 a large number of flint weapons and tools were unearthed in Graiglwyd Quarry, giving rise to the belief that in the Stone Age the place was the site of an important manufactory of those articles.

6. To Bwlch-y-Ddeufaen and Llanfairfechan. Walk up the Green Gorge and past the Druids' Circle, and continue half a mile farther along a green track winding westwards, where a sign-post directs to the Bwlch, about 2½ miles distant. The walk may be continued to Tal-y-Cafn, in the Conwy Valley or the Roman Road (now but a track) followed towards Aber or Llanfairfechan (*see* p. 136).

7. Llangelynin Old Church (3 miles) **and the Conwy Valley.** The route is through the Green Gorge, and then to the left and over a stile from which the path runs across the Fairy Glen stream to a derelict cottage a short distance beyond which the Church will become visible. It is said to have been built in the year 1350, stands 927 feet above sea-level, and is used only for a service at 6 p.m. last Sunday in each summer month. The keys are kept at a cottage near the church. (The last cottage on the right—"Garnedd Wen"—*refreshments*.) The return may be varied by either of the routes described under Walks from Conwy.

8. Ascent of Tal-y-Fan. The summit is 2,000 feet above the sea. It may be reached by striking across the tableland from the Druids' Circle, the time required for the walk between the two points being about three-quarters of an hour. But a better route will be found by making for the ruined cottage mentioned in the last route, and then ascending the hill (Cefn Maen Amor) on the slopes of which the cottage stands; thence keeping along the ridge until the final ascent begins. To the right is an upright stone, called for some unknown reason the *Stone of Games*. The summit of Tal-y-Fan is marked by two cairns, and by this route is about 4 miles from Penmaenmawr.

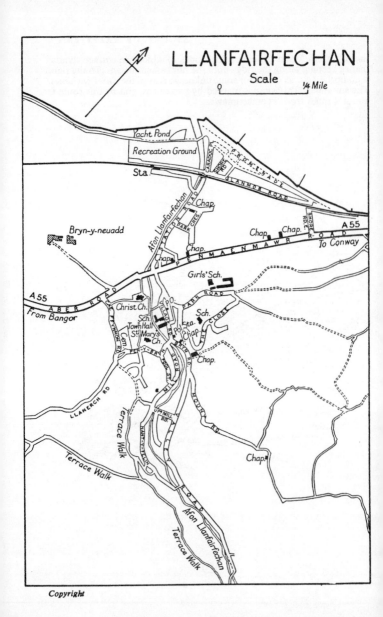

LLANFAIRFECHAN

Scale

0   ¼ Mile

Yacht Pond

Recreation Ground

Sta.

PROMENADE

CARANDA

GLANMOR ROAD

Afon Llanfairfechan

Chap.

PARK CRES.

Bryn-y-neuadd

Chap.

Chap.

Chap.

SHORE RD.

A 55

To Conway

PENMAENMAWR

Chap.

Girls' Sch.

A 55

ABER ROAD

From Bangor

PARK ROAD

Christ Ch.

CEFN

Sch.

P.O.

Sch.

Cem.

Town Hall

St. Mary's Ch.

Pol. Sta.

Chap.

CLOSE

MOUNT RD.

LLANERCH RD.

Chap.

Terrace Walk

UP MILL RD.

MARY-Y-BRYN

Terrace Walk

Terrace Walk

Afon Llanfairfechan

Chap.

Terrace Walk

Llanfairfechan

Access.—By the L.M.R. Chester and Holyhead line. Through expresses, during the season, from London, Birmingham, Liverpool, Manchester, etc. Connection at Chester with the Western Region Line.
Road Routes.—See pp. 8–10.

Amusements.—Mountain-walking, boating, bathing and fishing; tennis, crazy golf and bowls. Children's playground and paddling pool.

Banks.—*Lloyds, Midland, National Westminster.*

Bathing.—On a firm, sandy beach.

Beach.—A belt of shingle succeeded by a stretch of firm, flat sands which the tide uncovers to a distance of half a mile. Ideal for children.

Bowls.—At the Recreation Ground, adjoining model Yacht Pond.

Buses to Aber, Bangor and Caernarvon, and to Penmaenmawr, Conwy, etc.

Distances.—Aber Village, 2; Aber Falls, 4½; Bangor, 8; Betws-y-Coed (*via* Glan Conwy), 23; Caernarvon, 15½; Colwyn Bay, 12½; Conwy, 7; Liverpool, 68; Llandudno, 12; London, 234; Manchester, 93; Penmaenmawr, 2½.

Early Closing Day.—Wednesday.

Fishing.—Freshwater fishing in the Three Streams, Llyn Dulyn and the Aber Lake (licences required). Sea-fishing is very good, especially at the "Swash," a mile out.

Golf.—9-hole course. Within a ten-mile radius there are six golf courses, including the Caernarvon Championship Golf Course, all accessible by local services.

Hotels.—*Llanfairfechan; Bryn Onnen; Min-y-Don; Myrtlewood; Bryn Celyn; Glasfryn; Plas Menai.*

Model Yacht Pond.—At western end of Promenade.

Places of Worship, with hours of services on Sundays.—*Christ Church,* Aber Road—8 and 6. Organ recitals on Sunday evenings during season; *Parish Church,* Pen-y-Bryn Road—Welsh services at 10 and 6 throughout the year; *United Reformed,* Station Road—10 and 6; *Methodist* (English), Penmaenmawr Road—11 and 6; *Baptist,* Penmaenmawr Road—10 and 6 (Welsh). English in August at 10.45; *Roman Catholic, St. Mary of the Angels,* Village Road—9.

Population.—3,800.

Post Office.—Village Road; branch office towards eastern end of Penmaenmawr Road.

Road Routes.—The Chester-Bangor road passes through modern Llanfairfechan and leads eastward to Penmaenmawr, etc., and westward to Aber, Bangor, etc. There is a gentle "potter" of a mile or so up to the head of the valley containing the old village.

Sailing.—Local sailing club.

Tennis.—Hard Courts at Victoria Gardens, towards eastern end of the Promenade, and hard courts at the Recreation Ground, near the Model Yacht Pond.

In its brief but merry course to the sea the little Afon Llanfairfechan dashes first through rocky, fern-clad gorges; then through the gradually widening valley in which the original village of Llanfairfechan stands, and finally, passing under the coast road, it rattles past the modern resort called into being by visitors who appreciated this airy, healthy site on the verge of the sea yet within a stone's-throw of the mountains. This charming contiguity of interests is well illustrated by the stream which bubbles beside the main street of the village, for although its source is some 2,000 feet above the spot where it runs into the sea, yet its length is scarcely three miles. The eastern side of its valley terminates abruptly in the prominent headland known as Penmaenmawr Mountain; its western side falls away gradually in green, wooded hills above which the giants of Snowdonia raise their heads to the sky.

The hills stand sufficiently far inland for their majestic proportions to be seen and admired without the observer being oppressed with their too immediate proximity. Yet they are near enough for the ascent to begin at the door of the village post-office, and from any of them views of great beauty and variety may be had.

As the site has a gentle slope towards the sea, no great amount of moisture can remain upon the surface. Consequently the air is dry and bracing, and through the shelter afforded by neighbouring hills the climate is genial, as is demonstrated by fuchsias, myrtles, and other tender plants and shrubs—including the pale butterwort, a plant very sensitive to cold—flourishing all the year in the open air.

The Sea Front

The front at Llanfairfechan is unpretentious, but bathing is good, and the wide expanse of firm sand revealed by low tide forms a wonderland for children. There is a **Green** on which games may be played and at either end of the Parade public **Tennis Courts, Bowling** and **Putting Greens**. A feature of even greater interest to juvenile navigators is the **Model Yacht Pond**. A sea wall has been constructed along the Promenade.

To reach the Pond go to the western end of the Promenade and cross a bridge over either a foaming torrent (the *Afon Llanfairfechan*) or a bone-dry avenue of boulders, according to the amount of rain that has fallen during the preceding twelve hours.

A feature distinguishing Llanfairfechan sea-front from many another is the **View**:—not the customary wide expanse of sea, but a charming panorama extending from the Great Orme's Head across to Puffin Island, with its striped lighthouse, and then along the variegated coast of Anglesey to the tall roofs of Bangor, Penrhyn Castle rearing its battlemented tower above the trees to the south-west, and then the eye travels round by the hills above Aber to remote Foel Fras and so round to the familiar scree-strewn face of "our mountain."

The path between the Yacht Pond and the Recreation Ground leads (walkers only) to the **Embankment Walk,** a sea-wall which is continued by a grassy path through fields, across the railway and back to the main road. The circuit (about 3 miles) forms a favourite short evening walk, the sunset effects over the mountains, the Strait and distant Anglesey being often indescribably beautiful.

This walk encircles the beautiful grounds of **Bryn-y-Neuadd,** laid out by the late Colonel Platt, who also built the charming mansion. The farmlands surrounding **Gorddinog** are the subject of many comments. Gorddinog is noted for its sheep and cattle.

Of the buildings in the village calling for notice, the chief are the two churches. **St. Mary's,** the "little church of St. Mary," stands on a knoll above the village and has all its services conducted in Welsh. **Christ Church** (English services), situated near the entrance to the village from the west, is a striking building with a spire that stands up from among the trees and is prominent from many a neighbouring mountain-side. The church has a good screen and one of the finest organs in North Wales. (Recitals Sunday evenings during the season.)

Excursions from Llanfairfechan

Situated almost midway between Bangor and Conway, from which roads run into the heart of the finest scenery in North Wales, Llanfairfechan is a better centre for road excursions than might at first appear. There are good bus services and various coach excursions. The railway facilities are referred to in the Introduction.

But it is on account of its walks that Llanfairfechan is best known as a centre. The neighbouring hills so abound with paths and tracks that any one route may be varied, extended, shortened, or taken as part of a longer excursion almost indefinitely.

1. An excellent introductory ramble is by the **Terrace Walk,** along the western side of the valley in which "old" Llanfairfechan lies. Turn up the lane between the Midland Bank and the School, opposite the Post Office. Cross bridge, turn left, and at end of path go up Bryn-y-Mor Terrace, facing. Where these houses end turn right for a few yards and then immediately léft, through a council housing estate which leads to the bottom of an incline which is the commencement of the **Terrace Walk.** Ascend this short incline and onwards for a mile or more into charming paths alongside the stream. As an alternative, return by the other side of the valley.

2. The **Meeting of the Three Streams.** The lane leading to this delightful spot is the southern continuation of Valley Road and the Terrace Walk. The "Meeting" is a place of rock and tree and fern at the foot of the bare, black rounded hill known as **Dinas.** Part of the east side of the stream near Dinas has been appropriately labelled **The Happy Valley.**

3. **Carreg Fawr** (the "big rock"), (1,167 feet). Turn up the lane between the Midland Bank and the School, almost opposite the Post Office. Cross bridge, turn left, and at end of path go up Bryn-y-Mor Terrace, facing. Where these houses end turn right and then soon left and pass through housing estate, up an incline to the Terrace Walk,

134

which is followed to a point about 300 yards beyond the open space
on left, with iron seats. Here are two iron gates: one leading to a sand
pit, the other crossing our path, which goes up for 200 yards to where,
just short of iron swing gate, a narrow lane on right leads up, past a
small hamlet and farm buildings, and between walls to an iron swing
gate, beyond which the way, with wall on *right*, is as clear as it is steep.
The ascent is beautified with bracken, foxgloves, gorse and countless
wild flowers. The path passes through a second iron gate on to a
grassy track contouring easily up to the left, round the hill. This may
be followed for a short distance higher, or the attack on the summit be
opened at once. The way is steep and although nailed boots are not a
necessity they ease the climb over the slippery grass. An alternative
route turns out of the Aber main road by Cae Ffynon road, about 300
yards west of the bridge. Disregard all left-hand turnings and follow
the lane for about half-a-mile, until a pair of cottages are reached on the
left (bearing legend Llanerch Road). Turn up lane beside these cottages
and on farther side of farm, 200 yards on, turn up to right. From now
on "upward" is the only direction required.

4. A charming little walk can be enjoyed by turning out of the Bangor
road by a narrow lane on the left about a mile from Llanfairfechan.
In ¼ mile turn right and almost immediately left. Follow lane past the
Kennels and a farmstead on the right and woods on left, until at the
corner of a pine wood it ends at a gate.
Bear up to the left, still skirting the wood; then cross the old Golf
Course to a gate, descend the lane and turn to the right for Llanfair-
fechan.

5. **The Roman Milestone.** Take road upwards from the Post Office
bearing right up the Penybryn Hill and onwards along Llanerch Road
upwards to where the road branches down to Gwyllt. From here turn
upwards in direction of the old golf course and on to Llys-y-Gwynt
Farm on the right. Passing the farm on its upper side by a grassy path
and out on to a stony road, keep upwards some yards to a field on the
right. The milestone (a replica of the original in the British Museum) is
set up on the site on which the original was found. Entry to the field
is by the small swing gate set in the wall. Llanfairfechan can be regained by continuing on and circling left.

6. **Bwlch-y-Ddeufaen,** a pass some 3¼ miles south-east of Llanfairfechan, owes its name to the presence of two stones near the highest
point (1,403 feet). They are about 9 feet high and 16 feet in circum-
ference.
The shortest and easiest route is to follow the road to the Three
Streams. When this place is reached, the cart-road up the hill to the
left of the central stream should be followed. After passing through
several gates open ground is reached, and a slight track, very wet in

places, leads straight to the Pass, which lies in the gap between the heights of *Y Drosgl* on the right and *Foel Llwyd* on the left. You are now on the old Roman Road that ran from Aber to Conovium. The walk can be continued along this road, and the descent made to the Conwy Valley. There are fine views eastward and to the south during the descent. At Tal-y-Cafn, 5½ miles from the Bwlch, the train can be taken to Llandudno Junction, and thence to Llanfairfechan, or bus *via* Conwy.

7. **To Aber Lake.** It is a most interesting walk, and not very difficult, to Aber Lake (from which Llanfairfechan's water supply is derived) by passing round Carreg Fawr and on by the path worn in the shoulder between Drum and Yr Orsedd, almost due south of Carreg Fawr. The lake comes into view down on the right as Orsedd is rounded, the sheer sides of Foel Fras and Llwydmor guarding it to south and west. Aber village may be reached by following the public path running parallel to the stream to the point where it joins the old Roman Road at a gate—an easy walk of perhaps four miles; or a return made over the hills to Llanfairfechan by following the track round the flank of Foel Dduarth at the point where the route to Aber takes to a grassy lane between two walls, down on the left.

Note.—The *Aber Falls* are on the *farther* side of Llwydmor, and are not seen on this excursion. The ridge walk around and high above the Lake is exhilarating and worth while, but exploration of the vicinity of the Falls from this side has led to several nasty accidents and is not recommended.

8. **Aber Falls.** One of the finest walks from Llanfairfechan. Cross the bridge on the Bangor Road and turn up beside Christ Church grounds by the Caeffynon Road. Follow this and its continuation, Llanerch Road, to the fork with Gwyllt Road. Here keep to the left, and where the lane goes up left to old golf course, take track on the *right*, which leads round the breast of the hill to a stony lane near the Kennels. Just above the house a gate in the lane wall opens on to a path descending across fields to stepping stones over a stream in the Gorddinog woods. Fork sharp left up a bank and over the wall by steps, thence up across the open to Bodsilin House, over the wall, and then to the top of the rise. Continue thence down a steep grassy track to the old Roman Road through an iron swing-gate, and on down to Bont Newydd, at the commencement of the field track to Aber Falls, and about half a mile from Aber village.

For description of **Aber,** *see* p. 138.

The walk of at least half an hour from Bont Newydd to the Falls is by an extremely beautiful path across fields fringed with graceful trees and watered by the burbling stream issuing from the Falls. On either hand rise high hills, glorious with heather and bracken and the shimmering green of closely-packed trees. Motorists may leave their cars in the car park at Bont Newydd.

There is no café at the Falls; nor are there automatic machines or a car park, and most visitors confess to a preference for nature unadorned.

There are two falls, of which the finer is that first reached. It is some 120 feet in height, projecting rocks breaking its waters into lesser falls of extreme beauty. The fall is worth seeing at all times—after rain or during dry weather; an interesting time to visit it is when mist shrouds the upper portions and the water roars down upon one from an unseen source. The second fall is reached by turning to the right, in a south-westerly direction, and walking along the foot of the hill for about five minutes.

9. To the Druids' Circle, Fairy Glen, Dwygyfylchi, Green Gorge Jubilee Walk, and Llangelynin Old Church. Take the village road past the Post Office. Turn up Mount Road, on the left, and continue along it, skirting Penmaenmawr Mountain, until the highest point of the road is gained. The **Druids' Circle** is on a small hill two hundred yards ahead, and slightly to the right. After viewing the Circle, join the road, and continue a short distance until sign-posts direct you to the places mentioned. (*See* pp. 126–29).

10. Llyn Dulyn (The Black Lake). This is the objective of a delightful mountain expedition, but it is suitable only for good walkers and in clear weather. From *Carreg Fawr*, a green track will be seen winding up and round the shoulder of *Yr Orsedd* (*the Thrones*) in a south-easterly direction. Make for this and follow it till it ceases on *Drum*. On the right the steep slopes of Llwydmor descend to Aber Lake, or *Llyn Anafon*, and we get a glimpse down the Aber Valley. From the end of the path the best guide is the wire fence running up to the right. Cross the depression between *Drum* and *Y Foel Fras* and climb a short distance up the latter mountain. About a third of the way up, cross the wire fence on the left, and descend the mountain-side diagonally in a southerly direction, passing below a steep rocky slope, until the lake is reached. It is backed by a fine precipice which decends sheer into the water, the edge of which can be reached at the exit of the lake.

If there is any foundation for an ancient legend concerning Lake Dulyn, visitors who desire fine weather must be careful where they spill water drawn from the lake.

The old story runs:—

"There is a lake in the mountains of Snowdon called Dulyn, in a rugged valley encircled by steep rocks. This lake is extremely black and its fish are deformed and unsightly, having large heads and small bodies. No wild swans are ever seen alighting upon it (such as are on all the other lakes in Snowdon), nor ducks nor any bird whatever. And there is a causeway of stones leading into this lake; and if anyone goes along this causeway, even in hot sunshine, and throws water so as to wet the farthest stone which is called the Red Altar, it is a chance if it do not rain before night."

11. To Carnedd Llewelyn and Carnedd Dafydd. This is a full-day's expedition, for which fine weather is essential, as it is easy for those whose experience of mountains is small to go astray should mist come on. While the weather may be calm and sunny down by the sea, it is no uncommon experience to find storm and mist on the summits of the Carnedds and their higher spurs. The route to **Llyn Dulyn** should be followed to *Y Foel Fras*, 3,091 feet, where, instead of crossing the wire fence, it should be followed as a guide up the steep grassy ridge. When it gives place to a stone wall, continue by the side of it and the summit of the mountain will be easily gained. From thence a slight indistinct track, marked by diminutive cairns the latter part of the way, leads in a more or less southerly direction to *Foel Grach*, whence the summit of **Carnedd Llewelyn**, 3,484 feet, is easily gained.

For Carnedd Dafydd descend due south to the *Saddle*, the ridge connecting the two Carnedds, and there is no difficulty in following it to the summit of **Carnedd Dafydd**, 3,426 feet.

The most direct descent to **Bethesda** (whence the return to Llanfairfechan can be made by bus *via* Llandegai) is to follow the north-west ridge of the mountain, keeping to the left side. When comparatively level ground is reached, a cart-track will be struck. Turn to the left along this, and after passing several small farms, a field-path must be taken which eventually leads to a lane. After crossing a bridge over the Caseg stream, turn to the left along a cart-road, whence a field-path leads to another lane, by which the main road will be gained a short way from the *Douglas Arms*.

Routes down to **Capel Curig** are described (in the reverse direction) pp. 120–21.

Aber

Buses to and from Llanfairfechan. Penmaenmawr, Conwy, Bangor, etc.

Fishing.—*See under* Llanfairfechan.

Hotels.—*Aber*, near Station; *Aber Falls*, Main Road.

Teas, etc., can be obtained in the village, though it is well to go prepared to save disappointment. There is no accommodation of any kind at the Falls themselves, 1½ miles from the Bridge. It is an ideal spot for picnics and it is pleasant to note there are usually fewer evidences of former visitors—in the shape of paper, tins and bottles—than is often the case in this land of beauty.

"Aber" signifies river-mouth, and it is at the entrance to a deep and romantic glen that we find the village of Aber. The erection of a footbridge over the river mouth has opened up a very pleasant walk along the shore to or from Llanfairfechan. Aber has not become a seaside resort, though there is good bathing. Its full name is Aber-gwyngregin, said to signify the Mouth of the Stream of the White Shells.

In the village is an artificial mound, called the **Mŵd**, on which once stood a castle built by Llewelyn the Great, Prince of Wales, who married Joan, daughter of King John. It was in this castle that the last native Prince of Wales, Llewelyn ap Gruffydd, received and declined the summons of Edward I to attend the English Parliament at Westminster. Attendance meant the voluntary surrender of the independence of Wales. The Prince's refusal was soon followed by the conquest of the Principality.

According to a very old tradition, Llewelyn the Great, having taken William de Braose prisoner at the siege of Montgomery, held him captive at Aber, where he won the heart of the Princess Joan, who for reasons of state and not through love had been wedded to Llewelyn. De Braose was ransomed before the prince knew what had been stolen from him, but by means of an invitation to an Easter banquet, Llewelyn got de Braose into his power again, and then, having hanged him, led his wife to a window from which she could see the suspended body.

For the **Aber Falls**, *see* p. 136.

OTHER RED GUIDES
to
WALES

NORTH WALES (Southern Section)

Includes Aberystwyth, Borth, Towyn and Aberdovey, Cader Idris, Dolgellau, Barmouth, Criccieth, Pwllheli, Llangollen and parts of Snowdonia.

SOUTH WALES

Covers the coast from Aberystwyth past Fishguard and St. Davids to Tenby, and on by the Mumbles and Porthcawl to Cardiff and Newport, and the district inland as far as Brecon and Abergavenny.

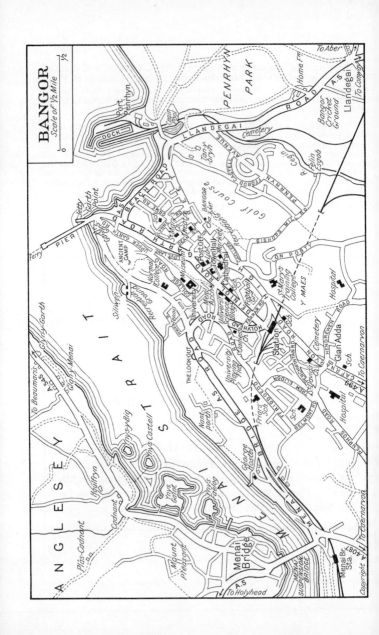

Bangor

Access.—By the main line of the L.M.R. *via* Chester.

Road route from Chester (60¾ m.) *via* Holywell, Rhuddlan, Colwyn Bay, Conwy and Llanfairfechan. From Shrewsbury (83 m.) *via* Llangollen, Corwen, Betws-y-Coed and Capel Curig (*see* pp. 8–10).

Banks.—*National Westminster, Lloyds, Midland, Barclays, Chester and North Wales Trustee Savings.*

Bathing.—Sea bathing safe at all times of the day. Indoor pool (heated).

Bowls.—Public crown greens near Town Hall, Heol Dewi, Garth and Glanadda.

Buses run all the year round between the Town Clock and Beaumaris and Llangoed. There are also services from Bangor to Menai Bridge and the whole of Anglesey; to Carnarvon, Snowdonia; to Bethesda, Capel Curig, and Betws-y-Coed; Conwy, Llandudno, Chester and Liverpool.

Car Parks.—Dean Street. From the High Street it is reached by turning down Garth Road at the Clock Tower, and bearing round to left. One-way traffic in High Street. Also in Ffordd Gwynedd, Dean Street, Deanhill, Garth (near pier), Kyffin Square, Canonry, Deanery and Sackville Road.

Clubs.—The *Conservative* and *Unionist Association* (Working Men's Club) are in Lower High Street. Visitors, members of other Conservative Clubs, can become affiliated members. *R.A.F.A. Club,* Holyhead Road. *Social Club* in Deiniol Road.

Distances.—Bethesda, 5; Betws-y-Coed, 20; Caernarvon, 9; Chester, 61; Conwy, 15; Holyhead, 24; Llanberis, 17½; Llandudno, 18½; Llanfairfechan, 8; Llanrwst, 26½; London, 235; Menai Bridge, 1½; Penmaenmawr, 10; Rhyl, 30.

Early Closing Day.—Wednesday.

Ferry across the Strait. According to conditions services are operated from Garth Jetty to Llandegfan and Beaumaris.

Fishing.—Ogwen and Idwal Lakes and the upper reaches of the Ogwen river are let to the *Ogwen Valley Angling Association*; the lower reaches are let to the *Penrhyn Fishing Club.* The Aber and scores of other streams and lakes are within easy reach. The deep-sea fisher finds excellent sport in the Menai Strait with bass, bream, conger-eel, pollock, etc. There is also good sea-fishing from the pier, where codling, plaice and whiting are taken.

Golf.—Excellent 18-hole course on the hill bordering the city on the south-east, facing the Snowdonian range and overlooking the sea.

Hotels.—*Castle,* High Street; *Belle Vue,* Upper Bangor; *Albion,* High Street; *British,* High Street; *Garth,* Garth Road; *Glanrafon,* Sachuille Road; *Gwynedd,* High Street; *Waverley, Nantlys, Greystones.*

Library.—In Ffordd Gwynedd, adjoining the Post Office. Open daily 9 a.m. to 7 p.m., except Wednesday. Lending Department open weekdays (except Wednesdays) 10.30 to 7 p.m., Saturdays, 6 p.m.

Market Day.—Friday.

Newspaper.—*North Wales Chronicle* (Thursday); *Weekly News* (Thursday).

Places of Worship.—For times of services see press and local announcements. *The Cathedral; St. Mary's,* Garth Road; *St. James's,* Upper Bangor; *St. David's,* Glanadda. Numerous Nonconformist Places of Worship, including—*United Reformed,* Upper Bangor; *Methodist,* High Street; *Baptist,* Glanrafon Hill; *Presbyterian,* Prince's Road; *St. Mary's Roman Catholic,* High Street. There are also several Welsh chapels.

Population.—16,750.

Post Office.—Ffordd Deiniol; branches in High Street, at Upper Bangor, etc.

Road Routes.—Bangor High Street is for one-way traffic only (west to east) and those bound for Holyhead or Caernarvon must turn off to the right along Beach Road, left into Garth Road and its continuation, Deiniol Road. Running up the valley this joins the main Holyhead road opposite the station, as it climbs to Upper Bangor. Thence it bears left for the run to the Menai Suspension Bridge.

For Garth, the Pier and the Ferries turn right at the junction of Beach Road and Deiniol Road.

Steamers.—During the season steamers run to and from Menai Bridge (reached by bus in about 10 minutes) to Llandudno and Liverpool. By taking train or bus between Bangor and Llandudno the fine trip round Anglesey can be joined; also those to the Isle of Man etc.

Tennis.—Heol Dewi Municipal Hard Courts; Glyndyl, Upper Bangor.

Bangor, situated on the southern coast of the Menai Strait, is one of the most ancient cities in Wales. Its authentic history begins with the erection of a monastery about A.D. 525, by Deiniol, who became the first bishop of the diocese. The name is by modern authorities derived from the "bangor" or wattle fence which protected the first monastic settlement.

It is a busy little town, and a good centre for the exploration of North-West Wales. From it there is easy access to the heart of the Snowdonian range, and to the popular spots in Anglesey. It commands delightful marine and mountain views; and is well served by railway and roads; it offers a large choice of hotels and good apartment houses; and facilities for various sports, as detailed at the head of the chapter.

Old Bangor, the commercial part of the city, lies along the valley through which runs the road to Caernarvon. On the opposite slopes are the buildings of the University College and beyond them lies Upper Bangor, the favourite residential quarter, commanding splendid views across the wooded Menai Strait.

Bangor Cathedral

Old Bangor is principally visited on account of the Cathedral, a rather plain building of low elevation situate in the little valley of the River Adda.

The church consists of an aisleless choir, transepts, and nave with aisles. It was founded by St. Deiniol, who had settled there in 525 A.D., becoming the first Bishop of Gwynedd (North Wales) in 546 A.D. when his church took on the status of cathedral. Deiniol was the son of Dunawd, whose father, Pabo, belonged to a North British reigning family. He founded a daughter house at Bangor Iscoed in Flintshire soon after his consecration as Bishop, and the daughter house came to enjoy for a time a greater fame than the original Bangor—the Bangor Fawr yn Arfon (The Great Bangor in Arfon). The cathedral itself,

however, closely bound up with the political fortunes of Gwynedd, became the mausoleum of many of its princes. It had an organ six hundred years ago.

Nothing remains of the original building or of many of its successors up until Norman times. The Norman church was built in the first half of the twelfth century, and all that remains of it is a walled-up window and a flat buttress in the south wall of the chancel. That Norman church was destroyed about a century later by order of King John, who is said to have repented immediately and to have contributed liberally towards its restoration. The Cathedral was, however, almost a total ruin, when in the closing years of the thirteenth century Bishop Anian undertook its reconstruction. Being liberally aided by Edward I, he produced a building more magnificent than any that had preceded it. In 1402 this fine Cathedral was damaged by Owen Glendower, when in rebellion against Henry IV. It remained in ruins until its restoration was begun by Bishop Deane in 1496. Further restoration was undertaken in 1532, by Bishop Skeffington, who, according to an inscription over the west door, rebuilt the west tower and the nave. After that, with the exception of much disfigurement due to repairers, the edifice remained practically unaltered until its restoration was begun in 1868, under the care of Sir Gilbert G. Scott.

At that time a central tower was commenced but left unfinished owing to the difficult nature of the sub-soil. The tombstones in the churchyard were laid flat, and the railings facing the High Street were put back and lowered—indeed everything that could be devised was done to lessen the effect of want of elevation.

Internally many improvements were made. In the core of the

fifteenth-century walls, where it had been embedded as mere rubble, Sir Gilbert Scott found much of the beautiful work of earlier date. To use his own words, the walls were "perfect mines of ancient details," so that, with the aid thus afforded, it was possible to reproduce in the transepts and the great arches of the central tower the structure of Edward's time, and some of the ancient stones were used again for the purpose for which they had been originally carved.

"We have been enabled," said Sir Gilbert, "to recover nearly the entire design of the transept, as erected in the days of Edward I, bringing to light again the work destroyed by Glendower, immured by Bishop Deane, and hidden for nearly four centuries; and that, too, without destroying any old features of subsequent date, except the very wretched windows which had been made up in place of those of the original transepts."

The choir was beautified without disturbing its main lines. The Perpendicular windows remained untransformed, but the roof was raised to a high pitch. It is of open woodwork, richly decorated with gold and colour. A new pavement was designed in accordance with ancient tiles found *in situ*. Other features of interest in this part of the church are the reredos and the east window. That which was the east window is now at the west end.

The restoration of the nave was not completed till 1884. The Cathedral was restored 1966–1971 when the central tower was completed and a short spire was added to the structure.

The monuments in the Cathedral are not numerous. Behind the stalls in the choir are two tombs of the Decorated period, that on the right belonging to one of the Tudors, while the other is probably the tomb of the second Bishop Anian (d. 1328). Under a pointed arch in the south transept (which forms a War Memorial Chapel) is the stone coffin, with a cross upon the lid, containing the remains of *Owain Gwynedd*, a valiant Prince of North Wales (d. 1169), whose father, Gryffydd ap Cynan, was the last to bear the title King of Wales. Owain's brother Cadwaladr was also buried in this church. On the west wall of the north aisle is the effigy of a lady, apparently dating from the fourteenth or fifteenth century, and discovered in 1897, under the floor of the chapter-house. A mural tablet bears the epitaph of Goronwy Owen, the eighteenth century poet. On the south wall at the western end of the north aisle is a pair of tongs for removing dogs from the church.

In the Cathedral is the original charter of Friars School, bearing the seal of the first Elizabeth; and one of its greatest treasures is the Mostyn Christ, a notable example of the "Bound Rood", portraying our Lord prior to crucifixion.

In what was formerly part of the Bishop's Palace Garden is laid out the well-known **Biblical Garden** (Handbook from Town Hall or City Library).

A couple of hundred yards along the High Street from the Cathedral gates, in the direction of Caernarvon, brings us to a steep narrow thoroughfare known as Lon Pobty.

Lon Pobty signifies "the lane of the oven"—a sufficiently apt

The Bridge at Llanrwst

Nant-y-Gwrhyd, near Capel Curig

Menai Bridge

South Stack Lighthouse, Holyhead

description on a sunny day, as those will agree who ascend the lane to—

Bangor Mountain

leased from Lord Penrhyn by the Corporation as a **Recreation Ground.** There are several approaches, the principal being near the upper end of Dean Street. The highest part commands views of great beauty and considerable extent. Walks have been laid out, paths made, trees planted, and seats placed in convenient positions.

From this retreat there is a pleasant walk southward to **Felin Esgob** ("The Bishop's Mill"), half a mile distant, on the River Cegin, but the mill from which the spot obtained its name is not now standing. Thence one can go across the fields to Llandegai, or may return to the city by a pleasant path, passed on the left just before reaching the mill.

In the opposite direction (eastward) from the Cathedral, High Street leads to the Market Hall (usually with a good display of fruit and vegetables) and the Clock Tower. Here Garth Road leads down left to the Welfield shopping centre on the right, and on the left to Ffordd Guignedd. The low building was formerly the Bishop's Palace but is now adapted to contain the **Municipal Offices.** To the right are the **Public Library** and the **Head Post Office.** Beyond the latter is the former Canonry which now houses the **Museum of Welsh Antiquities** (*free. Daily except Sundays and public holidays, 10.30–4.30.*) and the **Art Gallery** where loan exhibitions are regularly shown. To the left of the Town Hall, Rhodfa'r Esgob (the Bishop's Walk) leads to the **War Memorial,** adjoining which is a bowling green. Across the wide, tree-lined thoroughfare called **Ffordd Deiniol** is the **North Wales Heroes' Memorial Archway,** (*see* below) leading to—

The University College of North Wales

This fine building stands on a commanding site overlooking the centre of the city. Designed by H. T. Hare in a style which combines late Gothic and Renaissance elements, freely treated, it was opened by George V in 1911. With the additions of 1963–68 it consists of two quadrangles, and houses the Arts departments, administration and library, and includes the Great Hall named after its donor Sir J. Prichard Jones. In the valley below, along Deiniol Road, are the main Science buildings, most of which belong to the period after the 1939–45 war, and on a separate site in Dean Street are the buildings housing the School of Electronic Engineering Science. At the foot of the park, adjacent to the Memorial Arch, are the Refectory, Students' Union and Theatre; the residential areas are to the North-East of the main buildings (Women's Halls of Residence) and about half a mile to the South-West (Men's Halls).

The University College of North Wales, since 1893 a constituent college of the University of Wales, opened in 1884 in what had been the Penrhyn Arms Hotel, a building of which only the porch now survives. In 1906 the former Bishop's Park was presented to the College by the City Council, and this, with some additional land, provided the site of the new permanent buildings.

The College opened with a Principal and five professors and 58 students. In the years between the wars the student numbers stood at about 600, but since 1945 they have risen to the present figure of about 2,600. There are now 36 Professors and 355 other academic staff. In addition to the usual Arts and Science subjects there are departments of Linguistics, of Agriculture (with an experimental farm at Aber) and of Marine Biology and Oceanography (housed at Menai Bridge, where the research vessel Prince Madog is based).

In Deiniol Road stands the **North Wales Heroes' Memorial Archway,** a Memorial to the men from North Wales who fell in the 1914–18 War. The names (they number 8,500) are inscribed on panels in the room above this beautiful Tudor archway. It is one of the most impressive War Memorials and the panelled room, with its bronze doors, is particularly worth a visit. This Memorial was erected by the North Wales Heroes' Memorial Council out of funds (totalling £95,000) collected in North Wales for the purpose. The balance of the Fund was utilized to provide Bursaries tenable at the College, and modern Science buildings, which have been erected in Deiniol Road. The Scientific departments are now housed in detached blocks, and all are supplied with modern and efficient equipment. In particular the buildings provided for the Agricultural Department are among the best for that purpose now in existence in the United Kingdom.

There are three hostels for men and two for women students. Several scholarships and exhibitions are offered for competition annually.

From the University gateway a bus or a five-minute walk along Ffordd Deiniol and Garth Road will take us to Garth Point and—

The Pier

No admittance at time of writing.

The Pier runs out two-thirds of the way across the Strait, being 1,550 feet in length. At several points there are landing steps for small boats. The pier is now closed for safety reasons.

The prospect from the Pier entrance is delightful. Across the Strait are beautifully wooded slopes and charming residences; westward, backed by the densely wooded shores of the Straits is the Suspension Bridge; eastward the neck of land on which Llandudno stands is almost lost below the horizon, so that the Great Orme rises from the sea like a great island; southward are the Carnedds Dafydd and Llewelyn, divided by the great Cwm Llafar, and the connecting ridge between the two mountains sharply outlined against the sky. Near at hand is **Port Penrhyn,** and just behind, **Penrhyn Castle** rears its tower above the surrounding greenery.

From Garth Point, Menai Road will take us in about a mile to Upper Bangor, the way lying very pleasantly through woods, with glimpses through the trees to the smiling shore across the Strait. A little look-out, with seats, is known as the **Eagle's Nest.** Below is a strip of shingle beach. On the left we pass below the lofty **Ancient Camp Park** and farther west pass the **North Wales Nonnal College,** for teachers of elementary schools, and are soon in the favoured quarter known as **Upper Bangor.**

It is worth while to continue along the Holyhead Road for rather more than half a mile beyond the **Nurses Hostel,** to a "look-out" called the **Crow's Nest,** commanding a wide view of the Strait and the opposite shore. It is a favourite summer evening resort.

Excursions from Bangor

Bangor is an excellent centre for excursions through North-west Wales, either by road or mountain-path. Bus services quickly take one to Bethesda for the wildly beautiful Nant Ffrancon Pass; almost equally accessible is Llanberis, with its pass and its access to Snowdon; Caernarvon and its great castle are within easy distance; and the whole of Anglesey lies literally at one's door, inviting excursions.

TO LLANDEGAI

The principal feature of the road to Llandegai is the long high wall surrounding the Park (it is 13 feet high and seven miles long) of **Penrhyn Castle,** rebuilt 1827–40 for the first Lord Penrhyn.

A National Trust property, this nineteenth-century castle is an outstanding example of Neo-Norman architecture situated in lovely grounds. The rooms open to visitors have most of the original furnishings. In addition to much of great interest in the castle, there is an excellent industrial railway museum, an exhibition of dolls from all over the world and a natural history display. Open daily April, May and October and all Saturdays and Sundays, 2–5 p.m. June to September and all public holidays 11–5 p.m. *Admission fee.*

The principal entrance to the **Park** in which the Castle stands, a splendid battlemented gateway, is at—

Llandegai

Lord Penrhyn's "model village," rebuilt for workmen employed on the estate. It lies to the east of Bangor, on the Conwy road, between two and three miles from the railway station, amid picturesque and grand scenery, comprising, on one side, a fine amphitheatre of mountains, and on the other a fine view of the Menai Strait. The village consists of a Church, schools for boys and girls, and some cottages which mostly stand alone or in pairs. To each is attached a large garden. The dwellings are of many designs, and very pleasing to the eye. The roads through the village are bounded by dwarf stone walls, surmounted by a trim thorn hedge. There is no public-house in the village. Indeed, in the whole of the parish of Llandegai, there are no licensed houses whatsoever.

The **Church** (*always open*) is supposed to have been erected in the reign of Edward III, and to stand on the site of one built by St. Tegai (to whom the present edifice is dedicated) at the close of the fifth century. It is approached through a fine avenue of yews, said to be at least 700 years old. Under a great yew tree on the east side of the church is displayed a slate coffin in a good state of preservation. Among objects of interest in the interior are a mural monument of Archbishop Williams, Lord Keeper of the Great Seal in the reign of James I— "hasty, hot Welsh Williams," as Carlyle calls him; his helmet is displayed near the monument; a monument by Westmacott to the memory of the first Lord and Lady Penrhyn; and a curious monument removed from the religious house of Llanfaes at the Dissolution.

TO THE PENRHYN SLATE QUARRIES

Routes.—By road to Bethesda. Visitors who walk from Bethesda should take the first turn on the right beyond the town, about half a mile from the station, and then first left along the river.

Motorists turn out of the Bangor-Conway road at Llandegai, and take the road alongside the Ogwen river, running down from the top of Nant Ffrancon. Mountains loom grandly ahead and the road is prettily wooded for part of the way to the town of **Bethesda** and the adjacent quarries.

Slates were obtained from the Penrhyn Quarry in the reign of Elizabeth, but it was not systematically worked until about 1782, when the Lord Penrhyn of that time undertook the development of the quarries instead of the prevailing practice of allowing the quarrymen to work on their own account. Then and later extensive and costly operations were entered upon to facilitate the production and transportation of the slates. For instance, a tramway was constructed from the quarries to Port Penrhyn at a cost of £160,000, and a breakwater at the latter place cost £15,000. Previous to 1780, the slates were carried on horseback to the mouth of the Ogwen; afterwards, when the mouth of the Cegin was adopted as the point of export they were taken down to the ships in carts. All slates now go by road.

The quarries are among the largest in the world, and in good times over 2,000 men and boys have been employed at them. Seen from a distance the succession of terraces on the mountain-side is striking.

TO THE NANT FFRANCON PASS AND OGWEN LAKE

Route *via* Bethesda (*see* p. 150), which lies at the foot of the Pass. *Buses* run *via* Nant Ffrancon and Capel Curig to Betws-y-Coed and Llanrwst.

The roads of North Wales contribute to many a notable scene, but Nant Ffrancon is a supreme example of grandeur. As the road leaves Bethesda and runs through the birch woods above the Ogwen there is little indication of the wildness ahead. Then woods are left behind and the road begins to elbow its way along the inhospitable stony flanks of Carnedd Dafydd and there comes into view the wonderful amphitheatre of craggy precipices forming the northern flank of the Glyders. This rocky corner can be visited again and again and every time with rich reward; but best of all is it seen after heavy rain when mists are swirling about the Devil's Kitchen and a defiant sun lights up from the west the jagged rock-pinnacles that top the gloomy and mysterious cliffs. Ages ago the valley was the bed of a glacier, as the marks of the ice upon the rocks testify. In the hills also are hollows due to the action of the ice, they being the beds of smaller glaciers, when that in the valley was wasting. Cwm Craninog, the most remarkable of these hollows, or cwms as they are called, is on the western side of the valley, $2\frac{1}{2}$ miles from Bethesda Station.

At the head of the Pass is **Llyn Ogwen** (984 feet above sea-level), famed for trout and eels. The Ogwen river issues from it in a series of **falls** which are best seen from a path which doubles back just below the *Youth Hostel*. Note also the old bridge under Ogwen Bridge and the old road—a wonderful piece of engineering.

For description of the climbs and mountain walks in the Llyn Ogwen district *see* pp. 116–21.

TO THE BRIDGES AND THE ANGLESEY COLUMN

The **Menai Suspension Bridge** is some two miles from Bangor by way of Upper Bangor and thence along the beautifully wooded shore of the Strait. Buses run to Menai Bridge.

The bridge, which spans the Strait at a point $1\frac{1}{2}$ miles from Bangor station, carries the road.

Up to the beginning of the nineteenth century, ferries, five in number, afforded the only means of communication with Anglesey; but owing to the inconvenience and danger to which travellers were exposed, the attention of the Government was seriously directed to the matter, and, Telford's plans for the bridge having been approved by Parliament, its construction was begun in 1818, and on January 30, 1826, it was opened. Its actual cost was £120,000, and the sum of £26,577 was awarded to the owners of the superseded ferries. The roadway is 100 feet above the surface of the water at the highest tides; the distance between the points of suspension is 560 feet, and the total length of the roadway is said to be 1,000 feet. Only four fatal accidents occurred among the workmen engaged in the erection of the bridge, and those who lost their lives represented the four nationalities included in the United Kingdom.

Unfortunately the bridge proved unequal to the very heavy loads imposed upon it by modern traffic (loads for which, of course, it was not designed); but in 1937 the Ministry of Transport made the welcome announcement that, by "rehanging," the Bridge could be made adequate to modern needs while retaining its familiar graceful appearance. The work was completed in 1939, the roadway being widened and raised and the whole structure strengthened without spoiling its design or closing it to traffic for more than a single day. It is now free of toll for foot-passengers and cars.

The **Britannia Bridge** is exactly a mile west of the Suspension Bridge and carries the railway across the Strait. The original tubular bridge was badly damaged by fire in May 1970 and has been rebuilt as an arch girder bridge.

The name is derived from a rock in the middle of the Strait, on which rests the central tower, 230 feet high. The original tubular bridge was constructed by Robert Stephenson with the co-operation of Sir William Fairbairn, between 1846 and 1850, at a cost of £612,865. The tubes were 104 feet above the water. Their total length was 1,513 feet, but the bridge was 328 feet longer. On the central tower the ends of the tubes were immovable, but on the shore towers and abutments they rested on roller beds to allow for the contraction and expansion of the metal due to variation of temperature. At each entrance is a pair of colossal lions, of limestone, 25 feet 6 inches in length, and 12 feet 8 inches in height.

Prominent on the Anglesey shore is the **Anglesey Column** (*see* p. 154).

Anglesey

The Isle of Anglesey, which forms one of the counties of North Wales, is the ideal resort for those requiring peace and quiet after the strain and stress of town life. Connection with the mainland is made by the railway to Holyhead, and the high road over the Menai Suspension Bridge.

The extreme length of the island is 21 miles; its extreme breadth is 19 miles. The Menai Strait, which separates it from the mainland of North Wales, is about three-quarters of a mile wide. North, west, and south-west of the island is the open sea.

The general aspect of the island is slightly undulating, and it is almost bare of wood, in this respect contrasting strongly with its appearance two thousand years ago, when it was covered with groves in which the Druids conducted the worship of their gods. By reason of its trees the bards, in their songs, were wont to call Anglesey the "shady isle."

The county contains five market towns, namely Amlwch, Beaumaris, Holyhead, Llangefni, and Llanerchymedd. The seaside resorts are small and mostly originated in small fishing hamlets. Trearddur Bay, near Holyhead, Benllech and Rhosneigr have developed very rapidly in recent years. The island, as a whole, is thinly peopled. Outside the towns, the people dwell in sleepy little hamlets formed of old-fashioned cottages and connected with one another by a network of winding lanes, decked in the floral season with honeysuckle and dog-roses. The greater part of the inhabitants draw their means of subsistence from their grasslands, farm animals being reared in large numbers. Many of the men in the coast villages engage in fishing. For long the island was noted for its mineral wealth, producing much copper and lead ore rich in silver.

The Name

which the island bears in English speech is said to have been originally *Angles'ey*, that is, the "Island of the Angles," telling of the time when, after the departure of the Romans, Britain was overrun by the tribes from beyond the North Sea. To the Welsh it is *Ynys Môn* (unnis mone), the Isle of Môn. The Romans made the Welsh name take the form of their language by adding to it the letter *a*, and so to them the island was known as *Môna*, and is so referred to by Tacitus. For a long period the name Mona was applied both to Anglesey and the Isle of Man.

From the earliest times Anglesey has been known among the Welsh as *Môn Mam Cymru*—Mona, the mother of Wales. Various reasons for this name have been given, but it is probably due to the island having been the headquarters of Druidism. (The name is still retained by a hamlet on the Holyhead road.) In the year 61, the Druidical power was all but destroyed by the Romans, who crossed the Strait in flat-bottomed boats. The island was again subdued by Agricola in 76, but it was soon deserted by the Romans. Early in the ninth century it was conquered by Egbert. It regained its independence, and then was often torn by rival Welsh chieftains, until it was finally subdued, with the rest of Wales, by Edward I, 1282.

ON THE MENAI STRAIT

Ferries across the Strait:
Bangor (Garth)
Port Dinorwic and Moel-y-don. At any time when required.

Anglesey is connected with the mainland by two famous bridges (described on pp. 151–52)—the Britannia Bridge carrying the railway and the Menai Suspension Bridge carrying the road.

Those who keep to the Holyhead road after crossing the Suspension Bridge soon come in sight of the—

Anglesey Column

It was erected in 1816 in memory of the first Marquis of Anglesey, who served with distinction in the Peninsular War, and was second in command at Waterloo. The column stands on a knoll 250 feet above the sea, and is surmounted by a statue of the Marquis. The top, which is 91 feet above the base, is reached by 115 steps, and commands a magnificent view. *A small admission charge is made. Large free car and coach park.*

Just beyond the statue is the village of—

Llanfairpwllgwyngyllgogerychwyrndrobwllllandysiliogogogoch

which literally means "Church of St. Mary in a hollow of white hazel, near to a rapid whirlpool and to St. Tysilio's Church, near to a red cave." The name in its entirety, however, is seldom used, but "P.G." is added to "Llanfair" to distinguish the place from other Llanfairs. It is also contracted to "Llanfairpwll."

The place illustrates the Shakespearian query "What's in a name?"; for except for the name the village is quite unremarkable. Beyond it the main road runs, with hardly a bend, westward to Holyhead, one of the straightest and fastest roads in North Wales.

A short mile south of the village is **Plas Newydd,** the seat of the Marquis of Anglesey. It is built of marble from the Moelfre quarries. George IV was entertained at Plas Newydd on his way to Ireland in 1821, and Queen Victoria was visitor for several weeks in the summer of 1832, before her accession.

On the water's edge, near the railway bridge, stands a colossal **Statue of Nelson,** sculptured by Admiral Lord Clarence Paget, a son of the Marquis commemorated by the lofty roadside monument referred to on p. 154.

At the Anglesey end of the Suspension Bridge is access to a lane that leads through a fir plantation and across a causeway to **Llandysilio Church,** on a small rocky peninsula. It is about 15 yards long and half as wide. The nave is of very early date—possibly sixth century. During summer, English service is held in the Church on Sundays, at 6 p.m.

The little cattle market near the bridge is a great sight on Mondays, when all kinds of beasts arrive from all parts of the island, shepherded by farmers and prodded and inspected by dealers who are at least as interesting to the onlooker from far away cities as the animals themselves.

Turning eastward from this end of the bridge we pass through the village of **Menai Bridge** (*Anglesey Arms*) with facilities for boating, and for sea-fishing, which is remarkably good. The Beaumaris road is delightfully shaded by trees, except near its northern end, and through openings in the woods the traveller continually obtains glimpses of the Strait and the coast of the mainland. On the shore below, exactly opposite the head of

Bangor Pier, is the landing-stage of a **Ferry**. Nearer Beaumaris is an entrance to the grounds of **Baron Hill** the gates of which were in the Paris Exhibition of 1851.

BEAUMARIS

Banks.—*Lloyds, National Westminster, Midland.*

Boating.—Town beach, ideal for children —Fryars Beach also very popular.

Bowls.—In Happy Valley.

Buses run from Bangor several times daily all the year round *via* Garth Ferry and Menai Bridge. The buses also run between Beaumaris, Llangoed and Penmon.

Early Closing Day.—Wednesday.

Fishing.—Plenty of flat fish and small codlings along the Straits opposite the town (baits: black bait, soft crabs and mussels). Between Menai Bridge and Tubular Bridge good for bass. Puffin Island for pollack, cod and lobsters.

Sand eels obtainable from Dutchman's Bank.

Golf.—A capital 9-hole course about half a mile from the town.

Hotels.—*Bulkeley Arms*; *Henllys Hall*; *White Lion*; *Bull's Head*; *Wern-y-Wylan*, Llandona.

Population.—1,920.

Lawn Tennis in the Castle Pleasure Grounds. Also three good grass courts in the Happy Valley.

Yachting and Boating.—Annual Regatta Week held at beginning of August. Yacht racing every week during season. Boats—rowing, motor and sailing, may be hired in the town.

Beaumaris, though rather small, ranks as a borough, and is the capital of Anglesey. Except for the Church and the Castle it has few buildings of architectural merit, but the place has an "air" that is very attractive to those from bustling and smoke-shrouded cities. The Green overlooking the Menai Strait is a broad expanse of turf, and at all times the views across the water to the mountainous mainland are a sheer delight. There is a **Pier.**

The chief object of interest is **Beaumaris Castle** (*admission charge. Open daily throughout the year except Sunday mornings in winter*) which has been carefully and skilfully restored by the Department of the Environment and is worth visiting both from the artistic and archaeological standpoint. It covers a large extent, but is not of great height. There is an outer octagonal wall, and an advanced work called the Gunners' Walk. On the outside of its walls are rings for mooring the vessels that came up to it by a marine canal. The main structure is nearly quadrangular in form, with a large round tower at each angle and two striking gate-houses north and south. The most beautiful room in the Castle is the Chapel, reached by a wooden stair near the site of the old racquet court.

The Castle was built by Edward I in 1295, who then changed the

name of the place from Bonover to Beaumaris, a French word descriptive of its pleasant situation on low ground. The only event of importance in the history of the Castle was its surrender to the Parliament in 1646.

In the grounds are tennis courts. Bowling greens in the Happy Valley close by.

The **Church** (Sunday services, 8, 11, and 6.30; daily service, 11) was erected in the early part of the fourteenth century. It contains some ancient stalls, with finely carved misericords brought from Llanfaes Friary at the time of the dissolution of the monasteries, monuments to members of the Bulkeley family (the best is in the vestry), a stone, on the south side of the communion table, in memory of the father of Sir Philip Sydney (d.1563), and a tablet in memory of David Hughes, a native of the island, through whose beneficence the town possessed a Grammar School, erected in 1603, and Almshouses. The north door is secured by a stout wooden bar drawn from a cavity in the wall. In the south porch is the sculptured sarcophagus of the *Princess Joan*, consort of Llewelyn the Great, and daughter of our King John. She was buried at Llanfaes, two miles distant, in a monastery erected by Llewelyn. In the beginning of the nineteenth century her coffin was rescued from use as a watering-trough and her effigy was discovered in a ditch. Other events in her life are related in connection with Aber (*see* p. 138).

Also of interest in Beaumaris is the ancient **County Hall** dating from 1614.

A curious custom, the origin of which is unknown, annually in November marks the close of the Angelsey Hunt. Five pounds' worth of hot pennies is shovelled from the balcony of the *Bulkeley Arms Hotel* into the waiting crowd below, who scramble eagerly for the coins.

Baron Hill

is delightfully situated in the vicinity of the town. The house was built in the time of James I, for the reception of Henry, the eldest son of that monarch, when on his way to Ireland, but the death of the prince so much affected Sir Richard Bulkeley, the then owner, that he gave up his original and magnificent plan, and used only the part that was then completed for his family seat.

Beyond the grounds of Baron Hill is the **Bulkeley Monument.**

The Baron Hill estate is connected with the Arthurian legend, for on it is a hill called **Bwrdd Arthur** (Arthur's Round Table), whereon are the remains of British fortifications. In the Church of Llaniestyn, some three miles north of Beaumaris, is a tomb said to be that of "Iestyn, son of Geraint, a noble knight of Arthur's Round Table, slain by Saxons at the Siege of London."

North of Beaumaris and overlooking the expansive Red Wharf Bay is **Wern,** a small but attractive settlement of modern buildings.

Penmon Priory

at the north-eastern extremity of Anglesey, is 4 miles from Beaumaris by road. (Motorists should note that the latter part of the road winds considerably and is narrow.) The road passes the **Penmon Transmitting Station** of the British Broadcasting Corporation.

Penmon Priory was founded in the sixth century. There are no Saxon remains and the most striking parts are the nave and south transept of the Norman church—a tenth-century cross stands in the south transept. The finely moulded arches and arcades are very impressive, though this (the Norman) end of the church is very dark. The vicarage was originally the Prior's Lodging and the ruined building on the seaward site of the little garden was the Refectory, above which was the Dormitory. A hundred yards east of the church is a very fine stone **Dovecot.**

The wishing well has been identified as being the original shrine used by Seiriol to baptize his converts. Close by are the remains of the hut where Seiriol lived.

A mile or so beyond the Priory is Anglesey's most easterly point. It is occupied by the residences of the coastguard men, and is a very popular picnic ground. Teas and light refreshments are obtainable.

The light is automatic and becomes operative when daylight falls below a certain level of intensity. In view of the possibility of sudden fogs, the fog-bell tolls day and night, fair weather or foul. It has a melancholy note which, however, harmonizes with the remoteness of the spot.

The lighthouse guards the passage between Anglesey and—

Puffin Island

also known as **Priestholm** and by the Welsh as *Ynys Seirio* (Seiriol's Island), because Seiriol, a holy recluse in the sixth century, had a cell upon it. It was called Priestholm by the Danes who destroyed the monastic buildings in the year 853. And, lastly, it is known as Puffin Island through being the resort of immense numbers of the puffin auk. About half a mile in length, it is separated from Anglesey by a strait about half a mile wide. Near the centre is an old square tower, the remains of a religious house or a church.

SOUTH-WEST ANGLESEY

Menai Bridge to Holyhead

The road from Menai Bridge to Holyhead is so good that only the most inveterate sightseer will feel inclined to leave it for the lanes and byways southward. For nearly the whole 20 miles it is broad and straight.

Yet a number of motorists do turn aside, and if they seek small, out-of-the-way seaside resorts they will not be disappointed. There are, for example, one or two little settlements around **Malltraeth Bay** with distinct possibilities for a quiet and enjoyable holiday; and the sandy heaths onward to **Aberffraw** approach very nearly to a natural and perfect golf course. Aberffraw itself is a small village near the head of an estuary, but

Aberffraw sands are glorious. Farther west are rock-bound coves, with sandy floors, such as Porth Tre-Castell; and then comes—

Rhosneigr

Fishing for trout, perch and roach in Maelog Lake and the river and also for trout in Llyn Coron, about 5 miles south-east. Permission required.

Golf.—*Anglesey Club's* seaside course.
Hotels.—*Bay*; *Glan Neigr*; *Maelog Lake*.

Rhosneigr is a small village on the south-west side of the island, with a station on the Holyhead line. It lies some 4½ miles from the main road and commands fine views. The shore is broken by rocks, but there are firm sands affording excellent bathing. Golfing, fishing and boating on sea and lake can be had in abundance. The air is bracing. There is a fine tramp northward along the sands to **Cymyran Strait,** and the trip can be extended by ferrying across to Holyhead Island, the nearest village being Rhoscolyn (*see* later). Southward from Rhosneigr is **Llangwyfan Old Church,** which can be approached on foot only at low water, as at other times its site is an island. Five miles south-east of Rhosneigr, by road or rail, is **Llyn Coron** (close to Bodorgan station), where excellent trout fishing is available by permission.

Holy Island

The island, 8 miles long by 3½ miles wide, lies off the west coast of Anglesey, from which it is separated by a sandy strait, crossed by a causeway, which carries the high road and the railway and has in its centre an arch for the tide to pass through; by another causeway a mile or so more to the southward.

Long known principally as the terminus of the steamer route to and from Dublin, Holy Island is gaining fame as a holiday resort.

Holyhead Town has an interesting harbour popular for sailing. There is a promenade and various open spaces for picnics and games. There is a good range of shops, cinemas and facilities for tennis and bowls in the local park.

Golf Course (18 holes) at Trearddur Bay. Reduced fees from October to April.

The principal public building is the Parish Church, dedicated to St. Cybi, who lived in the early years of the sixth century. It is in the Per-

Cemaes Bay, Anglesey

Caernarvon

Llanberis Pass

Beddgelert

pendicular style and consists of nave with north and south aisles, shallow transepts, a long and narrow choir, a western tower, and a fine south porch. The wall which bounds three sides of the churchyard is considered by some antiquaries to have been built soon after the departure of the Romans. The oldest part of the Church is the chancel, mostly rebuilt in the fifteenth century on thirteenth-century foundations. The battlemented parapets of sixteenth-century work with their interesting carvings, should be noted.

The **Harbour of Refuge,** constructed by the Government a century ago, is one of the most complete works of the kind in Britain. Its **Breakwater,** the result of twenty-eight years' incessant labour, is about 1½ miles in length, and consists of a solid masonry wall, rising nearly 40 feet above low-water mark and backed by a strong rubble mound. It is used as a promenade, and affords a fine view of the rugged coast. Looking northwards across the Harbour, one sees on the horizon, about 8 miles away, the islands which the English call the **Skerries,** and the Welsh, *Ynysoedd y Moelrhoniaid,* the Islands of Seals.

The **Salt Island,** on the east side of the Harbour, is another promenade. In spite of its name it is a promontory, an artificial one. It owes its name to having been the site of works for extracting salt from the sea-water. The manufacture was established in the reign of Queen Anne, and continued until Holyhead began to acquire its present importance, about a century ago. The Stanley Sailors' Hospital occupies a site on Salt Island.

Holyhead Mountain is a mass of rock, 710 feet high, on the western side of the island. Its summit unfolds a lovely panorama, including the heights of the Isle of Man, the Cumberland hills, the mountains of County Down, and the Snowdonian range from end to end. Around the mountain, 60 or 80 feet from the top, is an ancient hill fort "Caer y Twr" traditionally ascribed to Caswallon, a Celtic chieftain of the sixth century. On the seaward side of the mountain is a deep chasm. At the top of it are the slight remains of a tiny *Chapel,* one of the six or seven sacred edifices that led to the isle being called Holy. Although the mountain is steep on the side nearest the town, it can quite easily be ascended by paths starting near the South Stack lighthouse. On the S.E. slopes of the mountain are found the **Cytiau'r Gwyddelod,** remains of the stone huts where lived the Gaidelic inhabitants of the district in pre-Christian days. They are circular in shape and are of great historic interest.

At the foot of the mountain is **Gogarth Bay.** Off its northern horn is the tiny islet of North Stack, and on the adjacent mainland is a Trinity House Station from which in foggy weather a gun and explosive are discharged. Off the southern horn is the islet called **South Stack,** famous for its lighthouse, its storm signals, and its bird sanctuary. The **Lighthouse** (*open to visitors*) was erected in 1809. A chain suspension bridge, 110 feet long, spans the Sound between the rock and Holy Island. The bridge is attained by descending Holyhead Mountain by a flight of 380 steps.

Buses run between Holyhead town and the Stack.

Overlooking the South Stack is **Ellin's Tower,** perched upon the edge of the cliff. It was erected by a former lord of Penrhos. Preserved in it are stone implements discovered on the site of prehistoric huts, near the foot of the mountain. The tower is in a dilapidated condition and care should be taken if entering.

On Trefignath farm, less than a mile south-east of the town, is a Bronze Age *souterrain,* of great interest to antiquaries, as is also a prehistoric grave mound, called *Gorsedd Gwlwm.*

The sands of **Rhoscolyn,** at the south end of Holy Island, are reached by a series of lanes that wind and twist in a most extraordinary manner. This keeps the crowd away, and those who persevere to the end of the lane generally find the place worth the journey. It is a semi-circular bay, about half a mile across; with low, grass-covered rocky headlands on either hand, which fall away to lower ground at the head of the bay. Bathing, boating, fishing, golf and tennis at Trearddur Bay or Holyhead: these are the amusements. The accommodation consists mostly of apartments in the houses scattered round the north-western corner of the bay.

Directly south of Holyhead town is—

Trearddur Bay

Access.—From the mainland, follow the Holyhead road to Valley, just short of the embankment; and here turn off to the left and cross to Holyhead by the Four Mile Bridge. Bear to right at fork.

Trearddur Bay is certainly not the least attractive, if the most youthful resort in North Wales. The bay is a wide inlet facing south-west and broken into numerous smaller bays by low ridges and piles of rock, between which are sands and pools. There is magnificent bathing, fishing, boating, tennis and golf links, and above all the atmosphere of a modern resort that is being developed on attractive lines. There is no promenade. The nearest cinema is at Holyhead, and doubtless the place has other shortcomings of an equally grave nature; but these matters do not appear to cause undue anxiety to those who come year after year for a jolly, open-air holiday. The Church, dedicated to St. Ffraid (St. Bridget), stands in the centre of Trearddur Bay (services in English).

ANGLESEY'S NORTHERN COAST

A good road leads northward from Valley and passes through a number of pleasant villages. **Llanfachraeth, Llanfaethlu, Llanrhyddlad** and **Rhydwen,** are each typical in their own way of the rural scene in Anglesey. Within a short distance of these villages are several charming coves and bays with miles of golden sands safe for bathing and other sports. The principal bays are **Church Bay, Borthwen** and **Silver Bay.**

Chief among the places on the north coast is—

Amlwch

Distances.—Bangor, 20; Beaumaris, 18; Caernarvon, 25; Holyhead, 20.
Hotels.—*Kings Head*; *Sportsman's Lodge,* Rhosgoch; *Hilary,* Penysarn.
Market Day.—Friday.

Amlwch is a seaport and market-town. Once it was of considerable commercial importance through the great development of the Mona and Parys copper mines, in the Parys Mountain, $1\frac{1}{2}$ miles south. Today modern tankers anchor offshore.

The mines were worked by the Romans, and there was a time in their later history when they yielded 80,000 tons of ore annually and commanded the markets of the world. In those days of prosperity (gone now, for the mines are deserted) Amlwch harbour was built, at great, but then warranted, expenditure. The harbour is tightly wedged between great rocks.

Those interested in architecture will doubtless seek out the Catholic Church—a concrete building in a clearly original treatment of the Romanesque style.

Records show that Amlwch is a very healthy place. The air is invigorating, being heavily laden with ozone, and though the town has a northerly aspect the climate is mild, through the moderating influence of the prevailing winds which blow over the warmed water of the ocean. Amlwch is a good centre from which to visit the numerous bays and beaches along the coast, such as Bull Bay or Llaneilian.

Bull Bay

Early Closing Day.—Wednesday.
Golf.—The *Bull Bay Golf Club* has an admirable 18-hole course, about midway between Bull Bay and Amlwch.
Hotels.—*Trecastell*; *Bull Bay*.

The place takes its name from a neighbouring inlet in the rock-bound coast. During summer, when south and west winds prevail, the Bay is usually smooth. Northerly winds lash its surface into great roaring waves. The village of Bull Bay is inconsiderable as yet, but numerous private dwellings are being built.

Shipping makes Bull Bay lively, for liners between Liverpool and America pass at a short distance, picking up or dropping pilots, and small vessels often come in for shelter.

The Bay is safe for boating, except in stormy weather; the numerous creeks are safe bathing-places, being quite free from dangerous currents. Good sea-fishing may be enjoyed from the rocks or from boats, whilst fresh-water fishing and rough shooting are close to hand.

Westward from Bull Bay, the cliffs become higher and more precipitous. At the end of $1\frac{1}{2}$ miles we reach **Porthwen Bay,** a small inlet with a heather-covered hill at its western point. Close to it is a natural arch projecting into the sea.

Westward again, and connected with Amlwch by bus, is **Cemaes Bay** (*Faraway, Castellor, Gadlys*), another interesting rock-bound bay, divided, as it were, into three "compartments.' Two of these have firm sandy beaches; the shore of the third is composed of small pebbles. Boating and fishing may be enjoyed without danger within the Bay. Cemaes village is rather reminiscent of some of the Cornish porths, but the resemblance of the coast is even stronger. Eastward between Cemaes Bay and

Porthwen, the coast is indented with rocky creeks, of which that known as **Hell's Mouth** is the finest as regards scenery. In the opposite direction, from Cemaes Bay to **Carmel Point,** the north-western extremity of the island, the coast is very wild.

Fresh-water fishing and shooting can be had by arrangement with the landowners or tenants.

Four miles from Cemaes Bay is the **Garn,** the highest point in the island, commanding a view of the whole of Anglesey, the Snowdonian Range, the Isle of Man, and parts of England and Ireland.

Cemaes contains the only ancient Church in Wales dedicated to St. Patrick. It was restored a few years ago by the late Lord Stanley of Alderley. An Ichthus stone may be seen at the west end, but the chief treasure of the venerable edifice is an Elizabethan communion cup.

At Wylfa is the new nuclear power station which generates over a million kilowatts of electricity. A viewing tower enables visitors to watch operations in progress.

Two miles eastward of Amlwch is—

Eilian Bay

a well-sheltered inlet with excellent sands and facilities for bathing, boating and fishing. **Lynas Point** is the eastward termination of the coast of Eilian Bay, and is a great resort of picnic parties. Besides the pilot station, it is the site of a modern **Lighthouse,** a Semaphore Signal Station and a Coastguard's Station. The light—bright 8 seconds, eclipsed 2 seconds—is visible 16 miles, and in clear weather the white-washed buildings can be seen from almost as great a distance. Near the Point is *Ogof y Saint,* or **Saint's Cave,** which penetrates the land for some distance. Near it, too, is the sandy gravel beach of a cove called **Porth-y-Cwrwgl,** a secluded spot for bathing, and where boats can be hired for picnic or shooting parties on **Dulas Island.** Another secluded gravel beach suitable for bathing is that of **Porth Ysgo,** a little farther from the Point. Still farther westward, but yet within Eilian Bay, is a third cove, *Porth yr Ychain,* or **Oxen's Cove.**

About 500 yards southward of Porth yr Ychain is **Llaneilian Parish Church,** a notable building. It is in two unequal parts, connected by stone steps. The smaller portion was originally built in the fifth century; the larger in the twelfth. The rood loft, with its screen, is in its original position. It is entered from a spiral staircase that also leads to the roof.

About half a mile to the west of Porth yr Ychain is the cursing well called **Ffynnon Eilian,** where, no more than a hundred years ago, were often to be seen corks containing rows of pins standing for the name of a person who had been cursed, and who would, it was supposed, suffer in health while the corks remained in the well.

Southward of the village is **Llaneilian Mountain,** 600 feet high, commanding fine views over land and sea. On its north-eastern side, near the summit, was the court of Caswallon, a Welsh prince of the last half of the fourteenth century, famous for his gallantry in the wars of his country.

Close to **Ceint** (keint) is a farmhouse which in George Borrow's day was an inn, and was the scene of that pleasant time described in Chapter xxxvii of *Wild Wales*. The road from Ceint to Penmynydd (meaning the "top of the hill") and on to Pentraeth, about 3½ miles, was travelled by Borrow, and his experiences there are related in Chapter xxxvi of the book just named. The view from the high ground of Penmynydd is grand and extensive.

About half a mile from Ceint is **Plas Pen Mynydd** (munnith), the birth-place of Owen Tudor, who married the Dowager Queen Catherine, widow of Henry V. Their son, Edmund Tudor, married Margaret Beaufort by whom a son was born, afterwards Henry VII.

Benllech

Benllech (*Glanrafon, Bay Court, Llanddwyn, Nantilus*) is a fast developing resort with sands and good sea views. There are good caravan sites here. It stands above a lovely bay, 4 miles in width, with firm sands on which there is safe bathing at all states of the tide and where children can paddle and play in perfect safety. There are facilities for tennis and bowls. The village consists of quaint rustic cottages and modern residences, and forms part of the parish of Llanfairmathafarneithaf. In another portion, locally known as *Rhosfawr*, is a small cottage called *Dafarn Goch*, notable as the birthplace in 1722, of the celebrated Welsh bard Goronwy Owen, whose pathetic history George Borrow graphically narrates.

The parish teems with carboniferous fossils. The Geological Survey collection contains over a hundred specimens, mostly corals, collected from Benllech cliffs. Northwards the coastline is chiefly formed of lofty rugged cliffs. But the narrow coast path is distinctly cliffy, and is not for everyone, particularly in a high wind. The cliffs are, however, indented by some delightful coves, some of which can be reached by car, and these are very popular with local visitors. **Traeth Bychan,** a couple of miles north of Benllech, is one such cove. There is a good caravan site here and sailing is popular in the bay. A mile or so farther north is the tiny village of **Moelfre,** built around a small cove and inhabited for the most part by fishermen and seafaring folk.

Charles Dickens spent the Christmas of 1859 at Moelfre.

About half-way between Benllech and Moelfre is **Marian Glas,** a pretty hamlet with good accommodation for visitors. Also easily accessible from Benllech and Red Wharf Bay are the old-world market-town of **Llanerchymedd; Bodafon Mountain,** 4 or 5 miles, the resort of picnic parties; **Llangefni,** about 6 miles, the principal market-town of Anglesey; at **Lligwy,** the remains of a Romano-British village enclosed within a low wall and covering half an acre, and the ruins of an ancient chapel; and **Arthur's Quoit,** one of the finest specimens of the Anglesey cromlechs, supposed to date from 1200 B.C.

Red Wharf Bay

is a wide inlet girdled by low hills and pleasant sandy beaches. At low tide the expanses of water give place to a waste of sand and small pools. Sailing is very popular and there is a flourishing club with headquarters at Red Wharf Bay. Sea fishing is also good.

The village is situated on the north side of the Bay, where is a pretty little cove, which forms (or used to form) a natural landing-place for the cargoes of small coasting vessels. Here are the Hotel and a few cottages. The Camping Club of Great Britain and Ireland have a site for canvas campers at Red Wharf Bay. There is also a good caravan site. The rock pools along the shore northward are extremely interesting and display fine specimens of anemones and other marine creatures. Overlooking the bay on the south side is the small village of **Llanddona** with its modern neighbour **Wern,** already mentioned on page 158.

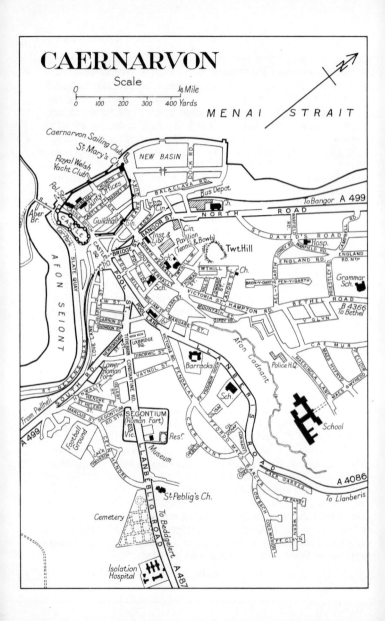

Caernarvon

Caernarvon (*Caer-yn-Arfon*, "the fortress in Arvon") stands just within the western entrance to the Menai Strait, at the mouth of the River Seiont. It is the ancient "metropolis of the hills"—the chief town in that mountainous stronghold known as *Eryri*, and the best view of the town (that from the path leading to the Baths) still shows the stout little fortress backed by the wild and rugged giants of Snowdonia. Caernarvon is the modern representative of the British fortress *Caer Seiont*, and of the Roman military station, *Segontium*, and in position, beauty and historic associations there are few towns, if any, in Wales to compare with it.

Of the thousands of persons who annually visit Caernarvon, the greater number are attracted by the Castle, but the town is an excellent centre for excursions by land or sea, and especially for tours through Snowdonia. Sea and river fishing, bathing, boating, golf, etc., can be enjoyed. Caernarvon was created a Royal Borough in 1963.

Castle Square is a meeting of ways, very busy with the coming and going of vehicles of all kinds. The entrance to the **Quay Car Park** is by the steep lane beside the Castle. The Square is an important bus terminus, and a stranger might be pardoned for supposing momentarily that the bronze statue of the late Earl Lloyd George was raising its arm in despair at the risks run by pedestrians. The statue was, however, erected for quite another purpose, being unveiled in 1921 by Mr. W. M. Hughes, then Premier of Australia.

In forcible contrast to the bustling scene below is the calm, stately Queen's Gate of—

Caernarvon Castle

Admission.—Charge; reduced rates available for parties over 11.
Open.—March, April, Oct., Weekdays: 9.30–5.30, Sundays, 2–5.30, May–Sept. 9.30–7 daily. Nov.–Feb., 9.30–4, Sundays, 2–4.

Caernarvon Castle is one of the finest in Great Britain. Dr. Johnson, who visited it in 1774, observed in his diary: "The Castle is an edifice of stupendous magnitude and strength. To survey this place would take much time—I did not think there had been such buildings; it surpassed my ideas."

It was largely during the last thirty years of the nineteenth century that a programme of repairs was undertaken at Government expense. King Edward VII took a great interest in the work. In 1911 the walls were further restored and strengthened. The Castle is now in the care of the Department of the Environment.

The walls enclose an area of about 3 acres, and are from 7 to 9 feet thick. The erection of the fortress was begun by Edward I in 1283, and completed by his son. It was twice unsuccessfully besieged by Owen Glendower. During the Civil War it was

garrisoned for the King, and, after changing hands more than once, was finally captured by the forces of the Parliament in 1646. In 1660 a warrant was issued for its demolition, but the order was never executed. The Castle is the scene of the historic Investiture of the Prince of Wales.

Among the prisoners immured in the Castle was William Prynne, one of the most notorious of the Roundheads. For an attack upon Archbishop Laud the Star Chamber fined him £5,000 and sentenced him to lose the *remainder* of his ears, to be branded on the cheeks and to be imprisoned in Caernarvon Castle for life.

The entrance is at the **King's Gate**, beneath a beautiful and lofty archway, over which is a statue of Edward I or Edward II. In front of the gateway are two eighteenth-century Spanish guns, trophies from the Peninsular War. On each side of the archway are portcullis grooves. In the towers flanking the gateway were the guard-rooms and other apartments, and over the archway an oratory and a small room used in raising and lowering the draw-bridge. The interior of the Castle separates itself into the Upper and Lower Wards, on our right and left respectively as we step clear of the entrance gate. Beautifully kept lawns are now spread where formerly there were halls and other apartments, but the scrupulous trimness of the whole makes it, at first, difficult to realize that this is a ruin and that its last occupants departed centuries ago—a difficulty that is not lessened by the modern flooring and sconces in the Eagle Tower.

Turning to the right, we have before us the remains of the **Kitchen**—fireplaces over which huge cauldrons rested, water-gullies and so on. The adjacent steps enable us to explore the interior of the **Well Tower,** and then we pass to the lofty **Eagle Tower,** at the western corner of the Castle. Its name is derived from the three stone eagles that are said to have decorated the battlements of the three lofty turrets. That on the west turret can still be seen. This majestic tower rises to the height of 124 feet. Access to the summit is gained by 158 stone steps. By following the narrow passage running round the tower wall at the first-floor level we come to an octagonal Chapel. Proceeding along the corridor, we reach a small dark room, measuring 12 feet by 8 feet, in which Edward II is said to have been born, although archaeologists assert that the tower was not built to this height at the time of his birth in 1284. The window has been filled with coloured glass exhibiting the arms of Albert Edward, Prince of Wales (afterwards Edward VII).

By keeping to the right on leaving the Eagle Tower, we come to the **Queen's Tower.** A door close to the curtain-wall gives access to a passage that leads to a corridor in the thickness of the wall. The windows opened into the **Banqueting Hall,** which was 100 feet long, 45 feet broad, and about 50 feet high. Nothing remains but the foundations of the outer walls. The corridor leads to the **Chamberlain's Tower.** Coming into the courtyard, and re-entering the Chamberlain's Tower by another door, we reach the **Black Tower,** which contains the smallest rooms in the Castle, and was probably the prison. From this tower we go to the entrance on the east side, called the **Queen's Gate,** because Queen Eleanor is said to have entered the Castle by it. Tradition also says it was here that the infant prince (Edward II) was presented to the people.

Beyond the Queen's Gate we come to a beautiful turret, generally known as the Watch Tower, which commanded a hillock that formerly occupied the site of the Castle Square. No name has survived for the neighbouring N.E. Tower. Further on is the Granary Tower, which contains a curious arch above a deep well.

An interesting feature is the multiple grouping of arrow slits on each side of the Granary Tower, enabling a great concentration of fire to be achieved.

The Walls

which formerly enclosed the whole town, are now around only a small portion of it. They had originally two principal gates; others were added as convenience required. The circuit of the walls can conveniently be begun by turning to the right on leaving the Castle, and again to the right on reaching the quay. In this way we are led past the river front of the fortress, and beyond the Eagle Tower reach a promenade running at the foot of the western wall, the towers along which house various institutions.

The **Town Church,** or St. Mary's, at the north-western angle, was founded in 1307 as a chantry chapel. Between 1810 and 1814 it was largely restored but the arcades are fourteenth century. Notable features include the memorial stained glass windows, military flags and the fine Investiture Cross. This was carried at the Investiture of Charles Prince of Wales in procession and at Caernarvon Castle on July 1 1969.

From the Church, the wall begins its eastward course. Its northern portion crosses High Street, at the top of which is the **East Gate.**

Twt Hill

a rocky eminence overlooking the town, is an excellent view-point.

The space beside the lane is scheduled for development of a civic centre.

Roman Caernarvon

There were two Roman forts at Caernarvon.

Segontium, the site of which lies across Llanbeblig Road (A 487) about half a mile from Castle Square, dates from about A.D. 75. It has been partially excavated and the foundations of buildings laid out so that the ground plan can be followed. It is now in the care of the Department of the Environment. There is a small Museum of finds from the site. (*Admission fee; opening times as for Caernarvon Castle*).

The **Lower Roman Fort,** a section of the wall of which can be seen in South Road (A 499) was built probably about A.D. 350. It was situated lower down the hill from Segontium within easy reach of the Seiont estuary, and its purpose was for defence against marauders from the sea.

Segontium is said to have been the birthplace of Constantine the son of Maximus, and of his mother, the Princess Helena. From her brother Publicus or Peblig the Parish Church of Caernarvon derives its name of **Llanbeblig,** *Peblig's Church*. This ancient edifice, half a mile from Castle Square, achieved the status of a royal chapel by the thirteenth century.

As such, the church was granted by Llywelyn ap Gruffydd (the last Welsh Prince of Wales) to the abbot and convent of Aberconwy. Much of the building is older than the fourteenth century. It has a beautiful oak roof, a holy water stoup, and a fine altar-tomb of the sixteenth century. This commemorates a son of Sir William Griffith, who was with Henry VIII at the siege of Boulogne. The tower is remarkable for its stepped battlements, a feature rarely seen except in Ireland.

The **Aber Swing Bridge** (*pedestrians and cycles only; toll*), at the mouth of the river, gives access to the open-air baths and two of the most pleasant walks in the neighbourhood of Caernarvon. By turning to the right after crossing the bridge, the path lies along the shore of the Menai Strait. At the end of rather more than a mile there is the disused church of **Llanfaglan,** a very small and ancient edifice, with Roman bricks in its walls.

the disused church of **Llanfaglan,** a very small and ancient edifice, with Roman bricks in its walls.

Lovers of the open sea should take the bus out to **Dinas**

Dinlle, on the Caernarvon Bay shore. The sands are of the best, and the views of Snowdonia and of the Nevin Rivals superb. The land between the main road and the sea is flat and uninteresting; but for this the site would doubtless develop rapidly. As it is, Dinas Dinlle boasts the inevitable cafés, a boarding-house or two and a small colony of bungalows.

The antiquarian interest, too, is considerable. Here Watling Street ended. Its modern representative is the stony track ending opposite the Coastguard lookout. On **Dinas Hill** is an Iron Age camp.

Five miles south-east of Caernarvon, on the Beddgelert road is **Betwsgarmon.** Here in the beautiful grounds surrounding a cottage called Hafodty are the Nant Mill Falls. Though the grounds are private, the owner permits free access to see these falls.

Snowdonia

Snowdonia National Park

Snowdonia became a National Park in 1951. Its 845 square miles extend beyond the boundaries of the former counties of Caernarvonshire, Denbighshire and Merioneth, stretching from below Conwy to as far south as the Dovey estuary. Only the well-known northern part, down to Beddgelert, its eastern boundary resting on the Conwy Valley, comes within the scope of this guide book. But what variety of scenery and interest is there, including the wild mountain climax of Snowdon itself!

By its designation as a National Park, this area has been marked out as standing in special need of preservation for public enjoyment. Here landscape beauty is safeguarded as a national asset against threats of spoliation. Here that same beauty is enhanced by measures such as the removal of unsightly structures or eyesores. Here also measures are taken to improve facilities for open-air recreation. But land in the park is still privately owned. So visitors must respect the Countryman's things, taking care to do no damage by following the maxims of the Country Code.

With the aid of the beautiful road linking Pen-y-Gwryd and Beddgelert, the two highways running south-eastward from Caernarvon encircle the mountain mass collectively known as Snowdon. The line of the former railway is now a by-pass road which affords a splendid view of Lake Padarn and the mountains.

LLANBERIS

Access.—By bus from Caernarvon, Castle Square (9 miles); buses or coaches also run from Capel Curig and Betws-y-Coed.
Road Routes.—See pp. 8–10.
Distances.—Betws-y-Coed, 16; Caernarvon, 7; Beddgelert, 14½; Capel Curig, 10½; Pen-y-Gwryd, 6½; Portmadoc, 22.
Early Closing Day.—Wednesday.
Fishing in the Seiont, Gwyfrai, and Llyfni rivers, Llyn Padarn and Llyn Peris, and numerous small lakes.

On Llyn Padarn boats can be hired.
Hotels.—*Royal Victoria*; *Castle*, High Street; *Dolbardon*, High Street; *Grosvenor Guest House*, *Padarn Lake*, *Erw Fair*, *Dol Peris*; *Prince of Wales*, *Glan-y-bala*.
Parish Church of St. Padarn's.—English services, 11.15 and 5. Communion, 8 a.m. On first Sunday of the month 11.15.

Llanberis is situated on the western side of **Llyn Padarn,** a lake two miles in length. This lake is connected with **Llyn Peris** by the rivulet called Rhyd-y-Bala. Boating can be enjoyed on both lakes,

176

and lakes and river alike afford sport for the angler. At the northern end of Llyn Padarn is a picturesque stone bridge leading to a Roman camp at Dinas Dinorwic, about a mile off.

A feature of Llanberis often overlooked is the **Ceunant Mawr** (the "big ravine") with its waterfall, well worth a visit after heavy rain, though less effective in dry weather. The fall is about 5 minutes' walk south of the village, and can be reached from the loop road which leaves the main road at Victoria Hotel, or by St. Padarn's Church. It is upstream from the point where the railway viaduct crosses the road.

At Llanberis begins the ascent of the magnificent **Pass of Llanberis.**

Here we may repeat that one of the best views of Snowdon is from the shores of Llyn Llydaw, some twenty minutes' walk from the main road by the Miners' Track (*nature trail*) starting at the car park opposite Pen-y-Pass Youth Hostel.

At the southern end of Llanberis is the lower station of the Snowdon Mountain Railway, *see* p. 183. Also in the old Quarry Yard is the terminus of the Llanberis Lake Railway, and the Museum of Industrial Archaeology featuring the slate industry of the area.

Overlooking Llyn Peris is *Dolbadarn Castle* with its stone walls and thirteenth-century tower.

BEDDGELERT

Access.—By *bus* from Caernarvon or from Portmadoc, also from Capel Curig and Llanberis.
Road Routes.—*See* pp. 8-10.
Distances.—Rhyd Ddu (South Snowdon Station), 4 miles; Betws-y-Coed, 17½; Portmadoc, 8; Caernarvon, 13.
Fishing.—Permits for fishing above Beddgelert Village and in Dinas Lake obtainable from Beddgelert Post Office. Permits for Glaslyn River obtainable locally. Price of permits, etc., from the Secretary, Glaslyn Angling Association, Portmadoc.
Hotels.—*Saracen's Head*; *Plas Colwyn*; *Tanronen*; *Bryn Eglwys*; *Sygyn Fawr*.
Road Routes.—The road to Aberglaslyn Pass and Portmadoc *crosses* the Bridge in the village; that to Caernarvon and Capel Curig keeps on the north side of the stream as it flows through the village.

The picturesque village of Beddgelert stands at the junction of three vales, near the confluence of the Glaslyn and the Colwyn, and amid lofty mountains, woods and murmuring streams. It is a favourite resort of anglers, artists, and climbers, and is a good centre for those wishing to explore the district by road. But to a large number of the visitors who come from all parts of North Wales during the season the principal attraction is the railed enclosure in the meadows south of the church—the **Tomb of Gelert,** Llewelyn's faithful dog, from which the place is said to have received its name (*bedd* = a grave). To reach the grave take the path running between the end of the Old Bridge and "Llewe-lyn's Cottage" and follow it alongside the Colwyn stream (here about to unite with the Glaslyn) as far as the footbridge, where take the footpath on the right. The grave is beneath a rail-surrounded tree in the large field on the right. There is no historical foundation for the story.

Beddgelert Church is on the site of an early Celtic monastery which was refounded later as a house of Augustinian canons. The present church incorporates part of the thirteenth century Priory.

Beddgelert is the centre for many charming walks, of which the chief is that alongside the conjoined streams to Point Aberglaslyn. Follow the riverside path past Gelert's Grave to the main road; cross the river by the Aberglaslyn bridge and thence follow the path as it winds through—

The Pass of Aberglaslyn

The final part of the walk is very beautiful, and looking back from the romantic Pont Aberglaslyn we have an uninterrupted view of naked brown precipices rising to the sky beyond the fir trees and the dashing stream at our feet.

Guarding Beddgelert on the west side is **Moel Hebog** (the Hill of the Hawk), where Owen Glendower hid himself when pursued by the English. The ascent (2,566 feet) may be made in about two hours from Beddgelert. Take a track on the north side of the Goat Hotel and strike up the mountainside to a gap in a wall which can be seen from below to the right of a stream. After crossing the gap, it is a stiff pull up to the ridge, to reach which it is best to bear to the right. Thence to the summit is only a few minutes' walk.

WALKS FROM BEDDGELERT

Those who have come to Beddgelert to ascend Snowdon, and find themselves cheated by mists, might take one of the following three walks in the neighbourhood:—

(1) Take the path which leads along the river past Gelert's Grave and follow it till the Portmadoc road is reached. At Aberglaslyn, cross the bridge and follow the main road for $\frac{1}{4}$ mile to a narrow turning on left leading up past Nantmor (Post Office). The lane continues between

walls and through woods, descending to cross a considerable stream beyond which is a white cottage (Bwlch-gwernog). Here turn left into a lane leading upstream and go past Cae Ddafydd. As the road descends steeply glorious views across to Snowdon and wooded Nant Gwynant open up. The main road is gained near a phone kiosk and the foot of the Watkin Path up Snowdon; turn left for Beddgelert, which is reached in about 3 miles.

(2) Follow the same route to Bwlch-gwernog; or, alternatively, go along the old railway track, which leads through a long tunnel and out to the Nantmor road on the further side of Pont Aberglaslyn. At Bwlch-gwernog strike up right along a steep path, past some pylons; at the top this turns to the left and winds among rocks, heather and bracken, the general direction being eastward. Exquisite views open up to the west-ward, and on reaching the eminence above Croesor there is a grand view southward across Cardigan Bay. To the left the steep peak of Cnicht rises majestically; one of the most beautiful mountain-forms in Wales. **Croesor** is reached by a steep descent. Go straight ahead, across the tramway, and the way is then unmistakable across beautiful moorland and through wooded dells until **Tan-y-Bwlch** station, on the Ffestiniog (narrow guage) Railway is reached. Hence bus from the foot of the hill may be taken to Portmadoc.

(3) An easier walk may be had by going up the Gwynant valley to the Power House below Cwm Dyli, about a mile short of Pen-y-Gwryd, and returning along the northern side of the stream, and through the woods clothing the lower slopes of the Snowdon mass as they descend to Llyn Gwynant. The path is easy to trace and leads through a locality having an air of remoteness that will remind many of the pastoral uplands of Switzerland.

The road is regained at the lower end of the "Watkin Path," from Snowdon, close to the bridge (Telephone box).

MOELWYN (2,527 ft.) AND CNICHT (2,265 ft.)

These mountains rise abruptly at the head of Traeth Mawr, and about midway between Beddgelert and Ffestiniog village. Cnicht from the neighbourhood of Portmadoc appears as a sharp and steep peak, and has, not inappropriately, been styled the Welsh Matterhorn. The summits of the two mountains are, as the crow flies, about 1½ miles apart, and those who do not object to a steep down-and-up course can proceed pretty direct from one to the other—a stiff hour's work. If, however, the intervening dip of Cwm Croesor is passed at its head, the additional mile or so in distance will involve no extra time, and save a good deal of fatigue. The walk from Bedd-gelert to Ffestiniog village, or *vice versa*, over both summits is about 13 or 14 miles, and the time required not less than 6 to 7 hours.

Moelwyn

From Tan-y-Bwlch Station cross the wall by the wooden steps, close to the down platform. The old mountain-road from Maentwrog—at best but a mule-track the greater part of the way—is then entered, and has to be followed for about 2½ miles. Moel Hebog is soon prominent in front, Moelwyn-bach is on our right, and on the left we get a wide view over Traeth Mawr to the sea about Portmadoc. Then, about two miles from the station, we cross the mouth of the great combe that runs between Moelwyn-bach and Braich-y-Parc (the western ridge of Moelwyn) and get a full view of Moelwyn. Still following our mountain-road, after the next steep, we turn to the right along the road that ascends the southern flank of Cwm Croesor to the Moelwyn slate-quarry. **Cwm Croesor** is a fine glen, but has lost much of its original wildness. A considerable collection of quarrymen's houses occupies its mouth, and a tramway runs up it. Cnicht rises almost precipitously on its north side, and is scarred by a quarry on its southern flank. After reaching the Moelwyn quarry the course bends sharply round to the right, and a steep but not difficult climb ends at the cairn on the top of the mountain.

From Moelwyn Mawn to Cnicht. The most direct way is to descend to the head of Cwm Croesor and climb the steep screes that rise from the cwm just east of the summit of Cnicht. There is no danger, though it is a stiff ascent to the ridge, which is gained a few hundred yards east of the top of the mountain. A longer, but easier route, is to descend Moelwyn Mawr by its northern flank—Moel-yr-Hydd to *Bwlch-cwm-Orthin*, the pass at the top of the cwm running up from Tan-y- Grisiau. Thence, climbing gradually to the lakelet-sprinkled and somewhat boggy watershed that divides Cwm Croesor from the Lledr Valley and is about 1¼ miles due north of the pass, we gain the northern ridge of Cnicht and have below us, close at hand, the uninteresting Llyn-yr-Adar. Turning left, along the ridge, we pass just above Llyn-y-Biswail and reach the summit of Cnicht in a few hundred yards more.

Cnicht (2,265 ft.)

From Beddgelert. By far the most interesting ascent is by the south-west ridge of the mountain. Leave Beddgelert by one of the two routes mentioned on p. 178, cross the Dylif stream into Merionethshire, and then climb on the end of the ridge, just short of **Cwm Croesor,** and by it we can ascend all the way. This ridge commands a fine view of that combe and of Moelwyn and on our left Snowdon rises to a noble peak. It is best, however, to bear to the right of the ridge and go over a wall which crosses the ridge in a hollow. The track then continues along the summit of the next long ridge, affording fine views on either side. The final climb to the summit is easiest made on the right of the rock face. Up this we make our way, and then attain a stone-strewn turf-slope. The summit is only a few minutes farther.

The Ascent of Snowdon

Access.—Motor-coaches run to and from Llanberis for the railway ascent of Snowdon. Some firms also provide lunch at Llanberis. Although the advertisements make a point of the fact that trains on the mountain railway will run only as far as snow permits, it may be stated that very little snow will be found on any of Snowdon's peaks after Easter.

The western walking routes up Snowdon are served by the buses between Caernarvon and Beddgelert and buses run to Gorphwysfa and Pen-y-Gwryd and past the foot of the Watkin Path.

For description of the **Road Routes** to and around Snowdon *see* pp. 8–10.

Refreshments.—At the summit is a large modern licensed restaurant, with windows commanding grand views—a very welcome development from the wooden shacks which served for so many years.

Snowdon, the highest and finest mountain in the southern portion of Great Britain, has five distinct peaks, viz., *Yr Aran, Lliwedd, Crib-y-Ddysgyl, Crib-goch*, and *Y Wyddfa*. But the name Snowdon is popularly reserved for the Wyddfa, the central and loftiest point, 3,560 feet above sea-level.

It may be well to summarize the five principal ascents:

1. That *from Llanberis* is the most popular, on account of its easy access by rail and road. It is rough and very wet in places, but is an easy walk considering that it climbs 3,000 feet in 5 miles.

2. Next in point of ease is the *Snowdon Ranger Path* from Llyn Cwellyn. It is inclined to be wet and the track is rather hard to find but it has the advantage of good views. The Caernarvon-Beddgelert buses pass its foot.

3. The *South Snowdon Route* (which incorporates the Beddgelert Path) is less easy than the others, but throughout commands grand views. There is a little ridge-walking towards the top, but nothing to disturb ordinary folk. The foot of this path is served by bus.

4. The *Watkin Path* presents one of Snowdon's most noble sides to the climber, and for two-thirds of the way the path is good and comparatively easy. The last part, however, zigzags across the precipitous face of Wyddfa by a path loose and narrow and the route should be left severely alone by all but the sure-footed and steady-headed, and even those should not attempt it in mist or when snow is lying. These same zigzags are a very disturbing factor to those using the route as a *descent*. This way is rather dull because it is shut in by the cup of the mountains.

5. The *Cwm Dyli* routes from Gorphwysfa or Pen-y-Gwryd. These converge above Llyn Glaslyn and then for more than a thousand feet zigzag steeply up loose stony paths that are not always easily traced in ascending; the most arduous of the ascents, but the best rewarded with views of mountain majesty. It is more frequently used as a descent, but the looseness of the path leaves few opportunities for looking at the view, and is apt to play havoc with optimistic time-tables and appointments for tea at Pen-y-Pass.

With the possible exception of the zigzags at the top of the Watkin Path, all these routes are free from danger and within the scope of the ordinary good walker.

As to the best "pair" of routes, much depends upon the facilities for reaching the various paths; perhaps the best round would be train to Caernarvon, bus to South Snowdon, walk over mountain, descending by Llyn Glaslyn and Llydaw to Pen-y-Pass, thence down Llanberis Pass to the bus back to Caernarvon; or bus from Caernarvon to Beddgelert, ascend by Watkin Path and descend to South Snowdon for bus back to Caernarvon.

For those who require something more ambitious there is the famous **Horseshoe**, "the finest ridge walk in Europe"—though "walk" is hardly the term to describe this exhilarating scramble up the steep south-eastern end of Crib Goch, along the ridge by the Pinnacles to the summit of Snowdon and then down by the Watkin zigzags to the magnificent ridge of Lliwedd (pronounced "Looeth") from which one descends eventually to the lower end of Llyn Llydaw (or to the south-ward from Lliwedd over Wenallt and so to Nant Gwynant). Through-out, the views are magnificent. It must be repeated that this walk is *not* for the new-comer to mountains and should in *no* case be taken without a companion.

BY CAR TO SNOWDON

Those who drive to the foot of Snowdon with the intention of climbing the mountain would do well to bear in mind that the ascent and descent are sufficiently tiring to make it desirable to leave the car as near as possible to the end of the descending route. It is, for example, a good walk from Rhyd-ddu over Snowdon to Gorphwysfa, at the top of Llanberis Pass—but enjoyment may be spoilt if someone has to go round by road to Rhyd-ddu to bring the car. Buses are useful—when running—and consultation of a time-table may solve what is really rather a problem for those to whom a five-mile walk is not an alluring climax to a climb over Snowdon. Another solution that is at any rate ingenious provides for the splitting-up of the party, one half being motored to, say, Rhyd-ddu and the other half taking the car round to Llanberis or Gorphwysfa, where it is parked and collected in due course by the climbers left at Rhyd-ddu. The party meets for lunch on the summit, and those who descend to Gorphwysfa drive round to Rhyd-ddu to pick up their friends who have descended on that side!

A simpler plan is to go up and down by the same route, but that is, to many minds, a waste of opportunity.

The Mountain Railway

The trains run several times daily from 9 a.m. The time occupied in ascending or descending is one hour.

The length of the line is 4¾ miles, the gauge being 2 feet 7½ inches. The rails are firmly bolted to steel sleepers, which are hollowed underneath so that they may be firmly embedded.

The mechanism for propulsion consists of a double steel rack, firmly bolted to the centre of the line, and in the deeply-cut indention of the rack the driving pinions of the engines work. There are four of these pinions, which are massive, and continually in gear; and, the whole power of the engine being available for braking purposes, the train can be brought to a dead stop instantly. As an additional precaution, extra lip girders have been provided, under which powerful brackets run, so that it is impossible for the engine or carriages to mount the rack without pulling up the rails and sleepers. The carriages have separate brakes, and during the ascent and descent the engine is at the lower end of the train.

Soon after leaving the Llanberis terminus, there is a full view of the Ceunant Mawr. Then, after passing the first of the three intervening stations, the line ascends along the east side of Cwm Brwynog until the ridge overlooking the pass is reached. From this point the view becomes even grander and more extensive.

Exceptional views require (alas!) weather somewhat exceptional. Disappointment would be less common if people would take the very obvious precaution of looking at the summit of Snowdon before starting. Many

183

consider Snowdon is seen at its best on a day when occasional clouds drift across its peak.

1. The Path from Llanberis

This, although somewhat wet, is the easiest route for walkers, and on that account is the most generally chosen. It is, indeed, so comparatively easy and gradual that motor-cycles and land-rovers have been driven all the way. Unfortunately, it is the least interesting. Its length is just under 5 miles, and may be accomplished in about 3 hours. To get to the path from the station, follow the main road to the Victoria Hotel and then take a road on the right to a small square. Go through the gate at the end of the road, and follow the winding road up the hill-side. At the first fork turn sharply to the left; thence the track is plain. At a height of 1,525 feet, about 2¼ miles from Llanberis, the path passes under the railroad. About a mile farther is a refreshment hut, generally called the *Halfway House*. Thence the track is steeper. At the height of 2,521 feet the path again passes under the railroad, and a fine view is afforded of the Llanberis Pass and Cwm Glas Bach, which lie immediately below. Some distance farther on the path meets the Snowdon Ranger route on the right and the Pen-y-Gwryd route on the left. The elevation of this spot is about 3,260 feet, and a steep climb for about a quarter of an hour completes the ascent.

2. The Snowdon Ranger (Cwellyn Lake) Route

The distance by this route is about 4 miles, and will occupy a couple of hours. The path commands fine views, but is very soft after rain. The ascent begins close to the Snowdon Ranger Youth Hostel (Caernarvon-Beddgelert bus route). Near the lower end of the path is a farmhouse, soon after passing which the path has a zigzag course, and leads through a gate. At the end of half an hour's walk there is another gate, and, the path becoming indistinct, the left shoulder of Snowdon must be taken as a guide until the track again appears. It leads along the crest of the ridge of Clogwyn du'r Arddu and finally joins the Llanberis path near the junction of that route with the path from Pen-y-Gwryd.

Those making the *descent* by this path should make for the Youth Hostel, situated in a clump of trees about the middle of the eastern side of the lake, and visible from the top of Snowdon. The path leaves the Llanberis route half a mile from the summit.

3. From Beddgelert or Rhyd-ddu

The distance to the summit from Beddgelert is 6½ miles (3 of which are along the road); from Rhyd-ddu it is 3½ miles. Some three-quarters of a mile from the high road the paths unite. The ascent from the road at Rhyd-ddu will occupy a good three hours. From Beddgelert follow the Caernarvon road for about 2¾ miles and there, just short of the

Pitt's Head Rock, pass from the road to the right through a farm (Ffridduchaf).

From beside the Post Office of Rhyd-ddu a path crosses the old line at the site of the disused South Snowdon Station. At fork in about 250 yards go to right, past ruined buildings and slag heaps. In about 20 minutes the Beddgelert path comes in on right. Look out for a narrow iron gate on the left. Take path beyond and strike across a depression. Near this point small cairns lead up to a gate in a wall, past a sheepfold and a large cairn to a piece of "staircase," from the top of which make for an iron gate in wall ahead. About here there are fine views westward to Nantlle. From the gate the path makes a wide sweep rightward, rejoining the wall above the grim precipices around the head of Cwm Clogwyn, which is skirted until the narrow path (known as the Saddle) on Bwlch Main passes to the other side of the ridge and we have a magnificent view of Lliwedd and the peaks and ridges eastward. The path now works round to the left, and then a final sharp ascent brings us to the summit.

For the **descent** pass the end of the restaurant farthest from the station. The track is unmistakable. In three-quarters of a mile it swerves to the right, and runs along the ridge of Llechog, near the end of which it passes through a wall and presently goes through the wall again. After a steep descent to the large cairn it crosses open ground to some sheep-pens, and through a wall, beyond which small cairns point the way to a small gate beside a big rock. For Beddgelert keep straight ahead, but for Rhyd-ddu follow the road to the right.

4. The Watkin Path

By this route the summit is $7\frac{1}{2}$ miles from Beddgelert and $4\frac{1}{2}$ miles from the high road, which is left by passing through a white gate a few yards short of the bridge over the river and close to a telephone box at Nant Gwynant. The route continues on past the late Sir Edward Watkin's house, the Gladstone Rock, and then some distance farther on the ruins of some quarry buildings. Here the path turns abruptly up to the right (an arrow in the ground indicates the route). This is the Watkin Path, and leads up to *Bwlch-y-Saethau* (Pass of the Arrows), the dip between Lliwedd and Y Wyddfa. Thence it runs along the ridge and then zigzags steeply up the final peak, but the zigzags are narrow and loose and should not be attempted by novices when covered with snow. In case of doubt, once the final zigzags have been entered, do not take apparent branches of the path leading downward. The real path leads steeply up all the way. At a cairn the Rhyd-ddu path is met near the summit.

The **descent** doubles back by these zigzags from the South Snowdon track a few minutes' walk below the restaurant. The actual point of departure is marked by two cairns on left where South Snowdon path makes turn to the right.

Mist is frequently encountered soon after leaving the quarry buildings, and only those thoroughly acquainted with the route, or accustomed to mountains, should proceed with the ascent. The return to Beddgelert can be varied, and a dignified retreat carried out, by striking westward from the quarry to the gap between Aran and Llechwedd (the wall is a guide). Beyond the gap are two tarns and a slate quarry. When these have been skirted (the left-hand side is easier, though sometimes wet), a track will be seen descending to Rhydd-ddu, by Llyn-y-Gader. This track, lower down, crosses the Beddgelert route up Snowdon, and by turning leftward along that the road will be reached near Pitt's Head; or one can descend to Rhydd-ddu and get refreshment while awaiting a bus.

5. From Pen-y-Pass

From this side is the wildest and grandest (and most arduous) of the approaches to Snowdon open to the ordinary non-climbing walker.

The "Pyg" Track (P.Y.G. = Pen-y-Gwryd, and is presumably a memento of the part borne in its construction by climbers from that headquarters). From the gate opposite the Pen-y-Pass Youth Hostel, at the top of Llanberis Pass, take the track running half right and climbing by the Bwlch Moch over the lower ridge at the foot of mighty Crib Goch. Llyn Llydaw comes into view as we cross the Bwlch and the track begins to hug the precipitous southern face of Crib Goch. Soon **Llyn Glaslyn** comes into view, and then the path suddenly becomes very steep on the zig-zags and not too easy to find, notwithstanding an occasional cairn. Keep well to the right at the copper mine, to find the path and avoid the worst of the scree. Patient plodding eventually brings the walker out on comparatively level ground where the Llanberis route and the railway are joined, and then ten minutes' comparatively easy walking leads to the summit. In a mist it would be a dangerous place for an inexperienced walker, as the scree is very loose in many places. From the top the path looks clear and simple; from the bottom and on the way up, it is by no means clear. The windings of the path as seen from above are simply lost owing to the vastness of the mountain-side.

Note.—The old route, starting by the bridle-path from the Pen-y-Pass Hotel Car Park, and crossing Llyn Llydaw by the causeway, is not always available owing to the raising of the level of the lake and the consequent submersion of the causeway. This is frequently exposed, however, and in case of need one can remove boots and stockings and paddle across. Those who ascend Snowdon by this route skirt the lakes and at the upper end of Llyn Glaslyn strike steeply up the scree. Hence it is a hard and uninteresting "slog" for an hour or so; and on the whole the P.Y.G. Track is to be preferred since the final scramble is decreased.

Llanberis to the P.Y.G. Track. Follow the Pass up past Dinas Mot, below which the road crosses the river. Some way above the bridge—which is about 4 miles from Llanberis station—look out for cairns indicating the path up to the Bwlch at the foot of Crib Goch. This is quite a good pull up, and generally speaking it is best to follow the road to Gorphwysfa and thence come back as already described.

To **descend** by the P.Y.G. Track, follow the Llanberis path alongside the railway for $\frac{1}{4}$ of a mile. Do not be in a hurry to get off the main ridge: the beginning of the track is marked by a cairn, and for the first few yards at any rate the way is quite a good path. The P.Y.G. Track keeps well up on the slopes and throughout is at a good height above the lakes. The Capel Curig path descends more steeply to the head of Llyn Glaslyn. In this case follow the cairned route carefully or you may come to grief in a disused mine. The greater part of the route is visible from the summit in clear weather.

6. The Cwm Glas Route

This route will appeal to those who wish to get a little off the beaten track and incidentally to enjoy some really fine scenery.

Leave Gorphwysfa by the P.Y.G. track, but instead of going up to the Bwlch keep down east side of Crib Goch. There are cairns and a fairly easy path follows, more or less, the electric supply lines. The immediate objective is to skirt the foot of *Dinas Mot*, the cliffs of which rise above the much humbler cliff overhanging the Pass road nearly a mile down. From the foot of the Mot bear upwards and slightly to the left. Cross the first stream and on coming to another follow it upwards (do not cross this stream).

N.B.—Those coming from Llanberis may reach this point by following this stream (the more northern of the two) up from the road, which is left at Blaenant Farm near Inys Ettws, the Climbers' Club, but it is a steep climb. From Gorphwysfa the best route is that we have outlined.

Following stream upwards one arrives by a fine moraine, beyond which rocks rise more steeply. The best course lies about midway between the two streams which course down the slope, keeping to left rather than right. Half an hour's steep climb brings one to the lower and larger **Llyn Glas,** with very fine views of the back of Crib Goch and the Pinnacles, and the beginning of Crib-y-Ddysgyl, with Clogwen-y-Person (the Parson's Nose at its base) projecting towards one, and on the extreme right the long ridge running steeply down to Llanberis Pass, beyond which Y Garn is a graceful mountain to left and the Glyders appear almost a moorland by comparison with Snowdon's constricted ridges.

There are two routes up from Llyn Glas. The easier contours up to the ridge on the right, on top of which is a wide grassy tract, providing an easy walk to the Llanberis track at a point commanding good views of the ridge down to Llanberis.

The finer route follows the shallow trough running from Llyn Glas to the dip below the Pinnacles. On reaching the ridge pass over Crib-y-Ddysgyl and so to the Clogwen ridge and the top.

The View from the Summit

The view extends to Ireland, the Isle of Man and heights in Cumbria, but the most magnificent portion of the prospect is that presented by the spurs of Snowdon itself, with the adjoining cwms and mountain-lakes. Due east at our feet Glaslyn and Llyn Llydaw lie enclosed by the fine crags of Lliwedd and Crib Goch, with Crib-y-Dydsgyl nearer at hand in the north, while farther to the left lies Clogwyn d'ur Arddu. Llechog rises in the south-west and Yr Aran almost due south. Beyond Llyn Llydaw, Moel Siabod rises, to the right of the Capel Curig lakes and the far distance is bounded by the Clwydian range. The Berwyn Hills continue the sky-line. The peak of Arenig Fawr shows up beyond Lliwedd, while on its right, but much farther off, Aran Bennlyn and Aran Mawddy present graceful outlines. South-south-east Moelwyn and Cnicht rise just beyond Nant Gwynant. The long line of Cader bounds the southern horizon, over the left of which there is a small strip of Plynlimmon visible under favourable atmospheric conditions. The Rhinogs are somewhat nearer, and to their right Cardigan Bay stretches away, St. David's Head at its southern extremity being visible in very clear weather over the far distance is bounded of Moel Hebog. Over Yr Aran, Harlech Castle can be located by the sea, while at the northern end of Cardigan Bay is the Lleyn promontory graced by the elegant peaks of the Rivals. The Nantlle Lakes lie almost due west, with Y Garn on their left and Mynydd Mawr on their right, Llyn Cwellyn reposing at the foot of the latter height. The Isle of Anglesey stretches away beyond Moel Eilio, with Holyhead visible Mountain easily distinguishable. There is a peep of the Menai Strait, and of the Railway Bridge. Due north Llyn Padarn is visible, with the peak of Elidyr Fawr beyond. Nearer at hand are Y Garn and the Glyders with the Carnedds beyond and a peep of Tryfan between the Glyders.

Index

Where more than one reference is given the first is the principal.